DISASTERS OF
THE DEEP

DISASTERS OF THE DEEP

A Comprehensive Survey of
Submarine Accidents and Disasters

by

EDWYN GRAY

LEO COOPER

First published as *Few Survived* in Great Britain 1986 by
LEO COOPER
in association with Secker and Warburg Ltd,
Reissued in 1996 by
Pen & Sword Books Ltd
47 Church Street
Barnsley, S. Yorks, S70 2AS

This third revised and updated edition is published in 2003 by
LEO COOPER
an imprint of Pen & Sword Books Ltd

A CIP record for this book is available from
The British Library

ISBN 0 85052 987 5

Printed in Great Britain by
CPI UK

Contents

To Vivienne with love

Author's Note to the Third Edition

During the seven years that have passed since the second edition of *Few Survived* was published many more Cold War accidents have been de-classified and are now in the public domain. Several make chilling reading. It has also been a period packed with unusual incidents such as the bizarre fate of the survivors from two North Korean submarine accidents, two fatal encounters between nuclear submarines and fishing trawlers, as well as similar but lesser incidents in home waters and abroad. The *Kursk* disaster, of course, dominated the first year of the new millennium and its aftermath rumbled on for nearly two more years. This Russian tragedy and some other accidents also brought political repercussions in their wake – the first time that politics has entered into the centuries-old saga of underwater disasters. And, worryingly, several other incidents in recent years suggest that the lessons gleaned from past tragedies have not been adequately assimilated.

Ongoing research continues to uncover new and additional facts which have a bearing on certain incidents described in the original text and I would like to take this opportunity to mention briefly some significant matters that require updating.

To begin with it has been established that, although John Day was the first man to lose his life in a 'submarine' disaster [see pages 19–21] his vessel, *Maria*, was the *second* pioneer submersible to sink. In 1719 a Turkish 'submarine' *Timsah*, designed by Ibrahim

Effendi, foundered in Constantinople harbour during a demonstration of its diving abilities. Happily her five-man crew escaped unharmed.

The puzzling double sinking of Russia's *Kambala* [page 62] has also now been resolved. The report in *The Times History of the Great War* of her loss at Kronstadt in 1909 proved to be erroneous and, on further investigation, was found to refer to the foundering of *Delfin* on 20 June 1904, an accident described earlier on page 50. *Kambala*, in fact, sank only once when she was rammed by a Russian battleship on 12 June 1909 and was never salvaged.

Due to a mistaken date details of *C.12*'s accident on the River Humber [page 82] were placed out of chronological order. The submarine actually sank on 6 October 1918 but was not salvaged until 2 February 1920. It should also be noted that an unintentional ambiguity in my account of the collision between *E.4* and *E.41* on 15 August 1916 seemed to imply that the entire crew of *E41* were saved [page 88]. Sadly this was not the case for sixteen crew members – mainly engine-room personnel – were posted as missing following the accident. I am indebted to Mr M.I. Frewer, a grandson of Leading Stoker Walter Frewer, one of those who did not survive, for bringing the correct facts to my notice.

The statistics of submarine losses in the First World War quoted at the beginning of Chapter Seven have been extensively revised and the reader is referred to Appendix Four which has been fully updated to reflect the most recent research available.

HMS Affray's tragic loss in 1951 [pages 200–205] continues to throw up surprises and attract media attention despite the passing of half a century. Some of the information that has surfaced in recent years helps to resolve the so-called mystery of her loss and is important enough to merit further detailed examination. This will be found in the new Chapter Fifteen.

Two other incidents need to be touched upon briefly. It has been confirmed that the attempted salvage of the Soviet Golf-class submarine, now identified as *K.129*, succeeded in raising the bow section of the submarine [see pages 217–219]. The bodies of six Russian sailors were recovered and buried at sea by the Americans. A movie-film of the ceremony has been screened on domestic and foreign television within the last five years. The wreckage was inspected by CIA experts and the intelligence obtained enabled the Pentagon to penetrate the Soviet Navy's world-wide communication systems. It was a coup equal in importance to the capture of Nazi Germany's Enigma coding machine in the Second World War and it is not therefore surprising that the United States laid down a smokescreen of disinformation to conceal their success from the Russians. It was a similar need for secrecy that allowed the myths and mysteries of how *Scorpion*'s wreck was located to develop [see pages 213–215]. The US Navy was anxious to conceal the extent of its network of oceanic sonar buoys (SOSUS) from its Cold War adversaries and it could not afford to publicize the fact that the lost submarine was found as the result of cross-bearings from these underwater sentinels. It was a secret the Pentagon kept concealed for some thirty years – long after the Russians and the rest of the world knew all about SOSUS.

A second new chapter has been added to cover the recently revealed details of Cold War incidents, the *Kursk* disaster, and other accidents that have occurred since 1995. As a result of this the original Chapter 14 has now been renumbered Chapter 16. In addition all the appendices have been revised and enlarged to reflect the very latest available information. In all, some 9,000 words have been added the text of the 2nd edition and numerous other corrections have been inserted.

My thanks are due again to all those correspondents who have assisted with information and other research material and I would like to acknowledge my debt to: Commander Jeff Tall, OBE, RN, the director of the Royal Navy Submarine Museum at Gosport, and especially to Margaret Bidmead, its curator, for her unstinting assistance in digging up vital facts and figures; and also to my Australian research colleague Denis Cahill who can always be relied upon to find the impossible at the drop of a hat. Thank you also Mrs Dorice Janzer of Florida (Project Jennifer and *CSS Hunley*); Innes McCartney of Periscope Books (*Affray*); Edward Mariott and Goldhawk Universal Productions (*Affray*); Grahame Currie for searching out internet websites; Dan Agardh and Bertil Skogsberg from Sweden (*Dumlupinar*); M.I. Frewer (*E.4* and *E.41*); Peter Haywood's *E.41 Newsletter*; Mrs W. Mogg; Eric Bugden (*Affray* and other British accidents); Jon Guttman of *Military History*, Leesburg, Va, USA: Barbara Davis (advice on radioactivity) and, of course, Charles Hewitt, Brigadier Henry Wilson and my friends at Pen & Sword Books Ltd.

Finally, all opinions expressed in this book are those of the author and do not necessarily reflect official views. Similarly the blame for any errors or mistakes must rest with me.

Edwyn Gray
Attleborough, Norfolk
December 2002

—ONE—

'Give us air'

On 29 January, 1917, the Royal Navy's new-fangled K-class steam submarines suddenly ceased to be a joke. From that day onwards *K* stood for *Killer*. And men of proven courage pleaded sickness, failed to report for duty on the flimsiest of excuses, and even mutinied to avoid serving in these gargantuan death traps. Of the twenty-one K-boats built* no fewer than sixteen were involved in major accidents and eight ended their careers on the bottom of the sea as rusting iron coffins.

The antics of these steam monsters and their reputation for elephantine cussedness had made them the butt of wardroom wit and a target for the mess comedian's latest obscenity for many a war-weary month. But the laughter came to an abrupt end on that fateful January morning in 1917 when the latest addition to the class, *K.13*, set off from Fairfield's yards on the Clyde for her final acceptance trials in Gareloch.

* * *

K.3, the first of the giants to go into service, had suffered more than her fair share of tribulation during her official trials. The temperature in the boiler room reached alarming heights even when the submarine was surfaced with her hatches open. And a tendency to push her bows down when meeting a head sea was not an encouraging trait to the discerning seaman.

---

*Including the M-class conversions.

She was equally unhappy under water. On one notable occasion the future King George VI, then serving as a very junior officer in the Grand Fleet, was invited aboard to watch her being put through her paces. But when her skipper, Commander Ernest Leir, proudly demonstrated the submarine's diving abilities, *K.3* simply dug her bows down hard like a recalcitrant horse refusing a fence and headed for the bottom at a steep angle. She hit the seabed with a resounding thump and stayed there with her bows buried in the mud. The water in Stokes Bay was only 150 feet deep and the submarine's stern remained poking up above the surface – her two huge bronze propellors spinning impotently in the sunshine.

Fortunately for the future of the British monarchy the crew managed to extricate the submarine from the mud without too much difficulty and, twenty minutes later, *K.3* was floating obediently on the surface once again. Prince George kept well away from submarines after that. In fact he went to the opposite extreme and took up flying.

The following January, on patrol in the North Sea and steaming at 10 knots, *K.3* again demonstrated her alarming tendency to bury her nose in the water. And when an unexpected sea suddenly crashed against her port side the water swept down the funnel intakes and swamped the boiler fires. Without power the submarine broached out of control and the sea, now on the beam and whipped into a steep chop by the strong breeze, cascaded down the funnels. By the time the hatches and funnels were finally closed the boiler room was knee-deep in water. Fortunately *K.3*, like the rest of her class, was equipped with a small auxiliary diesel engine, and Leir used this barely adequate power unit to bring the submarine's bows into the wind so that he could regain control and coax his charge safely back to Scapa Flow.

K.2 did even better than her flotilla mate: she caught fire in a spectacular manner during her initial diving trials in Portsmouth dockyard. The submarine had just submerged in one of the harbour basins when a sudden explosion sent a sheet of flame searing through the engine-room. Her skipper, Noel Laurence, surfaced hurriedly and ordered the crew to their fire stations. To the astonishment of the onlookers watching from the dockside the men tumbled out of the hatches, scooped water out of the basin with large iron buckets, and then dashed below again to help quench the flames. With an incredible lack of foresight someone had forgotten to fit the submarine with fire extinguishers and it was fortunate that this otherwise farcical incident did not develop into a major tragedy.

Not to be outdone in the comedy stakes, *K.6*, carrying out a similar submergence test at Devonport, stubbornly refused to return to the surface when the order was given to blow the ballast tanks and the fifty men inside the submarine were trapped for more than two hours before a dockyard inspector traced the trouble to a fault in the compressed air system. Not surprisingly the local dockyard workers had experienced quite enough of the K-boat's odd quirks and many of them refused to go down for a second time and further tests had to be postponed for nearly a week.

And so the saga continued. *K.4* ran aground on Walney Island during trials, while *K.11* ruined a generator when, like *K.3*, she shipped water down her funnel intakes during surface trials in heavy weather. It was hardly an encouraging beginning for a new and completely revolutionary type of submarine.

There is little doubt that many of these incidents were still fresh in the mind of Commander Godfrey Herbert DSO as he edged *K.13* out into the Clyde with the aid of two tugs. Not that he had any fears concerning his own boat. *K.13* had already carried out two test dives without trouble and, on 18 January, had reached a surface speed of 23½ knots over the measured mile to gain the honour of being the world's fastest submarine. But the K-boat jinx was never very far away. A rope entangled itself around the propellors, causing a short delay to their departure. And a potentially more dangerous incident was to occur within minutes of leaving the builder's berth when someone accidentally switched off the starter of the steering gear and put the helm out of action.

Veering out of control, *K.13* swung to the left and immediately grounded herself on a mudbank. This indiscretion was bad enough in itself, but worse was to follow. The strong ebb tide began dragging the stern downstream and, pivoting from the bows, the submarine was soon broadside on and almost completely blocking the river. The steamer *Sonnava* tried to squeeze through the narrowing gap between *K.13*'s stern and the dredger *Shieldhall* which was moored to a quay on the other side of the river. There was a shriek of rending metal as the steamer got herself sandwiched between the two boats and, after several minutes of swearing and confusion, *Sonnava*'s skipper pulled the steamer clear by going full astern.

3

Herbert tried a similar solution. *K.13* came off the mud with a shuddering lurch and then proceeded to move down the river *stern first*! It was an undignified mode of progress for one of His Majesty's ships but Herbert had no alternative and *K.13* was forced to steam backwards until she reached the junction with the River Cart where there was sufficient room to turn the submarine around and point her bows downstream in a more conventional manner.

K.13 was well loaded. In addition to her regular crew of fifty-three officers and men, she was also carrying fourteen directors and employees of her builders, Fairfields; eleven other civilian and Admiralty officials; plus the captain and engineer officer of her sister-ship *K.14*. She picked up another of Fairfield's directors and Professor Percy Hillhouse, the Company's senior naval architect, at Craigendoran Pier and by noon was heading for the placid waters of Gareloch. A short test dive en route revealed a leak in the boiler room but it was not regarded as significant and the VIPs adjourned to lunch aboard the tender *Comet* undismayed by the morning's alarming sequence of events. The leisurely meal finished at 3.15 pm and, having left two of the civilians behind on the tender, the submarine moved slowly towards the head of the loch for her final acceptance dive with exactly eighty men aboard.

The K-class design had been evolved out of fear – fear that the German Navy was building submarines capable of 20 knots on the surface – and the Admiralty demanded a submarine of even greater performance for operations with the Grand Fleet. But the primitive diesel engines then available were incapable of producing the tremendous power required to achieve the speeds desired by Whitehall. And, almost as an act of desperation, Sir Eustace Tennyson d'Eyncourt, the Director of Naval Construction, decided to use steam engines – the only form of propulsion capable of producing the horsepower necessary to thrust nearly 2,000 tons of inert steel through the sea at a surface velocity of 23 knots or more.

It was a revolutionary design, a morganatic marriage between the steam engine and the submarine, a union that had been tried several times before and had always failed. But there was no viable alternative to the shotgun wedding forced upon the unfortunate designer, and d'Eyncourt was no fool. Despite the carping of ignorant critics, many experts now consider that his steam-powered creations gave satisfactory service when due allowance has been made for their inherent limitations.

Displacing 1,883 tons the K-class were almost three times as big as any previous submarine and, with an overall length of 338 feet, they were not easy to handle. The main engines, two steam turbines fed by two oil-fired boilers, produced 10,500 horsepower and these were backed by four electric motors for underwater propulsion plus an 1,800 hp diesel unit for use on the surface while the boilers were building up pressure.

Each boat cost over £300,000 to produce and needed a crew of fifty-three men to run it efficiently. And in those halcyon days you could build a destroyer for £133,500. But in wartime money was no object and men were expendable.

Steam was, of course, only used on the surface. When diving the boilers were shut down and an ingenious system of double-acting levers first tilted the funnels over and then retracted them into special wells to clear the boiler uptakes. The resulting and rather ominous holes were then covered by circular watertight shutters. Four ventilators, shaped like giant mushrooms, helped to disperse the heat from the boiler room and these, too, could be lowered and sealed when the submarine submerged. The entire operation took four minutes to complete as against the thirty seconds diving time required by a conventional diesel-engined submarine.

Of equal importance to the crew, however, these complex design problems meant that the K-boats had six extra apertures to contend with – six more places where something could go wrong. As one matelot observed: 'A K-boat has got more holes to fill than a French whore!'

Commander Herbert, however, was easy in his mind as he took *K.13* into Gareloch for the final test dive. A careful check of the dials and instruments showed everything functioning correctly. One indicator, it is true, was seen to be flickering but Engineer Lieutenant Arthur Lane said this was due to faulty wiring and a bad contact. And Herbert had accepted the explanation. It was, however, a vitally important indicator. *It showed whether the boiler room ventilators were fully shut before diving.*

As the executive order was given *K.13* dipped under the waters of the loch and Herbert instructed the coxswain, Chief Petty Officer Oscar Moth, to trim her for twenty feet. Suddenly the quiet routine was broken.

'The boiler room is flooding freely, sir!'

Almost simultaneously Lane shouted up through the voicepipe: 'Surface at once. The boiler room is flooding.'

5

Herbert was an experienced submariner and he had already survived an earlier disaster.* He wasted no time asking questions. He rapped out an order to blow Nos. 2 and 3 tanks and surface.

The crew responded to the emergency with an efficiency born from long months of arduous training. Wheels spun, valves closed and levers were pulled. Compressed air hissed into the for'ard ballast tanks but *K.13* failed to respond. In fact she was sinking steadily by the stern and Coxswain Moth, seated in front of the depth gauges, confirmed Herbert's worst fears.

'She's out of control, sir.'

The ears of the men in the control room began to pop as the air pressure inside the submarine increased. And they knew what the sudden change in pressure signified. *K.13* was flooding at a dangerously rapid rate.

'Close watertight doors.'

'Drop for'ard keel.'

'Blow all tanks, 'planes hard a'rise.'

But the emergency measures were of no avail against the terrifying power of the sea. Nothing could arrest the downward plunge and *K.13* finally came to rest with her stern on the bottom of the loch, fifty feet down, at an angle of four degrees. As Herbert gave the order to stop motors a jet of water shot out of the voicepipe and it had to be quickly plugged to prevent the control room from suffering the same fate as the stern compartments. As

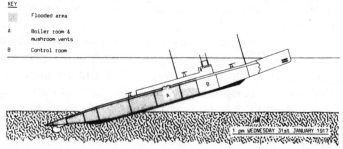

KEY

Flooded area

A   Boiler room & mushroom vents

B   Control room

1 pm WEDNESDAY 31st JANUARY 1917

if this was not enough, a fire broke out in the main switchboard which the men had to beat out with their bare hands. Other electrical circuits smouldered and flamed. Vivid blue flashes added an eerie dimension to the terrifying inferno. Choked and blinded by the fumes and smoke, and jolted by fierce electric shocks, the crew struggled to extinguish the flames and regain control. It was a race against time for the fires were consuming precious oxygen.

*See Chapter 3.

But against all the odds, with torn and bleeding hands, aching heads and smoke blackened faces, they finally succeeded.

There was an urgent knocking on the rear bulkhead of the control room and two shocked civilians tumbled through the hatchway as someone cautiously opened the watertight door. They told Herbert that all compartments aft of the midships torpedo room were flooded. Seeking confirmation, *K.13*'s captain tried to raise Lane on the telephone. But the line was silent. It was obvious that the men in the flooded stern section were already dead and Herbert wondered how much longer the rest of them would survive. The bulkheads were only designed to withstand a pressure of fifteen pounds per square inch – and the pressure of the sea at a depth of fifty-five feet was nearly twenty-five pounds per square inch. How long would the bulkheads hold?

Herbert remembered that *E.50* was also undergoing diving trials in the loch that day and, almost as a forlorn hope, he tried to communicate with the other submarine by using *K.13*'s Fessenden apparatus. But the underwater signalling device had been damaged by the fire and it failed to work. Nor was that their only problem. The rear drop-keel and the remaining half of the compressed air reserves were controlled from a panel in the engine-room and this meant it was impossible to make use of either. They were trapped. Their only hope of survival depended on the prompt action of the men on the surface. How long would it be before they realised that the submarine was in trouble?

Before ordering further emergency measures Herbert held a roll-call. Only forty-nine of the eighty men who were aboard *K.13* when she headed out into Gareloch answered to their names. Thirty-one of their shipmates were already dead, and the merciful swiftness of their end stood in sharp contrast to the probable fate of the stricken submarine.

Professor Hillhouse added to the gloom when he produced a slide-rule and began working out how much air was left and how long it would take to consume it. His answer was scarcely encouraging: eight hours at most. And further calculations showed that even if Herbert could blow every single drop of water from the forward tanks there would still be insufficient buoyancy to refloat the stricken submarine.

The dismal news filtered through the forward compartments where the men sat quietly in odd corners trying to avoid excessive movement in order to save oxygen. They were shaken by the accident but were outwardly calm and seemed to accept the verdict with resignation. Coxswain Moth, addressing no one in particular, summed up their unspoken thoughts.

'What a bloody rotten way to die.'

* * *

By four o'clock the men waiting on the surface were getting worried by *K.13*'s failure to reappear and Michell, the captain of the *E.50*, sent an urgent wireless message to the Senior Naval Officer, Clyde, reporting a probable accident and requesting immediate assistance and salvage apparatus. Six hours later the gunboat *Gossamer* set out for Gareloch, followed, shortly afterwards, by the salvage vessels *Tay* and *Thrush*. No one, it seemed, was in much of a hurry, despite the urgent nature of the emergency.

Michell had already noted an unusual rush of air when *K.13* first dived and he had taken the precaution of testing the water for the presence of acid. If the sea had entered the battery compartment the crew would have perished from chlorine gas poisoning within a few minutes. But his test proved negative, although he observed a thin stream of air bubbles rising from the depths of the loch together with small patches of floating oil. Michell was sure he had found *K.13*'s resting place and he sent two men to circle the spot in a dinghy as night closed over the grey waters. At least the salvage vessels, when they arrived, would not have to waste precious time searching for the missing submarine; and every minute saved could equal a human life.

Inside their steel tomb the survivors waited quietly – not for rescue but for death. Some settled down to write farewell letters and make-shift wills. Others tried to sleep. Sandwiches were passed around but, not surprisingly, no one felt hungry. The foul air, however, had given everyone a raging thirst but the sea had contaminated the fresh-water tank and there was nothing to drink. Herbert, wanting to conserve power, had turned off the radiators and the men were shivering with cold. Some wrapped themselves in blankets. Others huddled together seeking mutual warmth. Those who could pray did so. Those who could not tried to shut the thought of death from their minds.

The rescuers, meanwhile, were in a state of utter confusion. The Royal Navy had no emergency organization to deal with a submarine disaster and success depended on the initiative and the improvising abilities of the men on the spot – two attributes for which, fortunately, the British sailor was universally renowned. The official reaction to the situation, however, proved to be dismally inept.

Gossamer did not arrive on the scene until after midnight. She carried a diving suit but no diver. And when a qualified diver was finally located the suit was found to have perished with age and nearly drowned its wearer. *Thrush*, too, had now reached the loch. But, although designated as a salvage vessel, she possessed neither a diver nor a suit.

After an eternity of waiting a civilian diver from Fairfields made the first descent into the freezing water and began inching his way along the slippery surface of *K.13*'s hull. A morse message tapped out from inside the submarine was picked up and relayed to the surface.

All well before engine room bulkhead.

The truth, unfortunately, was less reassuring. Conditions inside the submarine were worsening. The air was slowly poisoning the trapped men and the rising level of carbon dioxide was slowing their reactions. Soon they would be unable to assist their rescuers, and most were already quietly waiting the inevitable end. According to the Professor's calculations their time had already run out.

Herbert, however, remained confident that, given the right equipment, it was still possible to salvage the submarine. His main fear was that the men on the surface would concentrate their efforts and resources on lifting the submarine instead of, first, supplying air and food to the trapped survivors. He discussed the problem in the privacy of his cabin with Commander Francis Goodhart, an experienced submariner and the captain-designate of *K.13*'s sister *K.14*, who was only on board to learn something about K-boat routine before asssuming command of his own boat. They agreed that someone should attempt to get to the surface so that they could advise the salvage team on the correct order of priorities.

They devised a plan to get into the conning-tower, build up the air pressure, and then open the hatch so that one of them could escape and float up to the surface. It was a technique that had been adopted in several previous underwater escapes, and, although dangerous, it held a good promise of success, given a modicum of luck. The two men agreed that Goodhart should make the attempt as it was Herbert's duty, as the captain of *K.13*, to remain with his crew.

A detailed report was prepared, setting out the exact conditions inside the submarine, to which Herbert, conscious of the worried relatives ashore, thoughtfully added a list of the survivors. The completed document was then sealed inside a metal watertight cylinder and fastened to Goodhart's arm. But, before the escape attempt could be made, certain preparatory work had to be carried out. A small hole would have to be cut in the side of the conning-tower and an improvised sea-cock fitted so that the flooding-up procedure could be controlled. Despite the appalling conditions inside the submarine, the work was carried out with skilful efficiency by some of the artisan workmen from Fairfields and at midday, some twenty hours after *K.13* had made her fatal dive, Herbert and Goodhart climbed into the tower and closed the lower hatch.

The success or failure of the mission was now totally dependent on the determination and nerve of the two young officers. There is nothing the Royal Navy cannot do. Or so they had been taught in their days as Dartmouth cadets. Now it was time to live up to that proud boast.

Goodhart opened the makeshift valve to let in the water and, gradually, the pressure built up as the incoming sea compressed the air inside the dark, cramped tower. When the water had risen to their waists Herbert reached forward and released the compressed air. Then, holding on to the steel supports of the ladder, he waited while Goodhart pulled the clips and opened the upper hatch.

The sudden surge of air swept *K.14*'s captain out of the compartment and Herbert caught a quick glimpse of his body streaking up through the water surrounded by a cloud of bubbles. Then, caught up by the power of the compressed air, Herbert found himself being forced upwards through the opened hatch in the wake of his companion. There was nothing he could do to resist the pressure and, releasing his grip on the supports and covering his face with his hands for protection, he allowed his body to be blown out of the conning-tower.

On board *Thrush* the first knowledge of the escape attempt was a tremendous upheaval in the water as the air rushed to the surface from the opened hatch. Suddenly, in the centre of the frothing maelstrom, a human head bobbed into view. Someone made a grab and a bedraggled and breathless Herbert was dragged to safety more dead than alive. There was, however, no sign of Goodhart.

Once he had been revived Herbert wasted no time in telling the salvage officers what conditions were like in the crippled submarine. Compressed air, he explained, was their only hope of survival – compressed air to help support the leaking engine-room bulkhead, to replenish the poisoned atmosphere inside *K.13* and, most important of all, to enable the trapped men to blow the forward ballast tanks and bring the bows nearer to the surface. The salvage men got busy.

High-pressure hoses were taken down to the stricken submarine but the divers were unable to find any means of connecting them into the hull and, while they searched for the external valves, the men on the surface weighed up the merits of several alternative plans. Captain Frederick Young, the Naval Salvage Adviser who had just arrived from Liverpool, suggested making an escape tube although he was more than a little vague how long this would take. Other salvage experts added their own pet theories. While they pitted their brains to find a solution the men inside *K.13* were slowly dying.

Hopes rose at six o'clock that evening when the divers finally managed to connect the air hose. But they were quickly dashed when it was found that, for some reason, the air was not getting through the valve. It was a heartbreaking disappointment after so much effort, and the despair of the rescuers was made all the more poignant by the series of regular morse messages being tapped against the hull plating by the entombed men:

'GIVE US AIR. GIVE US AIR.'

Conditions inside the submarine were now impossible. The poisoned air dulled the men's reactions and slowed their brain responses. Breathing was difficult and painful, and there was so little oxygen in the atmosphere that striking a match produced only a puff of smoke and no flame. Even Lieutenant Singer, upon whom command had devolved after Herbert's involuntary escape, was prostrate in his bunk suffering from delirium. But progress was being made. A hydrophone had been placed against the hull by the divers so that the men on the surface could hear what was happening inside the submarine, and a signal lamp had been rigged to pass messages through the periscope.

Soon after midnight the trouble in the air-hose was located. The experts discovered that it was blocked by several inches of ice.

11

With the temperature at freezing point the possibility should have been obvious, but working under stress at high pressure no one had stopped long enough to give the problem rational thought. As a result they had wasted seven more vital hours.

Once again the divers descended and fastened the air-hose in place. A signal was passed through the periscope and, moving with difficulty, two of the men inside the submarine cautiously opened the inboard air valve. There was a sharp hiss and moments later the life-giving compressed air was sweeping through the boat. Like men awakened from the dead the comatose survivors rose from their resting places, took deep breaths of the clean fresh air and felt their strength and determination returning. They even found the energy to cheer. And they had good reason. It was thirty-five hours since *K.13* had made her fatal plunge and they were all miraculously still alive.

Now that the atmosphere inside the hull had been revitalized the men turned their attention to the problem of getting the submarine to the surface. The compressed air was diverted to recharge the exhausted air bottles to the maximum pressure of 2,500 pounds per square inch and, as soon as they were full, orders were given to blow all available ballast tanks. At first nothing happened and the survivors were on the point of giving up hope when, suddenly, the bubbles in the depth indicators began to move. A few moments later they felt the deck tilt gently as the bows slowly rose upwards.

There was mounting excitement on the salvage vessels as the rescuers saw a surging froth of bubbling foam erupting on the surface. And at 3 am the forward periscope poked up through the tumult of white water. *Thrush*, working in unison with one of the trawlers, immediately steered through the maelstrom and passed a 6½-inch wire under the bows of the submarine to prevent it sinking back again. But, to Michell's disappointment, *K.13*'s bow section remained some eight feet or so below the surface and any immediate hope of bringing the survivors to safety via the torpedo tubes were dashed.

The rescuers now planned to rig a second pipeline through which food, drink, air and messages could be passed. And Herbert, in anticipation, had already instructed the divers to remove the brass plate covering the ventilator to the submarine's wardroom and bring it up to the surface. Expert fitters soon secured the second hose to the salvaged plate and the divers went back down into the freezing waters of the loch to replace it in position. But despite signalled instructions the men inside *K.13* seemed incapable of helping themselves. Still suffering from the effects of their terrifying entombment they could not understand what the men on the surface wanted them to do, and those who were still fit enough to think coherently were busy working in the midships torpedo room where water leaking through the engine-room bulkhead was threatening to flood the compartment.

The solitary bilge pump which they had been using to clear the water was no longer operative because of the high angle of the bows and, although they found a solution to the problem by lifting a manhole cover to an empty fuel tank which could be utilized to drain away the water, the work took two hours to complete. In normal circumstances three men could have unbolted and lifted the cover in five minutes flat.

It was dawn before the trapped men realized that they were being told to open the wardroom ventilator hatch. Gasping for breath, they reached up and pulled the clips. The poisoned air rushed up through the outlet pipe and there were sharp screams of agony from the survivors as the sudden decrease in pressure sent shafts of pain through their eardrums. Herbert, sitting in a bosun's chair slung beneath the bows of the trawler, waited for the foul air to disperse and then put his mouth to the surface end of the hose.

'Can you hear me down there?' he shouted.

'Yes – loud and clear.' It was William McClean, Fairfield's submarine manager, who answered.

'Is everyone all right?'

'We're holding out but we badly need air. And water. Has anyone seen Commander Herbert?'

'This is Herbert speaking.'

A cheer filtered up through the pipe. Herbert managed to find some words of encouragement and then passed an airline down the wide-bore hose. This was followed by brandy, milk, coffee, chocolate and beef essence. The men swallowed the drinks with the eagerness of parched camels. They had had nothing to drink for nearly forty hours.

Now that the second pipe had been safely secured the salvage officers considered that time was on the side of the rescuers. The men inside the submarine had food, drink and air in unlimited quantities. And preparations to lift *K.13* could therefore proceed slowly and methodically so that every conceivable precaution could be taken to avoid further mishaps. But Herbert and Michell both disagreed with the experts' plans. The vital engine-room bulkhead was still leaking, and, in Michell's opinion, it was likely to collapse before much longer – especially as the pressure inside the submarine had now been reduced. If it did, no power on earth could save the trapped men from the flood of water that would follow in the wake of its collapse.

While the salvage team was arguing another setback occurred when a soda bottle jammed and blocked the second pipe. All efforts to clear the obstruction failed and at 11 am the men inside *K.13* were instructed to close the inner ventilation hatch so that the pipe could be dismantled and returned to the surface for inspection. Meanwhile, and oblivious to this latest crisis, Michell was still trying to persuade his fellow-rescuers to raise the submarine's bows above the surface so that the survivors could crawl to safety through the torpedo tubes. It was only when Herbert added his support that the others reluctantly agreed.

At noon *Thrush* and the trawler, now assisted by two barges, began to haul in the wire. It was a tense moment for there was the ever-present danger of the hawser snapping under the strain. But their efforts were rewarded. The submarine's bows gradually inched upwards until, finally, they broke surface and came to rest ten feet clear of the water. Michell jumped into the skiff and rowed out to supervise the last stage of the rescue operation. And then disaster struck again!

K.13 suddenly lurched and began to slide back as her flooded stern settled deeper into the mud on the bottom of the loch. Frantic teamwork and superb seamanship by the salvage men succeeded in arresting the sinking movement. But the jinx of the K-boats had won, despite their efforts, for when the submarine came to rest the lower lips of the torpedo tubes were two inches beneath the surface. The only certain means of escape had now been rendered useless and it is not difficult to imagine the despair of the trapped survivors when they were given the news through the voicepipe. To compound their despondency a fuse blew on the main switchboard extinguishing all but one of the interior lights. Apart from the glimmer of illumination offered by three emergency hand torches the submarine was now in complete darkness.

After a great deal of heated discussion the experts finally agreed to accept Herbert's suggestion that a hole should be cut into the bow section with an oxy-acetylene torch.

'Damned bad salvage,' was the view of the senior salvage

adviser Captain Young. 'You can close the torpedo tubes if the need arises but you can't close a hole cut by a blow-torch.' He himself, favoured trying to lift *K.13* again so that the torpedo tubes were clear of the water. But that would have entailed more delay while heavy lifting gear and floating cranes were obtained.

Another expert warned that the accumulation of gases in the ballast tanks could explode when they came into contact with the flame of the torch. But desperate situations demanded drastic remedies. Time was now firmly against them. And, reluctantly, everyone agreed that risks would have to be taken.

Once again there were further delays and setbacks and it was three o'clock in the afternoon of the second day before the preliminary hole, just two feet square, was cut through the plating of the forward deck. There was a further hold-up when the space between the outer and inner hulls was found to be flooded and it was some time before the men inside the submarine were able to open the valves to drain off the water. A suction pipe was sent down to speed up the process and finally, at eight o'clock that evening, the task of cutting through the pressure hull commenced.

The dazzling flame of the blowtorch threw an eerie blue light over the scene and the roar of the pressurised oxy-acetylene gas was magnified by the echoing walls of the cramped working space. The steel plates glowed redly as the flame bit into the metal and the eyes behind the dark goggles narrowed with concentration as the rectangular hole was slowly completed. The anxious men watching from the salvage ships saw the crouched figure suddenly straighten up and push back the protective goggles. Then an arm waved vigorously.

'The hole's cut,' he shouted.

Inside *K.13* discipline still prevailed. Lieutenant Singer moved across to examine the narrow aperture and ran his fingers along the heat-blackened edge. Looking upwards he could see the stars twinkling. Turning away, he faced the assembled survivors,

'Civilians first!'

It was just after nine o'clock when the first of the entombed men climbed out through the hole and a tremendous cheer greeted his appearance. Large arc-lamps had been rigged on the rescue ships and the area around the protruding bows of the submarine was as brightly lit as a scene from a searchlight tattoo on Navy Day. One by one the survivors came through the jagged opening where they were met by the rescuers who were waiting to shepherd them to the warmth and safety of the *Thrush*. Herbert himself squatted on the casing to give a welcoming hand to each man as he appeared in the opening.

It took nearly an hour to bring out the forty-seven survivors and, in accordance with tradition, the senior officer, Paris Singer, was the last to leave the boat. He looked pale and drawn in the stark glare of the searchlights but, despite his terrible ordeal, he managed to conjure up a smile. His relief was understandable. The submarine had been on the bottom for an incredible fifty-seven hours. According to every scientific textbook on the subject he should have been dead. Yet, in spite of the impossible odds, the Lieutenant and his companions were still alive. Even today the experts do not know how they survived.

Not surprisingly, for all its muddle, confusion and inefficiency, the saga of the *K.13* ranks as one of the most successful rescue operations in submarine history. In the pages that follow we will encounter many disasters. Some end in triumph, some in tragedy. But none, for sheer endurance, can equal the story of *K.13*.

A full-scale salvage operation began the next day but the water which had been leaking through the damaged engine-room bulkhead partially flooded the torpedo compartment within a few hours and the additional weight over-strained the lifting wires, causing them to break and *K.13* sank slowly to the bottom. And Michell's earlier fears about the bulkhead were proved to be justified. When the divers went down the following morning they located Goodhart's body trapped under the roof of the wheelhouse. They also found that all four of the great mushroom ventilators were open to the sea and that, for some reason, they had not been sealed off when the submarine began its dive. Even more alarming, their investigations revealed that the indicators in the engine-room clearly showed that the ventilators were open. The Engineer Officer *must* have been aware of the danger even though he apparently chose to ignore the warnings given by his own instruments. And in the course of their examination the divers made another and even more puzzling discovery. The engine-room hatch was unfastened.

Faced by such overwhelming evidence, the Admiralty Court of Inquiry, which was convened on 19 February, had no hesitation in placing the blame for the disaster squarely on the shoulders of Engineer Lieutenant Arthur Lane. As he had died in the aft section of the submarine he was unable to defend his reputation.

Despite the young officer's excellent record and previously exemplary reports the Court's President, Captain Godfrey Corbett, pronounced the Inquiry's unanimous verdict: 'Engineer Lieutenant Lane was solely responsible for the accident.'

While the Court was considering the evidence, the salvage operation continued and, in the course of their work, the divers found a probable explanation for the mystery of the partially opened engine-room hatch. A careful search of the flooded stern section revealed only twenty-nine bodies; and one of the missing victims was Engineer Lieutenant Lane.

After a reconstruction of the events immediately following the disaster, the Navy's experts concluded that Lane and the other missing man, John Steel, had managed to open the engine-room hatch and make their escape before the compartment was completely flooded. It was assumed that both men had drowned before reaching the surface. This theory was confirmed two months later when Lane's body was found on the banks of the Clyde. And after an inquest he was laid to rest alongside his fellow victims in the cemetery at Faslane. The body of John Steel was never recovered.

K.13 was raised to the surface six weeks after her fatal plunge on 29 January. In mid-March she was towed into Fairfield's yards for refitting. Some months later, with minimal ceremony, she was recommissioned into the Royal Navy as the *K.22*. Less than a year later the *K.22* was to feature in another and even more terrible disaster, but that story will be told in a subsequent chapter.

In the sixteen years between 1917 and 1932 over 300 men lost their lives in K-class and converted K-class submarines; and all died as the result of accidents. Not one single man was killed by enemy action. In fact only one K-boat ever attacked a German ship. On 16 June 1917 *K.7*, under the command of Lieutenant-Commander Gilbert Kellet, fired a spread of four torpedoes at the *U-95* when she ambushed the U-boat on the surface. Three of the torpedoes missed the target and the only one to strike home failed to explode. It was a typical example of the jinx that haunted the K-boats.

Admiral Sir John Fisher once commented, 'I have not yet mastered on what basis our submarines harm the enemy more than themselves.' The K-boats did not exist when Fisher made that remark in 1914, but so far as these steam dinosaurs of the sea were concerned it proved to be remarkably prophetic.

—TWO—

'Into perpetual night'

Doctor Cornelius Van Drebbel, a Dutch physician working in England under the patronage of King James I, built and demonstrated the world's first practical submarine in 1620 when, so it is recorded, 'he calmly dived under the water' while the King and several thousand Londoners lining the banks of the Thames at Whitehall waited to see if he would come up again. Fortunately he did, and became the hero of the hour.

Modern historians now doubt both the validity of Van Drebbel's claims and the veracity of contemporary chronicles. The boat, they say, was no more than a semi-submersible. And, allowing that there is an element of truth in the account of his trip from Westminster to Greenwich, they conclude that the vessel merely ran awash and was carried downstream by the current rather than by the exertions of the four rowers inside. Bearing in mind that Van Drebbel's 'submarine' was constructed of wood covered by greased leather and propelled by two pairs of oars that verdict is probably near to the truth.

William Bourne, in 1578, had designed a similar craft. This, too, was powered by oars but his screw-operated bilge tank ballast system for obtaining positive or negative buoyancy was considerably more sophisticated than Van Drebbel's water-filled pigskin bags. But as Bourne's design never got beyond the drawing-board the honour for producing the first 'submarine' must remain with the Dutchman.

Other inventors followed. The Frenchman De Son – basing his

design on a book written by the English divine, Bishop Wilkins, in 1648 – went to Rotterdam to build a submarine in 1653. It was never properly tested at sea as De Son could not obtain a sufficiently powerful clockwork motor to operate the boat's internal paddle-wheel. Having spent all his money, he was reduced to exhibiting his creation at local fairs and markets in an effort to recoup his investment.

While there was no dearth of would-be submarine designers few had the temerity to convert their paper dreams to reality. Those that did took great care not to tempt fate by taking their inventions beneath the water despite their often wildly exaggerated claims.

In 1747 Nathanial Symons, described by a contemporary writer as 'a common country carpenter', built a submarine which he successfully demonstrated on the River Dart in front of several hundred people. Like the two earlier practical submarine builders, Van Drebbel and De Son, Symons based his vessel on the theoretical drawings of another person – in this case the Abbe Giovanni-Alfonso Borelli whose plans were published posthumously in his *De Motu Animalium* in 1680. It is, however, somewhat difficult to understand how an illiterate country craftsman could chance upon and, even more puzzling, understand a learned work that had been published abroad and was written in Latin.

It is even stranger that, while Borelli had thought in terms of goatskin bottles for altering the buoyancy of his boat along similar lines to those adopted by Van Drebbel, Symons dipped further back into the past and used a variation of Bourne's bilge tank ballast system.

The fact that the only reference to Symons appears in a contemporary periodical, *The Gentleman's Magazine*, may help to explain these apparent oddities. For journalists then, as today, often possessed vivid imaginations and were not beyond dressing up a story to suit the requirements of their readers. Suffice it to say that, according to the magazine's account, Symons successfully submerged his vessel for forty-five minutes and returned to the surface none the worse for the experience. The age of the submarine disaster was yet to come. And, in the time-scale of history, it came rather sooner than expected.

In 1774, nearly thirty years after Symons' experiments, a Suffolk wagon-maker, John Day, built a watertight compartment inside an old fishing boat, ballasted the vessel with large stones, and submerged in thirty feet of water in a convenient village pond near Yarmouth. After what he considered to be an appropriate period of time – he later claimed it to be twenty-four hours – he released the stones and returned to the surface unscathed. 'Elated with success', he decided to stage a public demonstration.

Day was an odd character. Apart from being both 'illiterate and indigent', it was said that 'his temper was gloomy, reserved and peevish, and his disposition penurious.' He was also said to be 'remarkably obstinate in his opinions and jealous of his fame.'

Certainly it was fame that he sought, and he went about it in an unusual manner. Unable or unwilling to use his own money to construct a larger boat Day wrote to a notorious gambler and man-about-town, Christopher Blake. The deal he offered was simple and straight-forward. If Blake would put up the cash he, Day, would build a new submarine and make them both rich men.

It was exactly the right sort of bait to attract a professional gambler and Blake closed the deal promptly. He advanced Day £350 and offered to give him 10% of all his winnings from the wagers he intended to take on the success of the inventor's enterprise. He tactfully omitted to explain that he was, in effect, betting on his protégé's life.

Day bought an old 50-ton sloop, *Maria*, and started work. He constructed a watertight compartment amidships similar to that in his original submarine and placed seventy-five empty hogsheads inside for additional buoyancy. Ten tons of ballast was packed into the hold and a further twenty tons was slung beneath the keel by means of ropes which could be released from inside the watertight compartment. He then painted the boat bright red and announced that he intended to take *Maria* down to 300 feet and remain submerged for twenty-four hours. Blake hurriedly amended Day's brash announcement to 130 feet and twelve hours.

On 20 June, 1774, *Maria* was towed out of Plymouth harbour to the strains of a local brass band and the cheers of the assembled crowd. While Day prepared for his demonstration dive Blake moved among the onlookers taking last-minute wagers on the success of the venture. In the early afternoon the little procession of boats located an area of water where soundings showed the required depth of 130 feet. Day, taking with him a wax candle, a box of biscuits and a bottle of water, climbed aboard the *Maria* 'with great composure' where eager helpers were waiting to batten him down inside the watertight compartment. The disposable ballast was added and the assistants had barely time to jump clear as the submarine sank out of sight, or, as one chronicler put it: 'Mr Day descended with her into perpetual night'.

Sadly, but not surprisingly, John Day never returned to the surface. Attempts were made to grapple the boat and raise it but the would-be salvers met with no success. Blake, sensing disaster, had vanished with the stake money. And a local doctor told the assembled crowd that 'considering the depth I can assure you that Mr Day froze to death'.

The learned physician was wrong. Water pressure increases by 15 pounds per square inch for every 30 feet of depth. At 130 feet Day's boat would have been subjected to a pressure of more than 60 pounds per square inch and it is highly probable that *Maria* broke up long before she ever reached the bottom of the sea. Certainly Day never released any of the coloured floats which he had said he would send up at intervals during his descent.

But, despite his ignorance and obstinacy, John Day was a brave man and he has earned an honourable place in history as the first person to lose his life in a submarine disaster. The first, sadly, of many thousands of other equally courageous men.

Fifty years were to pass before the next submarine fatalities, although experiments continued and pioneers like the Pennsylvania-born David Bushnell, who built the *Turtle* in 1775, and another American, Robert Fulton, made considerable progress in the science of submarine design and underwater warfare. Records, however, are irritatingly scant until the middle of the nineteenth century.

The Spanish inventor, Cervo, built a spherical submarine which he demonstrated to the public in 1831. The vessel performed well on the surface but disappeared without trace on its first dive. Equally unfortunate was a French physician, Doctor Petit, from Amiens. He tested his submarine at St Valery-sur-Somme in 1834 and, satisfied with its capabilities on the surface, decided, literally, to take the plunge and test it underwater. Some hours later, when the tide went out, the anxious spectators found Petit's self-made coffin resting forlornly in the mud of the estuary, tilted to one side and full of water. The submarine had claimed its third victim.

A more successful venture also ended in tragedy some seventeen years later in 1851. An American shoemaker, Lodner D. Philips, built and tested two 40-foot submarines of cylindrical design with cone-shaped ends. Both were powered by hand-operated propellers and the trim was regulated through a series of manually controlled ballast tanks. One boat, equipped with a saw, was intended for underwater survey and exploration while the second, armed with a primitive gunpowder limpet mine, was constructed for military purposes. Unlike their two immediate predecessors, both submarines worked.

Large crowds assembled to watch Philips diving in Lake Michigan and ample evidence exists to confirm that his boats were capable of prolonged submergence. On one occasion he sawed through a 14-inch block of wood underwater and, on another, he produced a detailed survey report on the formation of the lake bed. His wife and two children often accompanied him on exploratory dives and there is little doubt that Philips produced a perfectly serviceable submarine, allowing, of course, for the limits imposed by the technology of the period.

Moving to Lake Erie, Philips carried out further experiments and set out to make another underwater survey. Unfortunately this time the submarine did not return to the surface and it is assumed that his fragile craft was crushed by the pressure of the water when he dived too deep.

The same year, 1851, also saw the first successful escape from a sunken submarine when Wilhelm Bauer and his two-man crew escaped from *Der Brandtaucher* as it lay crippled and flooded on the bottom of Kiel harbour.

Although a Bavarian by birth and a carpenter by trade, Bauer was a corporal in the Prussian Light Horse Artillery. In 1850 he found himself stationed in Kiel during one of the frequent Schleswig-Holstein border disputes. When Danish warships began blockading the harbour, Bauer, who had been studying the problems of underwater navigation for some years, approached the authorities and offered to build a submarine which, he claimed, would destroy the enemy fleet.

His project was approved and, with the aid of a local ironsmith, Bauer set to work to build his machine. *Der Brandtaucher*, or *Sea Diver*, was constructed from sheet-iron boiler plates. When completed it proved to be a slab-sided monstrosity weighing some 38 tons. It measured 26½ feet in length with a beam of 6 feet and a depth of 9 feet. It had four large glass observation windows set in its sides. There was no engine and motive power was provided by a handwheel geared to a propellor in the stern. A large weight fitted to a threaded bar which ran almost the full length of the boat was used to control the horizontal trim and, although only a rudimentary device, it worked adequately. Ballast tanks operated by a manual pump adjusted the submarine's buoyancy and its offensive capability consisted of two leather 'gloves', which, operated from inside the boat, could be used to attach explosive mines to the keels of enemy ships. That, at least, was the theory.

Bauer's extraordinary vessel was never seriously tested in action for as soon as the Danes saw the submarine creeping towards them on the surface they hurriedly abandoned their blockade and fled. It was a moral rather than a military victory but it showed that the mere threat of a submarine attack could be as potent and effective as the attack itself – a fact of life that remains evident even today and which played an important part in determining the dispositions of both British and Argentine surface ships during the Falklands War.

The Danes, however, quickly renewed the blockade from a safer distance. The Prussian authorities asked Bauer to frighten them away again and, accompanied by two crewmen, Freidrich Witt and Wilhelm Thomsen, he set out across Kiel harbour on 1 February, 1851, for a second and more decisive confrontation with the enemy.

All went well at first. The hatches were secured, the valves were opened to admit water into the ballast tanks and, as the balance weight was moved towards the bows, *Der Brandtaucher* dipped slowly and obediently beneath the surface. The water in the harbour was shallow and safe for diving but, unfortunately, there was an uncharted hole in the seabed some 60 feet deep at the precise spot Bauer had chosen to submerge. So, instead of gently settling on the bottom, *Der Brandtaucher* continued sinking with accelerated momentum. Witt lost control of the balance weight and the submarine plunged deeper and deeper. Water began to pour into the hull through a dozen leaking seams, rivets popped on all sides, and the sheet-iron plating buckled ominously under the intense pressure. The manual pump could not cope with the inrush of water and, to make the situation even more dangerous, the pig-iron ballast in the bilges broke free and slid down the canted deck to add even more weight to the already over-heavy bow section.

Completely out of control *Der Brandtaucher* dropped like a stone until she came to rest in an almost vertical position with her nose buried in the muddy bottom of the harbour. No one could possibly survive such a disaster. The forward section of the boat was flooded, the hull was in imminent danger of collapse, and the air that remained was trapped in the stern.

Bauer realised that the pressure of the sea on the hatch would prevent him from opening it. But his rudimentary knowledge of theoretical physics suggested a solution. If the air inside the submarine could be compressed until it equalled the pressure of the water outside the hull, the hatch could be pushed open with ease and, given a modicum of luck, they could swim to the surface.

Rather foolishly Bauer omitted to explain his scheme to Witt and Thomsen, and when he began unscrewing one of the valves to admit more water into the submarine to compress the air his two assistants thought he had gone mad. There was a wild fight in the darkened boat which ended with Bauer being pinned down on the deck by the two brawny seamen. He tried to explain the theory that lay behind his apparently crazy scheme, but the two sailors took a great deal of persuasion and it speaks volumes for Bauer's forceful personality that they finally allowed him to get up. Then the three men huddled together in the darkness to discuss the pros and cons of Bauer's plan.

Four hours later no agreement had been reached and the air had become dangerously contaminated by the rising level of carbon dioxide. Breathing was difficult and their heads ached. But Bauer still failed to convince his two companions that his apparently suicidal scheme would work. Witt and Thomsen were simple men and the concept of compressed air was beyond their comprehension.

Suddenly the arguing voices were stilled as the men heard the clatter of a grappling hook scraping against the hull: the worried rescuers on the surface were trying to locate and lift the submarine to safety. Their initial relief, however, quickly turned to terror when they realized that the heavy steel hook might break the glass windows in the side of the vessel. In the face of this new threat, Witt and Thomsen agreed to try Bauer's plan.

Fumbling in the darkness, they located the valve wheels and slowly flooded the boat. The growing increase in air pressure threatened to burst their eardrums as, inch by inch, the water crept up their bodies. Bauer carefully positioned them beneath the after-hatch and waited to see if his theory would work. As the water began lapping under his chin even *he* started to entertain doubts.

Yielding suddenly to the immense pressure the heavy iron hatch burst open without warning and the three gasping survivors found

24

themselves being swept to the surface in a giant bubble of air. Wilhelm Bauer, Thomson and Witt had gained their place in the pages of history as the first men to escape from a sunken submarine. But Germany's tentative flirtation with the *Unterseeboot* had come to an inglorious end.

Der Brandtaucher was left to rust on the bottom, an abandoned and useless hulk. But in 1887 an enterprising salvage team succeeded in raising the relic and it was taken to the Naval School at Kiel. In 1906 it was removed to the Berlin Naval Museum where it remains on display to this day.

Undeterred by adversity, Bauer continued his experiments. Refused further financial support by his Prussian masters, and rebuffed in Austria, he set out for England in 1853 to look for a new patron. There he obtained an introduction to the Prince Consort, who was impressed by the claims of the young Bavarian. At the time of the Great Exhibition Prince Albert had become acquainted with John Scott Russell, one of the members of the Royal Commission that had organized the event. Russell, a business associate of the legendary Isambard Kingdom Brunel as well as a leading engineer and shipbuilder, seemed the most likely person to help.

A great deal of nonsense has been written about Bauer's sojourn in England and the submarines with which he was involved. And, as one of these boats met with a disastrous end, this seems an appropriate place to set the record straight.

By an arrangement with the Admiralty, although it is not clear how this august body came to be a party to the scheme, Scott Russell employed Bauer at his Millwall shipyard on London's Isle of Dogs and gave him a free hand to develop his ideas. All went well at first. Bauer was happily at work perfecting his drawings while Scott Russell was busily arguing with Brunel over the construction of the *Great Eastern* which was being built in the Millwall yards at that time.

Bauer, however, was an odd character and his inability to speak or understand English made him unduly suspicious. He convinced himself that someone was examining his drawings while he was absent from his office. And when, in April, 1854, he read a newspaper report about a submarine that Scott Russell was building he accused Russell and Sir Charles Fox, an eminent harbour engineer, of pirating his work.

The inventor left England as a result of this fracas and, taking his drawings and a working scale model of his new boat the *Diable Marin* with him, he made his way across Europe to Russia in search of a new patron.

He had however been right in one respect. Scott Russell *was* building his own submarine at Millwall. But it was a very different conception to Bauer's new design and, to be honest, greatly inferior. Russell's biographer described it as 'a diving bell shaped like an inverted boat and propelled by a two-man crew walking along the bottom of the sea, pushing against the thwarts fixed to the underside of the vessel. The idea of blowing out the ballast tanks with compressed air ... was introduced but control required a cool head and the operation a good deal of nerve.'*

Palmerston's government approved an appropriation of £7,000 for the development of the boat and even Disraeli got wind of the experiments, writing to Lord Derby on 20 November, 1855: 'Palmerston is for blowing up Kronstadt having got a discoverer who builds submarine ships worked by submarine crews who are practising on the Thames with, they say, complete success.'

The Admiralty observer, Sir Ashley Cooper-Key, did not share Disraeli's optimism and his reports suggest that, far from being a success, the trials were disastrous. According to one contemporary account 'the boat went directly to the bottom with nine of her crew' – a difficult feat for a two-man submarine. Another report claims that the boat never surfaced from its first dive and that three men were lost.

It is clear that Scott Russell's submarine was unsuccessful and there is official evidence that an unspecified number of fatalities occurred. But the end of the Crimean War meant that there was no longer a demand for a military submersible and Russell quietly abandoned his creation.

Bauer, however, had now arrived in St Petersburg where, with the backing of the Grand Duke Constantine and based on the plans he had prepared at Millwall, he built *Le Diable Marin* – his most successful boat to date. Like *Der Brandtaucher* it was constructed from sheet-iron boiler plates and was 52 feet long with a 12-foot beam. Propulsion was provided by a treadwheel which operated a three-bladed screw at the stern and Bauer also devised an improved method of depth-keeping. The boat was launched in May, 1855, and between then and October 1856 Bauer, with his 13-man crew,

*_John Scott Russell_ by George S. Emmerson. John Murray 1977.

carried out 134 dives reaching depths of up to 150 feet – proof, if such was needed, that the submarine was well constructed and able to withstand the tremendous pressures that had destroyed earlier vessels.

On one well-publicized occasion Bauer shipped a four-piece orchestra aboard *Le Diable Marin* and serenaded Tzar Alexander II from beneath the surface of Kronstadt harbour in celebration of the Emperor's coronation. But the Russian admirals, aware of Bauer's lowly army rank, regarded him as an ignorant upstart and they seethed with indignation when they saw the inventor basking in the glow of the Tzar's favour. In an attempt to bring him down a peg they demanded that Bauer should stage a demonstration of *Le Diable Marin* in its proper role as a naval vessel and not as an underwater musical-box. Kronstadt harbour, the scene of Bauer's previous triumph, was chosen as the venue and the Bavarian was ordered to sink a ship to prove that his submarine had an offensive capability.

The Russian 'dirty tricks' brigade were apparently involved in the admirals' scheme for, unknown to Bauer, the target vessel was carefully moored behind an invisible submerged mudbank.

All went well during the initial stages of the dummy attack and *Le Diable Marin* was running beneath the surface as she approached her prey. Bauer, however, was steering blind and, with only a compass as his guide, he was in blissful ignorance of the obstruction that lay ahead. Suddenly, just a hundred yards short of the anchored target ship, the submarine shuddered to a halt as it ran into the mudbank. Fortunately Bauer was already an old hand at underwater disasters. Ordering the forward ballast tank to be pumped clear, he told the four men working the treadwheel to go into reverse. But strands of seaweed had become entangled in the propellor and the submarine stubbornly refused to back off the mudbank, although the bows were slowly rising as the ballast tank emptied.

Bauer released the keel weights and, to the surprise of the watching admirals, the bows of the submarine broke surface like a vast sea monster coming up for air. The forward hatch flew open and moments later the crew were clambering out to safety. Bauer, as befitted his position, was the last to leave. But as he tried to close the hatch *Le Diable Marin* slid back slightly and the sea quickly engulfed the helpless vessel before the hatch-cover could be replaced. Bauer was dragged clear in the nick of time as the submarine sank to the bottom. It was a serious setback for Bauer's ambitions but he had proved, once again, that escape from a crippled submarine was possible.

Le Diable Marin was raised four weeks later but sank off Ochda shortly afterwards, fortunately with no casualties. Exactly what happened is uncertain but several accounts suggest that the Russian admirals deliberately scuttled the submarine in deep water where salvage would be impossible.

This episode was virtually Bauer's last contribution to the evolution of the submarine. His plans for yet another boat vanished in a welter of bureaucratic red-tape and, disillusioned with Tzarist Russia, he went to France to seek the support of Napoleon III. The Emperor was sympathetic but unhelpful and Bauer continued his travels in search of financial backing for several years before finally returning to his native Bavaria where he died, almost penniless, in 1875.

In the meantime, on the other side of the Atlantic, the American Civil War had produced a renewed interest in submarines and, in an attempt to balance the greater naval strength of the Northern States, the Confederates turned their attention to underwater weapons, notably mines – or torpedoes as they were then known – and submersibles.

Their first designs were not true submarines but their partial success in the attack on the *USS New Ironsides* during the blockade of Charleston was ample proof of their potential. These semi-submersibles, generically classified as *Davids*, were steam-powered and armed with a spar torpedo. Forty feet in length, with a cigar-shaped hull, they steamed towards the target with their upperworks awash so that only a small observation turret and a spindly smokestack showed above the surface. The moral success of these semi-submersibles turned Confederate thoughts in the direction of a *real* submarine, and this led to the construction of the *H.L. Hunley*, without doubt the most jinxed submarine the world has ever seen.

The story of the *Hunley* began in New Orleans in 1862 when two Confederate naval officers, Horace L. Hunley and James R. McLintock, together with a civilian engineer, Baxter Watson, designed and built a small submarine which they named *Pioneer*. The three men applied for a Letter of Marque on 29 March, 1862, and appended details of the boat to the relevant document: 'the said vessel ... is 34 feet in length, is 4 feet breadth (and) is 4 feet deep. She measures about 4 tons; has conical round ends and is painted black ... She will carry a magazine of explosive* and will be manned by two men or more.'

The necessary letter of authority was issued two days later and *Pioneer* began a series of tests in Lake Pontchartrain. According to some sources the little submarine and her crew of three were lost in the lake during diving trials. Other accounts say that it was scuttled to avoid capture when Captain Farragut's Union fleet threatened the city. Sixteen years later the rusty remains of the *Pioneer* were located on the lake bottom by two young swimmers and the historic relic is now on display at Presbyterre.

The *Pioneer* was the Confederacy's first true submarine, as opposed to the semi-submersible *Davids*, but the records show that the Union Navy had produced an underwater vessel, based on the designs of a French engineer called de Villeroi, almost a year earlier. The *Alligator*, as she was named, was armed with a spar torpedo and her motive power was provided by a crew of sixteen men working a hand-cranked propellor. She was lost in a storm while under tow from Philadelphia to Chesapeake Bay on 2 April, 1863.

Hunley, McLintock and Watson managed to escape from enemy-occupied New Orleans and gain the relative safety of Mobile. It was here that they set about building an improved version of the *Pioneer* in the workshops of Parks & Lyons. The new boat, also designed by McLintock, was 25 feet long and resembled an ungainly oblong box with tapered ends. Just how successful it might have been will never be known, for, like the enemy's *Alligator*, it sank in a storm as it was being towed from Mobile to Fort Morgan in readiness for operations against the North's blockade fleet. Fortunately, no lives were lost.

When the authorities refused to countenance the cost of a third boat, Hunley, a true Southern patriot, offered to construct a submarine, to be built to his own design, which he was prepared to finance from his own resources. Not surprisingly his offer was accepted.

Joined by W.A. Alexander, the *Pioneer* team returned to Parks & Lyons and began working on what was fated to be known for ever afterwards as the *Hunley*. The design was based on a 25-foot

---

*So far as can be ascertained the explosive charge was in the form of a towed similar in function to the British Harvey weapon.

long and 4-foot diameter boiler cylinder which was cut into two horizontal lengths. An iron strip, twelve inches wide, was inserted between these two halves, one on each side, and the four sections were then carefully riveted together to form the main body of the boat. Bulkheads were added at both ends of the modified cylinder and the hull was completed with slightly pointed bow and stern sections. When finished the submarine measured 30 feet on the fore and aft line with a beam of 4 feet. But the headroom, despite the addition of the iron strips, was only five feet and it was impossible for the crew to stand upright.

Two small hatchways for access to the interior were provided in the bow and stern ends and their circular cast-iron covers could be bolted shut from within the boat, rubber gaskets around the rim of each opening ensuring a watertight seal. Both hatches were mounted in low conning-towers fitted with glass observation ports and, lying along the centre-line between the two hatches, was a primitive snorkel tube, a hinged 1-inch diameter pipe, some four feet in length, through which air could be drawn from the surface while submerged. Although rudimentary, the *Hunley* was a well-conceived design and it was certainly a great improvement on its predecessors.

Propulsion was, like other pioneer submarines, manual. Eight men, seated lengthwise down one side of the vessel, turned a cranked shaft which rotated a helical propellor in the stern. The captain stood with his head inside the forward conning-tower while a second officer, who also acted as the eighth member of the cranking

CSS HUNLEY (1863)

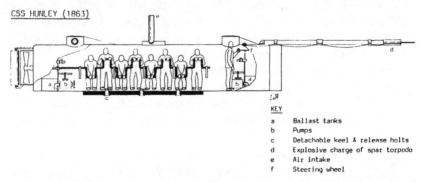

KEY

a	Ballast tanks
b	Pumps
c	Detachable keel & release bolts
d	Explosive charge of spar torpedo
e	Air intake
f	Steering wheel

team, was positioned under the rear hatch next to the controls of the stern ballast tanks. It was a tight fit for nine men. And once the officers had taken up their stations inside the conning-towers there was absolutely no avenue of escape for the rest of the crew.

Navigational aids, too, were conspicuous by their absence. The captain, apart from a mercury depth gauge, was only provided with a small magnetic compass. For illumination of the boat's gloomy interior after it had submerged the crew had to be content with candles.

The new submarine was completed by September, 1863, and, after a series of diving tests in the Mobile River, she was pronounced seaworthy. But Hunley felt that the vessel's potential would be wasted in the Mobile area and she was shipped to Charleston where there were better opportunities for attacking the enemy.

John Payne, a Lieutenant in the Confederate Navy, was appointed in command and a suitable berth was found for the South's secret weapon in the Chapel Street dock. But tragedy struck with unexpected swiftness. Within hours of his arrival in Charleston, Lieutenant Payne was ordered to take the *Hunley* for a trial run so that her crew could gain some experience before going into action. Their training programme must have been one of the shortest on record. For as the submarine was being carefully cranked away from the quayside the wake of the paddle-steamer *Etiwan* surged over the half-submerged boat. Water rushed into the still-opened hatches and the *Hunley* went to the bottom like a stone. Payne, stationed in the forward hatchway, managed to scramble clear but the other eight men were drowned. It was scarcely an encouraging start.

Raising the submarine presented few difficulties although the subsequent removal of the bodies was a gruesome experience. A new crew was quickly recruited and, with Payne at the helm, the *Hunley* set off for a fresh series of trials. But disaster struck again. A sudden squall blew up while the boat was outside the lee of the harbour and, caught on the surface with both hatches open, the submarine was swamped and sunk by the heavy seas. Payne was fortunate to escape with his life for the second time and on this occasion two other men also managed to struggle free as the boat went down. But *Hunley* had claimed six more victims and she was beginning to acquire an unenviable reputation.

A few days later the submarine was raised and towed back to Charleston. And even while the six coffins were being carried to the cemetery, notices were posted calling for further volunteers.

Although Payne was probably to blame for causing the first two disasters by his failure to close the forward hatch, he could not be held responsible for the next tragedy. *Hunley* was secured to another ship in the Fort Johnson dock when it happened. Without detailed records it is difficult to know what went wrong. The other vessel began to swing at its moorings, possibly as the result of tidal currents, and smashed against the side of the submarine. With little lateral stability, and only marginal reserve buoyancy, *Hunley* listed sharply under the impact. She was struck again and her vulnerable hatchways, which were open to ventilate the interior, dipped beneath the surface as she heeled over further. Within moments the sea had flooded her from stem to stern and she vanished, yet again, into the depths of the harbour. Incredibly John Payne escaped for a third time and three other members of the crew were able to get clear. But five more men had died and the *Hunley*'s evil reputation was confirmed.

The death toll from accidents had now risen to nineteen and General Beauregard, Charleston's commander, was so shocked by the tragedies that he refused to let Payne raise the submarine again. But McLintock, like Payne, retained his faith in the boat and he pleaded with the General for permission to salvage it. He blamed the accidents on bad handling – a reflection, surely, on Payne – and told Beauregard, 'If I can bring my own men down from Mobile, the men who built her, we'll prove that she can fight.'

Beauregard reluctantly agreed. His task was to defend Charleston no matter what the cost, and men, after all, were expendable. Having obtained permission, McLintock sent a message to Mobile and a few days later Hunley and some of the men from Parks & Lyons arrived to crew the salvaged boat. After all that had happened they must have been very brave men indeed.

The submarine was thoroughly checked and, with Hunley replacing Payne as captain and Thomas Parks acting as the Second Officer, the boat was taken to the Stone River for further trials. The original crew from Mobile seemed to understand the eccentricities of the vessel and, in the course of the next few days, she performed a series of successful diving tests in full view of the crowds lining the waterfront.

At 9.25 am on 15 October, 1863, the submarine cast off from the jetty and was cranked into the estuary. Hunley, apparently wanting to check the boat's behaviour in a steep dive, opened the sea-cock to the forward ballast tank but, for some reason, subsequently forgot to close it. Water lapped over the top of the for'ard bulkhead and within minutes it was swirling around the ankles of the men operating the cranking apparatus. What happened after that can only be a matter of guesswork.

According to the official *Journal of Operations* the submarine 'left the wharf at 9.25 am and disappeared at 9.35. As soon as she sank air bubbles were seen to rise and from this fact it is supposed that the hole (sic) in the top ... by which the men entered was not properly closed'. Subsequent examination of the submarine after it had been raised showed that the tragedy had been caused by the forgotten sea-cock and not by an insecurely fastened hatch.

General Beauregard was present when she was brought up. 'The spectacle was indescribably ghastly,' he wrote afterwards. 'The unfortunate men were contorted into all sorts of horrible attitudes, some clutching candles . . . others laying in the bottom tightly grappled together. And the blackened faces of all presented the expression of their despair and agony'. Experts who examined the boat considered that some of the trapped men had drowned in the first few minutes while the others, including Hunley and Parks, had probably lived for an hour or so before dying from suffocation. They had certainly tried to escape for both officers were found with their arms raised as if trying to open the hatches.

Hunley should have been left on the bottom of the river as a memorial to the twenty-eight men who had sacrificed their lives, but in time of war human lives count for little and another crew was recruited from the receiving ship *Indian Chief*, although, before volunteering, each man was warned of the submarine's terrible record.

During a familiarization work-out the new crew was ordered to make a dummy attack on the *Indian Chief*. A Confederate officer has left an eye-witness acount of what happened: 'Lieutenant Dixon and myself stood on the wharf as she passed and saw her dive, but she did not come up to the surface again. After a week's efforts she was brought to the surface and the crew of seven were found in a bunch near the manhole. Lieutenant Dixon said they had failed to close the after valve (to the stern ballast tank)'. The inexperienced crew, however, may not have been entirely to blame for the tragedy as other reports suggest that the submarine fouled a cable hanging down from the target ship and that this jammed the controls and prevented her from surfacing. But whatever the cause another seven men were dead and thirty-five lives had been forfeit in a boat that, as yet, had never seen action against the enemy.

Although the details of the *Hunley*'s last mission are outside the limits of this narrative the story must be told if only to complete the saga of the submarine's ill-starred career. On the night of 17 February, 1864, and now under the command of Lieutenant George E. Dixon, the *Hunley* set out from Charleston with orders to attack the blockading Union squadron. Aided by an ebb tide she approached the darkened warships on the surface and Dixon chose the 1,240-ton corvette *Housatonic* as his target. The submarine dived and, without a periscope to guide his course, the Lieutenant was forced to estimate his progress by reference to a small compass and a pocket-watch in the dim light of a guttering candle.

At 8.45 pm the Acting Master of the *Housatonic*, J.R. Crosby, sighted a strange object in the water and, with commendable promptness, gave orders to raise the anchor and go astern. Moments later *Hunley*'s spar torpedo lanced the corvette's hull and a tremendous explosion echoed across the bay as gunpowder charge detonated the ship's magazine. The *Housatonic* reeled to port and sank rapidly by the stern leaving her bewildered crew clinging to the rigging as she went down. In the circumstances it was a miracle that only five Union sailors were killed.

But the *Hunley* had vanished as completely as her victim and her ultimate fate was only discovered some weeks later when divers, searching the shattered hull of the *Housatonic*, found the submarine and its seven-man crew tangled up in the mangled remains of the corvette's wreckage. Forty-two men had died to achieve this final success. But they had not given their lives in vain for the *Hunley* had become the first submarine in history to sink an enemy ship. And that fact alone is an everlasting memorial to their sacrifice.

Strengthened by the events of the American Civil War, the search for a successful submarine continued at an ever-increasing pace. In 1863, while the *Hunley* was still drowning her hapless crews in Charleston Bay, two Frenchmen, Simeon Borgeois and Charles-Marie Brun, built an advanced type of submersible driven by an 80 hp compressed air engine. Displacing 140 tons in surface trim, and 140 feet in length, she was christened *Plongeur* and launched at Rochefort in April of that year. The two designers, thoughtfully concerned for the safety of their crew, fixed a large hollow cylinder to the upper hatch through which the men could escape should anything go wrong during the initial dock trials. It proved to be a wise precaution. For when *Plongeur* submerged for the first time water entered through one of the scuttles and the boat was quickly flooded. But, thanks to the foresight of the designers, every man aboard managed to climb to safety through the escape cylinder. The submarine underwent a number of relatively successful sea trials but, for some mysterious reason, she lacked horizontal stability and was ultimately broken up.

In 1886, during the war between Spain and her former colonies of Peru and Chile, a German inventor living in Valparaiso, Herr Flach, offered to design and build a submarine for use against the Spanish fleet. His boat was hand-propelled but appears to have been fitted with rudimentary hydroplanes to control its diving angle. It also carried a cylinder of oxygen to replenish its air supply when submerged.

The Admirals naturally demanded a demonstration of the boat's diving ability before any money changed hands and Flach was so confident of success that he took his son and six other persons on board for the evaluation trials although the admirals wisely decided to observe the tests from the safety of the shore. A large crowd watched the submarine move out into the bay and there was a ragged cheer as it dipped beneath the surface for the first dive. Unfortunately it also proved to be the last, for the vessel never came up again. An officer on board *HMS Leander*, which was anchored in the bay, saw a stream of bubbles rising to the surface near the spot where the submarine had gone down. But that was the only clue to its fate. Herr Flach and his passengers were never to see the light of day again.

British naval divers subsequently located the boat in 27 fathoms of water and reported that its bows were buried in the soft mud of the bottom. *Leander*'s crew managed to get ropes around the hull but an Admiralty signal forced the cruiser to leave the scene on another errand and no further salvage operations were undertaken.

As the race to develop the first successful submarine gained momentum there was, inevitably, a corresponding increase in the number and frequency of underwater disasters. The limitations of space make it impossible to record every accident in detail. But before recounting the story of John Philip Holland, the 'father' of the modern submarine, two more boats are worthy of mention.

The first is that of the Russian inventor Alexandrowski who constructed a 600-ton monster at St Petersburg in 1868. It was 120 feet long and, like the *Plongeur*, was propelled by a compressed-air engine which, it was claimed, could drive it through the water at five knots. It rejoiced in the curious name of *Potpourri*

Alexandrowski insisted that he had made several successful dives in the submarine but when he demonstrated the boat to the public it dived too deeply on its first outing and both submarine and designer were crushed by the pressure of the sea.

The other boat was conceived in the United States and was originally intended to be the North's answer to the Confederate *Hunley*. But although building began in 1862 during the Civil War it was not completed until many years later. Quaintly named the *Intelligent Whale*, it was financed by General Hoxey and built at Newark to the plans of the New Jersey inventor Oliver Halstead. Shaped like an American football, the vessel was only twenty-six feet in length and its stubby hull had a maximum span of nine feet. Carrying a crew of thirteen it was driven by a manual crank similar in principle to that employed by Horace Hunley and required the muscular effort of six men to achieve optimum performance – an alleged speed of 4 knots when submerged.

The initial tests of the *Whale*, carried out in 1872, were so impressive that the US Government agreed to buy her for $50,000. But it turned out to be a bad bargain for, like the ill-omened *Hunley*, Halstead's submarine seemed intent on devouring its crews at an alarming rate. During prolonged trials, she foundered three times and took her entire crew to the bottom on each occasion. Within a few months the Government had had enough. There was no war in progress to justify such a waste of human life and the *Intelligent Whale* was hauled ashore and laid to rest on the close-clipped lawns of the Brooklyn Navy Yard.

As one wag observed at the time: 'Intelligent? By heck – whoever heard of a whale being put out to grass?'

—THREE—

'The best tradition of the Service.'

For some reason submarines have exercised a strange fascination for men of religion. Bishop Wilkins in 1648 and the Abbe Borelli, some thirty years later, both produced designs for underwater vessels. So it is not surprising to find at least one clergyman amongst the host of eager inventors who crowded the scene in the latter part of the nineteenth century.

The Reverend George William Garrett, a clerk in Holy Orders in the City of Liverpool, began his experiments in 1878 when he successfully tested a small egg-shaped submarine in the local docks. Ballast tanks were used to control buoyancy and a hand-operated propellor supplied the motive-power. But despite the inherent disadvantages of manual propulsion the design showed that Garrett, a burly and bearded man who would have looked more at home on the bridge of an Antarctic whaler than in the pulpit, was an accomplished and original engineer. Within a year he had embarked on a more ambitious project.

Devising a means of mechanical propulsion had defeated the early pioneer inventors for two centuries. Van Drebbel and Bourne both relied on oars; Bauer used the treadwheel principle; while Hunley and Halstead put their faith in a manually operated crank. The Russian designer Alexandrowski was the first to exploit the new technology with his compressed-air engine, and this system was also successfully adopted by Robert Whitehead for his revolutionary 'fish' torpedoes. But Garrett took a giant leap forward by turning to the steam engine.

The *Resurgam,* his second boat, was fitted with an ingenious adaptation of the Lamm fireless locomotive boiler. Sufficient head of steam could be raised while running on the surface to provide enough latent heat to power the engine for ten miles while submerged. He had, in fact, solved the problem and had produced a submarine that could be propelled beneath the surface by mechanical means. Reliance on human muscular exertion was now only a curiosity of the past.

Resurgam was built by Cochrane & Company at the Britannia Engine Works in Birkenhead for an all-in cost of £1538. She weighed some 30 tons when completed and was launched, ready for sea, on 26 November, 1879. Garrett, anxious to try out his new toy, took the submarine for a quick test-run that very evening, and two days later the little steam-powered vessel submerged successfully for several hours.

The boat performed moderately well on its initial trials, although the midships location of the diving planes created problems with depth-keeping and the large boiler made movement inside the cramped interior unduly difficult. Shifting his base from Birkenhead to Rhyl, and purchasing the steam yacht *Elfin* to act as the submarine's tender, Garrett continued his experiments until he was satisfied with the boat's performance. In the early weeks of 1880 he decided to take *Resurgam* to Portsmouth where he could demonstrate it to the Swedish armaments tycoon, Thorston Nordenfelt. The necessary arrangements were made and at 10 pm on the night of 24th February *Elfin* steamed out of Rhyl harbour with the submarine in tow.

The weather deteriorated rapidly as Garrett headed west along the coast of North Wales and the little convoy spent the next day battling with the gale-force winds and rising seas. Finally the yacht's boilers gave up the ghost and the submarine's crew were hurriedly brought across to the *Elfin* to assist with the repair work. The recall of the crew proved to be providential, however, for at 10 am the following morning the tow-rope parted and *Resurgam* was quickly swamped by the waves and sank to the bottom.

Garrett's misfortunes were not yet over. Still stunned by the untimely loss of his precious submarine, he suffered a further blow when the *Elfin*, struggling to reach the Welsh coast, was rammed and wrecked by another vessel which was, ironically, coming to her rescue.

Despite these twin disasters, Garrett's achievements had not passed unnoticed and he was approached by Nordenfelt who asked him to design a commercial submarine which the millionaire offered to finance. Garrett accepted and the first boat, built in Stockholm in 1882, was sold to Greece four years later for £9,000. *Nordenfelt 1* was the subject of many trials and tribulations not least being the frequent near asphyxiation of its crew by carbon monoxide poisoning caused by leaks from the furnaces and smoke-boxes of the steam engine. Garrett himself was ill for three weeks after breathing the tainted air.

Two further boats were built for the Turkish Government but neither proved very successful and they never became operational – although for a period Garrett served as commander in the Imperial Ottoman Navy and was even photographed resplendant in his new gold-braided uniform topped by a red fez.*

Despite the existence of these two intervening boats the next submarine, constructed as a private venture in England, was known, confusingly, as the *Nordenfelt II*. Built under Garrett's supervision this new vessel was sold to Russia but ran aground off the coast of Jutland while being towed to the Baltic by Garrett's yacht *Lodestar*. Although salvaged a few weeks later the Tzarist Government refused to accept delivery and she was written off as a constructive loss and scrapped. Garrett threw in his hand and emigrated to the United States following this latest débâcle but Nordenfelt continued his interest in underwater craft and subsequently built *W.1* and *W.2* for the German Navy which, although unsuccessful, can be justifiably identified as the first U-boats.

Before returning to America to trace the development of the Holland submarine mention must be made of one other mishap. In 1886 two English engineers, Campbell and Ash, designed the 60-foot *Nautilus* which was built at the yards of Wolseley & Lyon on the Thames. The vessel is worthy of note as being one of the first submarines to use electricity as its primary means of propulsion and it is a pity in many ways that her design was faulty in various other important details.

Nautilus was publicly demonstrated at Tilbury in January, 1887, when, amongst the distinguished guests invited on board, were

---

*Another famous submarine man, Admiral Karl Doenitz, also served briefly under the Turkish ensign in 1914.

Lord Charles Beresford and Sir William White, the Chief Constructor of the Royal Navy. The diving trials were held in one of the docks which, as it turned out, was a fortunate precaution. For, like so many experimental submarines, *Nautilus,* having submerged, refused to return to the surface. And the only thing visible to the anxious onlookers as they stared down into the waters of the dock was a tell-tale stream of bubbles rising up from the bottom.

According to Lord Beresford: 'I suggested rolling her by moving the people quickly from side to side. The expedient succeeded, none too soon; for by the time she came to the surface, the air was very foul.'

Sir William White's version differed from that of his lordship and according to his wife: 'White took charge of the machinery for raising the vessel; and sent all the men to the end of the ship that was higher, hoping their weight would pull the other end out of the mud; and though he, with one other, strained every nerve; and though he described the sensation of his head growing larger and larger, and his breath coming in short gasps, as if each would be his last, and not in the end realising what he was doing, the vessel began to move. Then the anxious crowd at the dockside saw the *Nautilus* come into view.'

Having made due allowance for Lady White's convoluted prose and unusual punctuation, the question remains, was it Sir William or Lord Charles who saved the *Nautilus*? Sadly we will never know the answer. But the hilarious scene inside the submarine with the illustrious passengers running hither and thither in response to the contradictory instructions of these two eminent Victorian gentlemen is certainly one to contemplate.

* * *

In 1873, a year after Halstead's *Intelligent Whale* was laid to rest in the Brooklyn Navy Yard, a frail and sickly-looking Irish schoolteacher arrived in Boston. John Philip Holland, a 32-year-old native of County Clare, had come to America in the hope of repairing his persistent ill-health and to escape from the political turmoil and poverty that plagued his home country. Like most Irishmen of the period he was fervently anti-British, and although a schoolteacher by profession he had already been bitten by the submarine bug. In fact the records show that, even as early as 1859, he had prepared some sketch designs of a diving vessel while living in Cork.

Within a year of his arrival he was working at a parish school in Patterson, New Jersey, and devoting his evenings to perfecting his submarine. The original *Holland I** was little more than a toy. Shaped like a stiletto, it was a mere 15½ feet in overall length, carried small torpedoes, and was operated by a pilot wearing a diving-suit. The motive power was provided by foot pedals and there is considerable doubt whether this particular design ever got beyond the drawing board.

One of Holland's students, whose parents happened to be friends of the Navy Secretary, George M. Robeson, saw some of the preliminary sketches and suggested that the plans should be submitted to the Government. After all, they had bought the *Intelligent Whale* only two years previously and were clearly shopping around for a practical submarine. Holland followed their advice and in February, 1875, detail drawings were sent to Washington. They were, however, rejected by Captain Simpson of the Torpedo Station on the grounds that the pilot would be unable to see where he was going once the little boat was running beneath the surface. Holland retorted with a snappy letter to the Captain reminding him that there were such things as compasses. To which Simpson replied that no one but an utter fool would dream of going beneath the surface in such a crackpot contraption!

Undeterred, Holland set to work on a new design. And now that his Irish temper had cooled he could, perhaps, see some justification for Simpson's criticisms. So, assisted by an engineer, William Dunkerly, who checked his calculations, Holland spent every spare hour of the day and night at the drawing-board while his brother, Michael, set out in search of financial backing. Having exhausted the more conventional sources of risk capital Michael approached the Fenian Brotherhood – a forerunner of Sinn Fein and the IRA – suggesting that they should build and buy John's machine for use against British seaborne commerce, a grandiosely impractical idea that immediately sparked fertile Irish imaginations.

*There is considerable confusion over the numbering of Holland's prototypes. Some authorities ignore this model and classify his next boat as *Holland I* while others omit the Zalinsky design or the 1888 competition entry. Following the numerical system adopted by most historians I have taken the 1874 prototype as *Holland I*. Thus the submarine finally taken into the US Navy as SS 1 in 1900 is identified as *Holland VIII*.)

After a series of clandestine meetings between Holland and the Brotherhood's senior officials it was agreed that the organization would finance the project from its Skirmishing Fund. And a phoney company, Jacobs & Co., was set up to conceal the true identity of Holland's sponsors before work began at a local New Jersey yard. *Holland II* cost the Brotherhood $4,000 to build and, when completed, its iron hull, tipping the scales at a solid 2¼ tons, was a mere 14 feet in length. The Irishmen were disappointed with their bargain but, in fact, the boat was not quite as primitive as it appeared and it marked an important breakthrough in submarine design. For, having realized the futility of pedal power and discarded the idea of steam propulsion, Holland broke new ground by fitting his little submersible with a two-cylinder Brayton gasoline engine.

The launch of *Holland II* took place on 22 May, 1878 – the same year in which Garrett tested his first experimental boat – and a team of horses dragged the little vessel to the Upper Passaic River where a convenient launching place had been selected near Spruce Street Bridge. A festive crowd cheered as the submarine slid into the river and bobbed gently in the water at the end of its mooring rope. But the plaudits quickly turned to jeers as *Holland II* began to sink slowly by the stern. As one newspaper reported, she 'went immediately to the bottom and this without even the assistance of the captain'. And one morbidly-minded bystander tagged the boat an 'iron coffin' – a description that has been irrevocably linked with submarines ever since.

As the tow rope was still attached to her bows the vessel was hauled back to the river bank without difficulty and a short while later, after being cleaned out, she was ready for her second trial launching. But *Holland II* seemed intent on disgracing herself and promptly sank again as soon as she hit the water. Even the inventor must have entertained a few misgivings as the submarine was dragged ashore. But his mind was soon put at rest. There was nothing wrong with his design – some idiot had forgotten to insert a pair of small screw plugs into the drain holes of the bilges on the underside of the hull.

Holland tried once more and this time, despite problems with the temperamental gasoline engine, he finally persuaded the boat to remain afloat to the relief of not only himself but also his Fenian backers who were beginning to think that their cash, like the submarine, was going to end up on the bottom of the river. Having made some further delicate adjustments to the trim Holland pronounced himself ready and, squeezing through the hatch, he closed the top scuttle and steered the vessel out into the Passiac River where, to the delight of his sponsors, he successfully submerged to a depth of twelve feet.

Satisfied that Holland could produce the goods the Brotherhood immediately ordered a larger boat which was to be built at the Delameter Iron Works on W 13th Street, New York City, for a maximum price of $20,000. The inventor accepted the offer but, before starting work on the new design, he removed the engine from *No. 2*, stripped the submarine bare of fittings, and scuttled the hulk in 2½ fathoms of water close to the Spruce Street Bridge. The little boat had served her purpose and Holland had finished with her. He did not believe in sentimentality.

Holland III, or as she is more commonly known, *The Fenian Ram*, was considerably larger than her two predecessors. The completed design drawings gave her a length of 31 feet with a beam of 6 feet and a height of 7½ feet. Requiring a crew of three, she displaced 19 tons and was powered by a 15 hp Brayton gasoline engine which, with typical ingenuity, Holland had rigged to work on compressed-air while the boat was submerged.

Encouraged by the new contract he gave up school-teaching and a short while later, as proof of his new-found vocation, he formed the *John P. Holland Torpedo Boat Co.*

The *Fenian Ram (Holland III)* was launched on the Hudson River on 1 May, 1881, and she proved to be a satisfactory boat in every respect. The first submergence trials took place in June, 1881, and Holland tested the vessel exhaustively for the next two years, to the growing impatience of the battle-hungry Irishmen. He also began work on *Holland IV*, a 16 foot mock-up for a larger design. The boat sank early in its career while being ballasted with the hatches open but it was subsequently raised.

Other problems were now bedevilling the Fenian Brotherhood. Several senior members considered that the inventor was spending too much money and, as a side issue, a court action was pending concerning the cash in the Skirmishing Fund. The dissident Fenians, led by J. J. Breslin, one of the original Jacobs & Co. conspirators, seized both *Holland III* and *Holland IV* on a dark November night in 1883 and, towing them behind a harbour tug, set out for the East River. The sea was choppy as the procession entered Long Island Sound and, as the waves washed over the hull, water soon began to leak into the insecurely fastened upper hatch of the 16-foot prototype. She settled deeper and deeper into the sea until, finally, the tow-rope snapped under the strain of the additional weight and she disappeared forever in 110 feet of water.

The *Fenian Ram*, however, survived the hijack and was hidden away at a brass foundry on the Mill River at New Haven. Holland naturally protested strongly to the Brotherhood but they were too engrossed in their own financial and legal problems to listen and his complaints were brushed aside. But he was now thoroughly disenchanted with the back-stabbing and intrigue that lay behind the outward mask of political respectability. Confident that he could stand on his own feet, Holland broke off his connection with the Fenians to make his own way as an independant submarine designer.

Deprived of his expert guidance, the Brotherhood soon found itself facing a further problem. For when Holland's former engineer, George M. Richards, was told to take *Holland III* on a preliminary trial run the excursion ended in near-disaster. The wake from the tug towing the submarine out into the Mill River surged over the half-submerged boat and swamped the open hatchway. The *Fenian Ram* sank by the stern as the river flooded her interior compartment and Richards, trapped at the controls, had a remarkable escape when the pressure of the air inside the hull shot him up through the hatch. Apart from an involuntary ducking he emerged from the disaster none the worse for his frightening experience.

Salving *Holland III* cost the Fenians $3,000 and the Irish amused themselves by cruising around New Haven Harbour waving half-empty bottles as they engaged and sank hundreds of imaginary British ships. But they remained sufficiently sober to make sure that the *Fenian Ram* never submerged. For that 'begorra' would be tempting Providence too far!

Finally, after angry complaints from other users of the harbour, the Authorities put a stop to the Fenian junketings. *Holland III* was hauled out of the water for the last time and was left to rust on the beach. Happily the remains of this historic boat are now on display in Westside Park, Paterson, New Jersey.

Without funds and almost bankrupted by the Fenian débâcle, Holland was forced to obtain employment as a draughtsman with the Pneumatic Gun Company in New York. It was here that he met Lieutenant Edward Zalinsky, the inventor of the dynamite gun. The two men got along well and within a few months Holland agreed to design and build a submarine which was intended to act as a floating platform for Zalinsky's assorted pieces of ordnance. When completed in 1886 *Holland V* was 40 feet long but was so overloaded with weapons that the wooden launching way collapsed. The impact opened the hull seams and the ill-starred submarine sank to the bottom for the first and last time. Exit *Holland V* alias the *Holland-Zalinsky* boat alias Zalinsky's *Nautilus*.

In the eleven years since 1875 Holland had designed and built no less than five submarines all but one of which had, at some time or another, ended on the bottom. But he was undeterred by misfortune and in 1888 he entered a Government-sponsored competition to design a submarine for the US Navy which offered a prize of $150,000 for the winner. Garrett's mentor, Thorsten Nordenfelt, was another of the entrants.

In the event no design was considered worthy of the prize although Holland's boat was adjudged the best of those considered. A newly elected Government shelved the competition in 1889 and *Holland VI* never progressed beyond the drawing-board. But Holland had proved that he was, at least in the eyes of the Navy, the world's foremost submarine designer.

When a further competition was organized in 1893 it was again the Holland Company that emerged triumphant, and although the Navy delayed for two years before making the necessary appropriation of funds, the $150,000 contract was finally signed on 13 March, 1895.

The keel of *Holland VII*, or *Plunger* as she was officially named, was laid down on 23 June, 1896, at the Columbian Iron Works. But she proved a 'technical and financial failure'. Navy engineering experts meddled with Holland's drawings and substituted, in place of the designed gasoline engines, two 600 hp and one 300 hp steam engines complete with boilers. The result was calamitous and the over-laden boat capsized on launching. Even after salvage and modification she was never able to steer a straight course. It was not Holland's fault but the Navy, rather unfairly, refused to accept the vessel and, in 1900, the contract was finally cancelled, although Congress approved a token payment of $15,000 towards the building costs.

In 1896, having realized that the *Plunger* would be a failure, Holland began work on a private venture which he offered to build for the Navy at his own expense. He was still desperately short of funds and his magnanimous offer was only made possible by the timely gift of $25,000 from an unnamed New York lady.

Completed in 1898 *Holland VIII* displaced 78 tons in submerged trim and her official dimensions are recorded as 53'10" x 10'3" x 8'6". She carried a crew of seven men and was armed with a single 18-in torpedo tube and an 8-in dynamite gun designed by Zalinsky. One torpedo was shipped inside the tube and there were two reloads. Surface power was provided by a 45 hp gasoline engine giving a speed of 8 knots, while an electric motor fed by a series of storage batteries gave the submarine a submerged range of 50 miles and a maximum underwater speed of 5 knots. A far cry from the primitive pedal-power of *Holland I*.

There was no proper periscope and the captain had to 'porpoise' the boat when approaching the target submerged – a distinct disadvantage which was soon overcome in subsequent classes. With very little reserve buoyancy she was difficult to handle on the surface, and submerged she was even worse. According to Rear Admiral Arnold-Forster, who commanded Britain's first Holland Submarine: 'She had none of those hydroplanes on either side which makes the modern submarine so easy to manipulate under water. There was simply a horizontal diving rudder in the tail which was used to steer the boat down to the depth ordered and keep her there by pointing her nose downwards at an angle which varied with her buoyancy and the skill of the coxswain at the diving rudder wheel'. But these were minor criticisms by comparison with the general success of the Holland design as a true underwater warship capable of tackling, and sinking, the largest battleship with its Whitehead torpedoes.

The US Navy purchased the boat on 11 April, 1900, for $150,000 and immediately ordered a further seven vessels of similar design. It should have been a triumphal moment for the former schoolteacher. But, two years earlier, in 1898, Isaac L. Rice, the owner of the company that supplied Holland with his storage batteries, had engineered a merger with the Irishman's business when the latter had been unable to pay his creditors. The new corporation, known as the Electric Boat Company, appointed Holland as its Chief Engineer but Rice made sure that *he* retained all financial and executive management control. And on 7 February, 1899, Rice tied up the loose ends of the transaction by acquiring Holland's patents. Sadly the Navy's decision to buy *Holland VIII* had come too late to save Holland's independence, for which he had fought so hard. In the course of the next few years, dogged by ill-health, his participation in the affairs of the new company gradually declined until, ultimately, he became no more than a non-executive figurehead.

In 1901 Holland and the Electric Boat Company began building another private venture, the *Fulton*. It proved to be a successful design but in April, 1902, while on passage from New York to Washington, hydrogen gas which had built up inside the boat, following an acid leak from the storage batteries, exploded violently and although the submarine itself survived most of her seven-man crew were badly injured by the blast. It is worth noting that they were the first casualties ever suffered in a Holland submarine over a period of more than twenty-five years of pioneering experiment, testament indeed to Holland's skill as a designer and his caution as a practical inventor.

Fulton was subsequently sold to Russia and was still in service at the outbreak of the Great War under her new name of *Som*. She was lost when she collided with the Swedish steamer *A.K. Angerland* in the Aaland Strait on 23 May, 1916. The submarine, in fact survived longer than her designer, for John Philip Holland, died at Newark on 12 August, 1914.

Several historians have challenged the claim that Holland was the 'father' of the modern submarine and consider that the honour more correctly belongs to Maxime Laubeuf. Their case rests on the fact that the Frenchman's *Narval* was the first submarine to be built on the double-hull principle, whereas Holland employed a single-hull design which was, in due course, universally superseded by the Laubeuf method of construction. *Narval* came into service in June, 1900, and thus pipped *Holland VIII* to the post by a few months for, although purchased in April, the American boat was not formally commissioned until 12 October, 1900.

However, although the *Narval* demonstrated better handling qualities when submerged, thanks to her bow-mounted hydroplanes, she incorporated many obsolescent features, notably in steam engines for surface propulsion and drop-collars for launching her torpedoes. And even the famous double-hull was not entirely original, for Simon Lake, another American designer, had constructed a primitive version of the system for his *Argonaut* in 1897, a full year before the *Narval* was even laid down.

Nevertheless 1900 was a watershed year for submarine development. The French, already well ahead of other navies, had a number of boats in service in addition to the *Narval*; the United

States had acquired *Holland VIII* and had ordered seven repeats; Russia was experimenting vigorously; and Britain had been reluctantly forced to order her first five *Hollands* from Rice's Electric Boat Company even though the diehards of the Royal Navy condemned the submarine as 'underhand' and 'a damned un-English weapon'. With such a sudden proliferation of boats manned, unavoidably, by inexperienced and only partly-trained crews, disaster was sure to be close at hand.

On the final day of the Spring manoeuvres, 18 March, 1904, Britain's pioneer submarine flotilla left harbour and sailed out into the Solent to set an ambush for the cruiser *Juno* which was returning to Portsmouth after completing her part in the exercises. The flotilla consisted of the five original Holland boats, ordered in 1900, and *A.1*, the first of a new British-designed class built by Vickers.

Juno was sighted coming down the Solent off the Nab Tower at noon and Submarine *No. 2* edged into an attacking position, fired an oblique shot but missed. Closing to within 400 yards *No.3* loosed off a practice torpedo and, to the surprise of her young captain and the consternation of the cruiser's officers, scored a direct hit. Delighted with this proof of his flock's capabilities Captain Bacon, who was directing the proceedings from the gunboat *Hazard,* made a visual signal for *A.1* to join the attack.

Lieutenant Mansergh, the submarine's Commanding Officer, with his eye glued to the periscope and all his concentration directed towards the impending attack, apparently failed to notice the liner *Berwick Castle* bearing down on him as he closed the target. It was a misty afternoon and by the time the Master of the passenger ship realized that a half-submerged object was lying across his path it was too late to avoid a collision. There was a screech of torn metal as the liner's sharp steel bows smashed into *A.1's* conning-tower. Rolled over onto her beam ends by the violent impact, the submarine disappeared in the flurry of spray.

Unaware of the tragedy that had occurred, and signalling that she had struck a practice torpedo, *Berwick Castle* resumed her voyage to Hamburg. Several hours were to pass before Captain Bacon realized what had happened. *A.1* was admittedly overdue but that, in itself, was not unusual, for most of the pioneer boats had poor reliability records. It was only when he was given the signal from the *Berwick Castle* that his worst fears were confirmed. *Hazard* was immediately despatched to the scene but on reaching the vicinity of the accident all she found was a large patch of white water created by air bubbles rising up from the shattered hull. There was no salvage equipment on board and nothing could be done to rescue the trapped men, if indeed, any were still alive.

A.1 had never been a lucky ship. Even before she had left her builders, Vickers Son & Maxim, she had suffered a serious explosion of hydrogen gas; and while being towed to Portsmouth to join her flotilla water penetrated her batteries when she encountered heavy seas off Land's End. The chlorine gas generated by the salt water coming into contact with the acid batteries overwhelmed the crew and they were forced to abandon the boat which was subsequently towed into Falmouth for repairs and cleaning. When she finally reached Portsmouth she was ignominiously berthed in a remote part of the harbour 'for safety'.

The accident, the first submarine disaster to be suffered by the Royal Navy, shocked the British public and remained headline news for many days. On Thursday, 24 March, for example, a week after the tragedy, the *Daily Illustrated Mirror* devoted half of its front page to a doleful photograph of the wreck marker buoy bobbing forlornly in the waters of the Solent with the caption: *Lonely buoy that marks the tomb of the A.1 heroes.* This was typical of the reaction of the national press to the accident.

Admiral Sir John Fisher, then serving as C-in-C Portsmouth before his appointment as First Sea Lord in October, sent a private report of the disaster to the Prince of Wales (later King George V) who had visited the *A.1* at Portsmouth a few days earlier. For public consumption he composed the following General Signal to his Command:

'Time has not permitted the Commander-in-Chief until now to express publicly his great personal sorrow for the grievous calamity that has befallen us. Practically our gallant comrades died in action. Their lives are not thrown away if we consider their splendid example in cheerful and enthusiastic performance of duty involving all the risks of war.'

It was a fitting epitaph for Lieutenant Mansergh and his crew. And with characteristic perception Fisher had made a very valid point. For a submarine, more than any other type of ship, is at constant war with the forces of the sea, and any man who loses his life as the result of a submarine accident has, truly, died in action in the never-ending conflict with the eternal enemy.

Although *A.1* had sunk in only 42 feet of water the treacherous tides and cross-currents of the Solent made salvage difficult. Divers going down to examine the wreck found a large hole in the conning-tower where the *Berwick Castle*'s bows had struck, and it was clear that Mansergh and his men had drowned almost immediately. The discovery was, at least, some consolation to their relatives.

Only three months later, on 20 June, 1904, the Russian Navy sustained its first submarine disaster when the *Delfin* sank in the River Neva just outside the Baltic Shipbuilding Yard in Kronstadt. She was lying on the surface trimming her ballast tanks when the wash of a passing tug entered her open hatches and she went down within seconds. Twenty-six men were lost but a fortunate half-dozen managed to fight their way through the swirling waters and were picked up by rescue boats.

The men of the American submarine *Porpoise* would have gladly given a year's pay for a similar opportunity to escape. For when their boat went out of control during a diving exercise and hit the bottom in 125 feet of water every hatch was tightly secured and they found themselves locked inside a steel tomb.

Porpoise, like all early Holland boats, was only designed for a maximum diving depth of 100 feet, and as the men took stock of the situation they could hear the hull plates groaning under the pressure. Fortunately no water had entered the boat so there was no danger of flooding but the cork packing sprinkling down from the deckhead like fine brown snowflakes showed that the seams were slowly yielding to the power of the sea. And every man knew that within the next few minutes the submarine's tough steel hull would be crushed like an empty egg-shell.

Technical reasons made it impossible to blow the ballast tanks once the boat was submerged below 50 feet, and the pressure of the sea prevented the electric pumping system from being operated. Their sole hope of survival rested with a small hand-pump intended for the clearing of bilges. Working in pairs for short periods, the men laboured at the pump until sufficient ballast had been expelled to restore the submarine's slender buoyancy and she rose slowly to the surface. The men of the US Navy had proved that dogged determination and steady discipline could still achieve miracles.

A similar incident in 1885 had demonstrated the opposite side of the coin although, fortunately, a tragedy was avoided. The *Peacemaker*, an experimental submarine built by the Submarine Monitor Company of New York for Professor Josiah L. Tuck, went to the bottom of the Hudson River when water leaked through the gasket of the clutch. One member of the crew became hysterical and Tuck solved the problem with simple directness. He knocked him out with a hammer! Then following the precedent set by Bauer, he allowed more water into the flooded hull and, when the pressure was equalized, the crew escaped through the hatch. Fortunately such extreme measures proved to be unnecessary in the *USS Porpoise*.

Apart from the French steam-powered boats the majority of early submarines used gasoline engines for surface propulsion. With a highly volatile substance such as petrol, accidents were inevitable. On 16th February, 1905, the British *A.5* was tied up alongside a tender filling her petrol tanks. It was a bitterly cold day and everyone was anxious to get the job completed as quickly as possible. Precisely what went wrong has never been fully established, but when the ignition switches were turned on a tremendous explosion ripped through the boat killing the Commanding Officer and six other members of the crew. A further twelve men were seriously burned. As the dead and injured were being removed a second explosion added to the chaos.

Petrol vapour ignited by an electrical spark was generally considered to be the cause of the disaster but, surprisingly, an inquest jury chose to blame the accident on carelessness. It seemed a harsh verdict on the Royal Navy's dedicated band of submariners who were only too aware of the danger of petrol vapour. As one consequence of the tragedy the Admiralty ordered that, in future, a cage of white mice was to be carried in every submarine. This precautionary measure was taken after an expert had assured Their Lordships that they squealed when their sensitive nostrils detected petrol vapour. Whether the expert was correct or not is a matter for debate, but they made excellent pets for the crews!

The Royal Navy suffered an equally serious accident only four months later when *A.8* was lost in Plymouth Sound on 8 June. According to a report in *The Times A.8*, together with *A.7* and the Torpedo-boat *No. 80*, had set off from Devonport dockyard at 9 am for diving exercises. It was a dull grey day with rain falling at intervals, although visibility was tolerably clear. Operating off the western end of the breakwater each submarine carried out two training dives and, at 10.30 am, both su᷊ ʿaced and closed the torpedo-boat to exchange three members of their crew for an equal number of ratings under instruction. The conning-tower of *A.8* opened and, as the three men to be exchanged climbed out, the three trainees stepped down onto the foredeck plating of the submarine.

Suddenly 'the bow of the vessel was seen to dip heavily causing her to ship a huge quantity of water through the conning-tower. Then, to the great consternation of those watching, she began instantly to settle down before it was possible to close the (hatch)'. The men standing on the forward casing were swept into the water and Lieutenant Candy, who had been supervising the change-over, and the other crewmen in the conning-tower leapt clear as *A.8* sank under their feet. Boats were immediately lowered by *No 80*, and also by *Commonwealth* and *Forth* which were in the vicinity, in a desperate bid to save the survivors.

A passing fishing ketch, the *Chanticleer*, scooped four men from the sea but, despite a long search, the other rescue boats returned empty-handed. The ships on the spot, especially Torpedo-boat *No 80*, had reacted with commendable promptness, and not a moment was wasted in getting emergency measures under way. But the suddenness of a submarine disaster is so overwhelming and so immediate that, even in these favourable circumstances, it proved impossible to save the lives of the fifteen trapped men.

The First Officer, Sub-Lieutenant Edward Fletcher, was amongst those lost but the survivors included *A.8*'s Commanding Officer, Lieutenant Candy, who, after a distinguished war record, retired as a Rear Admiral; and Petty Officer William Waller, an underwater veteran who had served as the original coxswain of the Royal Navy's first submarine *Holland No 1*.

A.8 was raised four days later and an inspection revealed a loose rivet in the bow plating. It was a tiny fault yet it had proved fatal and it typified the dangers which faced the men who went down to the sea in the early submarines. For that small hole in the plating could, under pressure, admit a staggering one ton of water in a mere ten minutes! Some accounts suggest that *A.8* sank following a battery explosion, but eye-witnesses confirm that the two explosions to which these sources refer occurred *after* the submarine sank and were probably the result of petrol vapour igniting when the sea shorted the electrical circuits.

Less than a month after the British disaster the French Navy experienced its first serious accident when, on 6 July, 1905, the 185-ton *Farfadet* was lost in Lake Bizerta. Completed in 1902 and powered entirely by motors feeding from electric accumulators she was regarded as a very successful boat and her sinking caused a considerable shock in naval circles. The accident happened while the *Farfadet* was exercising in the vast sea lagoon to the east of Bizerta in French North Africa. She submerged before her hatch was fully secured – an error due, almost certainly, to the inexperience of her crew – and, overwhelmed by the rush of water, she went to the bottom within seconds. But those few fleeting moments were sufficient to save the lives of three men. The Commanding Officer and two of the petty officers were still in the conning-tower when the error was made and, like Engineer Richards in the *Fenian Ram*, they were blown clear of the sinking submarine when a pocket of trapped air blasted them through the narrow hatchway. Their fourteen shipmates were not so lucky.

Fortunately the waters of the lake were shallow and salvage operations began without delay. Divers descending to inspect the sunken boat heard tapping sounds from inside the hull and, having confirmed that the trapped sailors were still alive, a floating crane was rushed to the scene. Lines were secured around the submarine and she was gradually raised. Success seemed within sight as the stern section emerged above the surface but hopes were brutally dashed when, unable to take the tremendous strain, the crane collapsed and the *Farfadet* slid back into the depths. Fourteen men were still alive when this failure occurred. All were dead by the time the submarine was finally salved.

On 16 October another of the British Navy's A-class boats found herself in trouble, although, on this occasion, thanks to the cool-headed reactions of her crew, there were no casualties. The submarine, *A.4*, commanded by Lieutenant Martin Nasmith, who was later to win the Victoria Cross in the Dardanelles with *E.11*, was carrying out an experiment in underwater signalling when the accident happened.

Nasmith planned to receive messages while submerged by means of an insulated megaphone which had been placed against the interior hull plates of the submarine. To test the device, Torpedo-boat *No 26* was ordered to steam in circles around the submerged *A.4* ringing a large brass bell. So that the officer in command of the torpedo-boat would know that the bell was audible Nasmith arranged for a boat-hook bearing a red flag to be pushed up through the ventilator tube, the upper end of which projected a few inches above the surface. This meant trimming the submarine down so that she was just, and only just, beneath the water. Nasmith considered that his crew were capable of such a delicate adjustment. Events, however, were to prove otherwise.

Whether the bow-wave from the circling torpedo-boat or the wash of a passing steamer was reponsible for the near-disaster that followed has never been fully established. It may even have been, as some have suggested, a handling error by *A.4*'s crew. But, whatever the cause, water entered the ventilator tube while the submarine was still adjusting its diving trim and the next moment the boat was heading for the depths with the sea pouring into her hull. Nasmith gave orders to blow all four main ballast tanks but it had no effect.

Both Nasmith and his First Officer, Godfrey Herbert, were aware of the fact that it needed eighty gallons of additional water to upset *A.4*'s precarious positive buoyancy. And it did not require a trained eye to see that there was considerably more than this already swilling about inside the boat.

A.4 sank to 90 feet – only 10 feet inside her maximum diving limit – and was down by the bows at an angle of 40°. Loose gear tumbled towards the front of the boat in chaotic confusion; the main switchboard fused and the lights went out. Herbert recalled that moment: 'I can well remember thinking how the Portsmouth evening newspapers would have a large headline: ANOTHER SUBMARINE DISASTER. It all seemed so inevitable.'

Realizing that the sea was coming in through the ventilator tube Leading Seaman Baker, *A.4*'s second coxswain, tried to screw the lower cup back into position. But the rush of water swept it from his grasp and he thrust his Navy-issue cap into the opening. Other caps followed and, finally a thick wollen jersey. The inrush of water eased slightly but there was now a new and more menacing danger. The sea, which had flooded the interior of the submarine, had washed down into the battery compartment and chlorine gas began rising up through the deck plating as the salt water came into contact with the acid in the accumulators. Choking fumes filled the boat but ingrained discipline kept the men steady at their diving stations as they waited in darkness for their next orders.

There was only one possible chance of survival. And Nasmith took it. If it failed *A.4* and her crew were lost.

'Blow main ballast, Number One. Put on full pressure.'

As First Officer it was one of Herbert's duties to vent the tanks and months of training made him familiar with every corner and crevice of the submarine so that, despite the blackness, his hands had no difficulty in locating the pressure valves. He turned each control wheel in sequence and the men heard a hiss as the compressed air was released. *A.4* rolled slightly and, as the tanks emptied, began to rise. Exactly three and a half minutes after she had sunk to the bottom of Stokes Bay she returned to the surface in a froth of white water.

'It was a relief to see daylight again,' Herbert recalled in a masterpiece of understatement. It had certainly been an experience that no man would ever wish to repeat but, as related in Chapter One, Godfrey Herbert found himself facing an identical situation nearly twelve years later when *K.13* sank in Gareloch. No doubt the memory of Nasmith's leadership in *A.4* inspired his own calm reaction to the disaster which faced him as Captain of *K.13* that January afternoon in 1917.

After the crew had clambered out on deck Nasmith took a roll-call and found two men missing. Although the submarine was in imminent danger of foundering he descended the conning-tower ladder again and found the two seamen standing patiently at their diving stations. In the noise and confusion of the final moments they had failed to hear the order to abandon ship.

A.4 continued to misbehave as the *Hazard* towed her back to Portsmouth and at 4.45 pm she shuddered under a violent internal explosion. A second followed half an hour later and a third blast as she reached the dockyard. While waiting to enter her berth, she settled gently and sank beneath the water.

In accordance with standard Royal Navy procedures after the loss of a ship Nasmith found himself facing a Court Martial on a charge of 'negligently or by default, hazarding His Majesty's Submarine *A.4.*' Evidence both for and against was submitted and Nasmith readily admitted to an error of judgement. He was found guilty of default but acquitted on the more serious charge of negligence. The Court sentenced him to an official reprimand after 'taking into consideration the prisoner's coolness and presence of mind under difficult circumstances after the boat had submerged.' Fortunately the verdict did not have any adverse effect on Nasmith's promising career and he went on to reach the rank of Admiral and was, at one time, Flag Officer Submarines.

The national newspapers had a field day as details of the story emerged at the Court Martial hearing. The *Daily Mail* blazoned banner headlines across its front page: FACING DEATH IN A SUBMARINE. STORY OF MAGNIFICENT BRITISH PLUCK. HEROISM IN INKY

DARKNESS. PERILOUS MINUTES ON THE A.4. Even *The Times* was constrained to comment: 'Nothing but the admirable steadiness of the men and the splendid presence of mind of Lieutenant Nasmith and Sub-Lieutenant Herbert could have saved the country from another appalling submarine disaster.'

But the statement most appreciated by the survivors was written by Admiral Sir Archibald Douglas, the Flag Oficer, Portsmouth. In a General Signal issued, significantly, two days after the Court Martial verdict he wrote: 'The Commander-in-Chief . . . wishes to make it known to all officers and men of the Fleet that he is deeply impressed with the behaviour of the officers and men (of A.4). Their pluck and devotion to duty under the most trying circumstances was most commendable and . . . worthy of the best traditions of the Service.'

A.4 was raised and refitted in the dockyard before returning to duty. And 'in the best traditions of the Service' Godfrey Herbert, now promoted to the rank of Lieutenant, was appointed as her new Commanding Officer. He was, perhaps, consoled by the thought that lightning never strikes twice. Well, hardly ever.

—FOUR—

'They feel very cold...'

The US Navy's purchase of *Holland VIII* in 1900 sparked off a frantic race between the world's leading naval powers. Suddenly every nation wanted its own submarine fleet, and the bigger the better. France, who had been assiduously developing her own designs since the original all-electric *Goubet* prototype of 1887, had built up a commanding lead. By June, 1901, she already had fourteen submersibles in service and twenty-five more under construction. And thanks to her concentration on the production of efficient storage batteries for electric propulsion she maintained her pre-eminent position throughout most of the decade. The submarines listed in *Jane's Fighting Ships* for 1905-6 indicate just how great a lead the French Navy had established by that time:

	Built	*Building*
France	52	6
Great Britain	20	15
Russia	17	?
United States	8	2
Italy	6	2
Japan	5	2
Brazil	2	2
Germany	1	1
Sweden	1	-
Spain	1	-
Argentina	1(?)	-
Chile	-	1

In view of the success achieved by her U-boat arm in two World Wars it is interesting to note Germany's lowly position in the league table, and, bearing in mind the Soviet Union's present massive strength in submarines, Russia's third ranking in the days of Tzar Nicholas II, with twice as many boats in service as the United States, is not without significance to those who see today's Communist régime as no more than an instrument of traditional Russian imperialism.

France, however, was to pay a heavy price for her underwater superiority. In the twenty-six months from August, 1906, to October, 1908, the French Navy lost no fewer than seven submarines in accidents while a number of others were seriously damaged as the result of collisions, internal explosions and, in some cases, sheer carelessness.

Following Japan's victory over Russia in 1905 four small *Perle*-class harbour defence submarines were shipped to the Far East to strengthen France's naval presence in Indo-China. On 13 August, 1906, one of them, the 68-ton *Estergeon*, sank while in dock at Saigon. The cause of the accident has never been established, no lives were lost in the incident and the boat was subsequently salved and restored to service.

Almost exactly a month later, on 16 September, the veteran *Gymnote*, whose service dated back to 1889, suffered a devastating hydrogen gas explosion caused by a leaking storage battery. Two men were seriously injured but, despite extensive damage, the submarine was raised, repaired and recommissioned. In the same year *Angouille*, a sister of *Estergeon*, suffered an almost identical fate. On this occasion the explosion was said to have been caused by an electrical spark igniting a pocket of petrol vapour. But she, too, was repaired and back at sea within a few months.*

Bonite, yet another of the accident-prone *Perle*-class boats, was more fortunate than her sisters. She was taking part in battle exercises with the French Fleet in the Western Mediterranean when she had a lucky escape. She had attacked and hit the cruiser *Conde* and the battleship *Ilena* with practice torpedoes and had then dived to 60 feet to avoid detection by the destroyer

---

*As *Angouille* was an all-electric boat it is difficult to explain the presence of petrol and it is probable that the records are incorrect and that she also suffered a battery explosion.

screen. Having allowed time for the excitement to die down *Bonite*'s captain brought his boat to periscope depth in search of another target. But, to his horror, he found the 12,750 ton *Suffren* only forty yards away and, a moment later, the great ram bow of the battleship crashed into the tiny submarine.

Bonite reeled under the impact but before the inrush of water could swamp the boat her captain released the detachable weighted keel and the submarine bobbed safely to the surface. With the gaping hole made by *Suffren*'s bows now riding clear of the sea *Bonite* was able to return to Toulon without assistance. A few months earlier Lieutenant Fraser had saved the Royal Navy's *A.9* in a similar manner. The British submarine collided with the steamer *Coath* off Plymouth while engaged on exercises and Fraser, who subsequently commanded *E.10* during the war, managed to get his boat back to the surface by dropping the emergency keel. Both incidents emphasized the value of highly trained and quick-thinking submarine captains.

But before 1906 was over there was one more disaster in store for the French submarine service. *Lutin*, a sister of the ill-fated *Farfadet*, was carrying out a diving demonstration of Bizerta in heavy seas for the benefit of some high-ranking Inspecting Officers and, in the circumstances, her captain was no doubt trying to impress them with his efficiency. The submarine made two successful dives but when surfacing after its third descent only the bows emerged from the water. She hung there for several minutes as the crew struggled to trim the boat level and then, without warning, she slid back into the sea stern-first.

The Authorities began salvage operations almost immediately and the Royal Navy responded to their request for assistance by sending a rescue team and a small floating-dock from Malta. The submarine was located in more than 100 feet of water and salvage presented a number of difficulties. But *Lutin* was finally brought to the surface and towed into the floating-dock where inspection revealed several serious leaks in her hull plating and a bent rudder, damaged when she struck the sea bottom. It was clear that the boat had partially flooded during her third dive and that she had lacked sufficient buoyancy to return to the surface. Her conning-tower hatch was also found to be slightly open but, in the opinion of the experts, this was probably the result of an abortive attempt to escape. The entire crew of *Lutin*, two officers and twelve men, lost their lives in the disaster – the first time a French submarine had gone down with all hands.

The New Year opened badly when the *Algerien* sank in Cherbourg Dockyard on 17 January. The 146-ton *Morse*-class submarine had been moored carelessly and when the tide rose the boat tilted away from the jetty wall and continued to heel over until her opened hatches dipped beneath the water and she was swamped by the sea. Fortunately her crew was ashore at the time and there were no casualties. Suffering only minimal damage from her involuntary immersion, she was pumped dry, cleaned up, and returned to her flotilla within days.

After surviving the battery explosion that had occurred a year earlier *Gymnote* was the next to be lost when, on 19 June, 1907, she sank in Toulon Dockyard while trimming her ballast tanks. 'Due to a confusion of orders,' the report reads, 'too much water was admitted to the tanks and the submarine sank when the sea entered the hatches which were open for ventilation'. Two members of the crew who were working inside the boat were lost. But the French Navy seemed reluctant to write off the old veteran and *Gymnote* was raised once again and re-commissioned.

The next to go was *Bonite*, the submarine that had already escaped disaster after her collision with *Suffren*. Living up to the evil reputation of the other *Perle*-class boats, she sank in dock while undergoing tests to check whether her hull seams were watertight after some refitting work. Unfortunately a nameless idiot had failed to close one of the internal valves and, flooded from stem to stern, *Bonite* ended on the bottom of the dock. But even then her good luck did not desert her for her crew was safely ashore and there were no casualties.

Detailed information concerning the remaining two accidents does not seem to be available. But, for the record, *Castor*, another *Perle*-class boat, was lost on 6 August, 1907, and *Fresnel* went down on 15 October. Both submarines were salved and there were apparently no lives lost in either incident. *Fresnel* went on to take an active part in operations against the Austrians in the Adriatic during World War I and she finally ran aground on the Albanian coast in heavy fog on 5 December, 1915. Despite strenuous efforts, the crew failed to refloat the stranded boat and she was ultimately destroyed by gunfire from the Austrian destroyer *Varasdinier*.

In contrast to the heavy casualties suffered in later submarine disasters it seems incredible that, although seven boats went to the bottom in those fateful twenty-six months, only sixteen lives were lost. Although never officially admitted, it is clear that the chain of accidents blunted French enthusiasm for under-water warships, and, though France continued to build sub-marines, the Royal Navy had already outstripped her by the time war was declared in August 1914 by 78 to 76. And the decline continued. According to *Jane's Fighting Ships* France had dropped to fourth place by 1918 behind Britain, the United States and Italy.

Italy also experienced her first submarine disaster in 1909 when, on 26 April, the *Foca* suffered a massive internal explosion caused by the hoodoo spirit that pervaded all the early boats – petrol vapour. Fourteen men were killed by the blast and another twelve seriously injured. The resulting damage proved so severe that the submarine was written off and scuttled.

The loss of the Russian *Kambala* on 12 June, 1909, is shrouded in confusion, the Tzarist Government being as adept at concealing information as its Soviet successors. The *Kambala* had an interesting history. Designed by a Spaniard, R. d'Equevillet, who had trained and worked in France, she was built by the Krupp-Germania shipyard at Kiel and was one of the three *Karp*-class boats bought from Germany by the Russian Admiralty who were unhappy with the weird products of their own designers. The Kaiser's first official U-boat, *U-1*, was also designed by d'Equevillet and was a very close relation to the *Karp* boats.

Displacing 196 tons in surface trim and fitted with Korting kerosene engines to avoid the dangers of petrol vapour *Kambala* was a highly successful submarine. She was armed with three torpedo tubes and was capable of a maximum 11 knots on the surface.

According to *The Times*; 'The submarine sank while being tested at Kronstadt, the Kingston valves being opened before the conning-tower hatch was closed. The boat flooded and sank. There was an instructional class on board at the time and one officer and twenty-three men were lost'.

But a schedule published by the highly respected *US Naval Institute Review* in 1972 shows the *Kambala* as being rammed 'and cut in half' by the battleship *Rostislav* when five miles from

Sevastopol. And the casualties are given as twenty men lost and four saved.

It is difficult to believe that these two widely differing stories relate to the same incident. In the first *Kambala* was sunk in the Baltic as the result of a human error while diving, and in the second she was rammed by a specifically identified battleship several thousand miles away in the Black Sea. Obviously both accounts cannot be correct. Or can they? Surprisingly, there *is* a plausible explanation for these apparently contradictory versions. It is quite possible that the unfortunate *Kambala* actually sank *twice* – in the Baltic while undergoing sea trials soon after she had been delivered by Krupps; and then, following salvage and transfer to the Crimea, as a consequence of her collision with the *Rostislav*. Circumstantial evidence in support of the submarine's presence in southern waters is provided by the careers of the other two *Karp*-class boats, both of which served with the Black Sea Flotilla during the war. It is a pity that the Soviet Navy, which could probably established the correct facts from its pre-1914 archives, failed to respond to enquiries.

In the five years since the sinking of the *A.1* in 1904 at least 122 men had lost their lives in submarine disasters and thoughts were now beginning to turn towards the development of more scientific escape systems. Despite the improvements in submarine design there had been no advance on the technique first demonstrated by Wilhelm Bauer in 1851, and it was clear that, without some form of breathing apparatus, only a handful of men could make their escape from a sunken vessel using such primitive methods. But was there a viable alternative ?

On Thursday 15 April, 1909, Ensign Kenneth Whiting entered the bow torpedo tube of the *USS Porpoise*. The rear door was secured and the young officer had to wait in the claustrophobic darkness of the narrow tunnel while it was flooded up before he could release the clip of the outer door and rise safely to the surface. Although, on this occasion, he was the only man to swim clear, it was apparent that, if the tube had been drained down again, every member of the crew could have made his escape in a similar manner. It was an encouraging and brave experiment which pointed the way to the escape chambers of the future.

Another officer, Ensign Carr, made a series of simulated

escapes from the *Shark* a short while later, but he went one better than Whiting by *re-entering* the submerged boat via the torpedo tube by reversing the procedures of flooding up and draining down. Acting on their personal initiatives and without official support Whiting and Carr had shown that there was, indeed, an alternative to the Bauer method of escape. But that, unfortunately, was only one part of the solution. There were other problems of survival to be faced, not the least being the presence of chlorine gas from fractured storage batteries and the slow but relentless build-up of carbon dioxide inside a sunken submarine.

The germ of an answer was already in existence in the shape of the Fleuss-Davis self-contained diving apparatus produced in 1878 by the internationally renowned firm of safety engineers Siebe, Gorman and Company. This apparatus was based on the closed circuit principle in which the carbon dioxide content of the exhaled breath is absorbed by a chemical cartridge while a small amount of oxygen is replaced into the system from a high-pressure cylinder. Although used successfully underwater in several mining disasters it proved too large for use inside a submarine. And even though Davis had succeeded in reducing its proportions by 1903 no one of consequence showed any interest.

In 1906 Commander S.S. Hall, the Royal Navy's Inspecting Captain of Submarines, visited Siebe Gorman's Neptune Works in South-East London and consulted Davis about a suitable escape apparatus. But, although he was suitably impressed by the new breathing kit which Davis had developed, the oxygen cylinder was still too bulky for submarine use.

A technical breakthrough was, however, just around the corner. While Davis was struggling to make his apparatus more compact a French chemist, Doctor Georges Joubert, discovered that sodium peroxide not only absorbed the poisonous carbon dioxide contained in the exhaled breath, it also gave off oxygen. But while this meant that the bulky oxygen cylinder could be discarded it did not entirely solve the problem. For, as is so often the case, theory did not translate smoothly into practice. The oxygen took an unduly long time to build up and it was necessary for the escaper to be enclosed in a waist-length diving suit complete with sleeves and a metal helmet. That was not the only drawback. Sodium peroxide is a highly unstable substance with an inclination to burst into flames when wet – hardly a suitable property if it was to be used in a flooded submarine. But, despite these inherent disadvantages it offered, as one Commanding Officer put it, 'a sporting chance of escape' and the Hall-Rees apparatus, incorporating sodium peroxide, was patented by the Admiralty in 1907 who funded further development and research with a generous £27,000.

But while the scientists worked to solve the problems of survival the toll of lost submarines continued to rise. 1909 had already claimed two victims - the Italian *Foca* and the Russian *Kampala*. Now it was the turn of the Royal Navy again. Four years had passed since the loss of the *A.4* and, although three men had been killed by an explosion aboard *C.8* in 1907, there was a general feeling in the Service that improved training methods and better designs had made the submarine safer. While it was true that the French, Italians and Russians had suffered a series of disasters the pre-1914 British Navy considered itself so superior to the fleets of other nations that comparisons were meaningless. But such optimism and conceit was subjected to a rude shock on 14 July when the new *C.11*, exercising off Cromer, was rammed by the steamer *Eddystone*. With an enormous hole punched into her side she plunged to the bottom with thirteen men still entombed inside her. Only three members of the crew who were in the conning-tower at the time of the collision survived. So much for improved training methods and safer boats. The submarine was still a killer.

On 15 April, 1910, Japan had her first encounter with disaster when Submarine *No 6* sank during diving trials in Kure harbour. It was, if such a thing is possible, a routine accident and the details are similar to many of those already described. But the extraordinary letter written by the boat's captain, Lieutenant-Commander Sakuma, as he sat waiting for death in the dark fume-filled interior of the submarine demands a fuller account of the tragedy. For while, in Europe, scientists were busy devising equipment to help survivors escape from the bottom of the sea, the fatalism of the Orient enabled men to accept their entombment with, to Western eyes, almost superhuman detachment.

No 6 was the first submarine to be built in Japan. Laid down in November, 1904, by the Kawasaki Shipbuilding Company of Kobe she was, in effect, a scaled down version of the original

Holland design, five of which had been purchased from the Electric Boat Company by the Imperial Japanese Navy. She was a small experimental vessel displacing only 57 tons on the surface and fitted with a single torpedo tube in the bows.

The submarine started her fatal dive at 10 am while exercising in company with a small steamer which also acted as the parent ship. For some reason the boat submerged too quickly and, as Sakuma explained in his letter, a ventilator slide valve malfunctioned. The sea poured into the submarine which sank stern-first and settled on the bottom in 60 feet of water.

At 11 am, alarmed by *No 6*'s failure to return to the surface, the parent ship sent an urgent wireless message to the naval base at Kure. The *Toyohashi*, accompanied by tugs and lighters, hurried to the scene. But despite an extensive search operation the would-be rescuers failed to locate the sunken boat and as dusk deepened the hunt was called off until the next day. It was 3 pm the following afternoon before the wreck was finally found but, even then, due to various problems with the lifting-gear, she was not raised to the surface until late the same night. Sakuma's letter was found when the bodies were removed:

'I am very sorry that, owing to my carelessness, I have sunk His Majesty's submarine and killed the officers and men under my orders; but I am glad that they have all faithfully discharged their duties with composure until the moment they died, and that we all sacrificed our lives for the sake of our country. What I fear, however, is that this mishap may cause public misunderstanding as to the safety of the submarine and check its future development. If you, my dear sirs, investigate the development of the submarine with more zeal and without this misgiving I shall be most grateful.

The cause of the accident

'While navigating under water with the gasoline engine we dived too deeply, and when we tried to close the slide valve of the ventilator the chain broke. Thereupon we endeavoured to close it with our hands but it was too late, the after part of the boat being flooded, and she sank stern first. The angle was about 25°.
'After the boat had settled, her inclination was about 13°. As the switchboard was submerged the electric light went out and noxious gas issued which made breathing difficult. The boat sank at about 10 am on the 15th. We tried to pump out the water in the boat with a hand pump. No sooner had the boat sunk than we pumped out the main tank and although we could not see the gauge owing to the darkness we think we succeeded. The electric current became unavailable, and although the solution in the cells overflowed a little, sea-water did not get into them, which prevented

the generation of chlorine. We depend upon the hand pumps entirely.

The foregoing was written in the conning-tower at 11.45 am. The clothes of the crew are nearly all wet with salt water and they feel very cold.

'I am always of the opinion that the crew of a submarine must be very calm and careful, but unless they behave boldly the progress of the submarine will never be accomplished, and therefore I have always warned my men not to be too cautious through timidity. Some people many laugh at my failure on this occasion, but I am confident that I am right in my opinion.

'The depth gauge in the conning-tower shows 52, and although we have done our best to pump out the water up till noon the boat is still fixed. I think we must be in about ten fathoms.

'The crew of a submarine should be composed of specially selected men lest they should suffer similar experiences to this one. I am satisfied that my officers and men have all done their duty. Whenever I leave my home to join my boat I feel that I may never return alive, and therefore I have made my Will and have left it in a drawer at my house, but it is not necessary to say more about it here as it only concerns my private affairs. I request that Messrs Taguchi and Asada will see my father about it.

To His Majesty

'Sire, I entreat you to look after the families of the officers and men under my orders so that they do not starve; this is the only thing that troubles me.

'Atmospheric pressure is increasing and I feel as if my eardrums have been broken. 12-30 pm. Respiration is extraordinarily difficult. I mean I am breathing petrol gas. I am intoxicated with petrol. Captain Nakano, it is 12-40 o'clock ....'

At that point the letter ends. Sakuma, who had by some miracle survived for more than 14 hours, was dead. And so too were the other thirteen brave men who made up *No 6*'s crew.

It is only rarely that the outside world is made privy to the thoughts and actions of the men trapped inside a submarine when it is lost with all hands, and for this reason Sakuma's letter has been reproduced in full. It is a testament not only to a courageous man but to all men, of whatever nationality, who have perished unseen in the depths of the ocean trapped inside the iron coffins that have taken them to their deaths.

At 10 am on 17 April, exactly forty-eight hours after the submarine had begun its last plunge, *No 6* was pumped out and her buoyancy restored. The torpedo hatch was opened and when the boat had been thoroughly ventilated the Senior Surgeon of the *Toyohashi*, with four assistants, descended into the submarine to remove the bodies of the fourteen men who had died. Each man was carefully re-dressed in a clean uniform appropriate to his rank and lowered into a waiting coffin. Then, with her ensign fluttering at half-mast, *Toyohashi* returned sadly to Kure.

1910 saw two further disasters. On 26 May the French submarine *Pluviose*, a steam-driven boat built in 1907, was rammed and sunk by the Channel-packet *Pas de Calais* two miles out from the French coast. Like *No 6* she was also lost with all hands. And her death-roll of twenty-seven men was the highest so far sustained in a single accident. The Russian *Forel*, which sank while in tow on 1 June, was more fortunate and her entire crew survived. In fact *Forel*'s only claim to fame rests on her reputed submerged displacement of just 17 tons, which, according to the reference books, makes her the smallest naval submarine ever to be lost in peacetime.

Germany, who had entered the submarine building race some time after everyone else, suffered her first loss on 17 November, 1911, when *U-3* sank in Kiel harbour with a class of officer-trainees aboard. The incident revealed that, despite their late start, German scientists had already designed some noteworthy items of equipment: a lifebuoy with a telephone that could be released and sent to the surface in an emergency; chemical cartridges which were able to purify the air inside a stricken submarine and prevent the build-up of carbon dioxide; and, finally, a monstrous double-hulled salvage vessel named, with Teutonic aptness, *Vulkan*.

With *U-1* acting as her surface escort, *U-3* had been carrying out a series of practice dives when the accident occured and the first intimation that something was wrong came when the U-boat's telephone-buoy bobbed to the surface. *U-1* steered alongside and grappled it aboard so that her captain could speak to his opposite number in the other submarine. Communication having been established, *U-3*'s commander reported that his boat was flooding and that chlorine gas was building-up as a result of sea-water mixing with the sulphuric acid in the battery cells. He would, no doubt, have said more but at that moment the telephone went dead and all contact with the sunken vessel ceased.

Using the distress buoy as a guide to the position of her lost comrade, *U-1* dropped anchor and her wireless operator transmitted an urgent signal to Fleet Headquarters at Kiel requesting immediate assistance. Then an extraordinary thing happened. The men trapped inside the flooded submarine managed to blow one of the forward ballast tanks and, almost before the wireless message was completed, *U-3*'s bow section suddenly emerged from the water.

An officer from *U-1* jumped onto *U-3*'s exposed hull plating and was quickly joined by the Engineer. The two men tapped a morse signal on the casing and instructed the trapped crew to open the submarine's bow caps so that they could escape by climbing up through the torpedo tubes. There was no response and it was uncertain whether the men had merely failed to understand the signal or whether they were already dead. The two officers tried once more, but again there was no answer.

While *Vulkan* and the main rescue team were still preparing to leave harbour a floating-crane, which had been working nearby, arrived on the scene and a wire was passed around the exposed bow of the U-boat to prevent it from sinking back into the water. Then, striking the plating with a steel wrench, the morse message was repeated and this time an answering tattoo proved that at least one of the entombed men was still alive. There was a brief pause, followed by the whine of a servo-motor, and, as the men watching from the deck of *U-1* shouted their encouragement, the bow-cap swung open. A rope was lowered into the torpedo tube and a sharp jerk from the inboard end showed that the first man was ready. The crew of *U-1* hauled on the line and slowly dragged the trapped seaman up the 28-foot tunnel. *U-3*'s first survivor had been saved.

The men of *U-1* did not spare themselves until they had dragged every one of their twenty-eight comrades clear. Most of them were in a pathetic state, choking and coughing from the chlorine gas eating into their lungs, and several were already unconscious as they were laid on the submarine's deck. But for some rescue had come too late. And the inert bodies were quickly covered with blankets brought up from below.*

A roll-call revealed that *U-3*'s captain and two other officers were still missing and, after questioning the survivors, it was established that they were trapped in the upper section of the conning-tower. The rescuers decided to await the arrival of *Vulkan* which was already in sight. No one doubted that, with the help of the special lifting gear carried by the salvage ship, the last three men would be released within a few hours. But, as on

*One of the rescued survivors was Otto Weddigen who, as captain of the *U-9* sank the cruisers *Aboukir, Cressy,* and *Houge* on 22 September, 1914.

so many other similar occasions, their optimism proved to be sadly misplaced.

In order to lift the sunken U-boat *Vulkan* had to straddle the wreck and raise it centrally between her two catamaran-type hulls. Before this delicate operation could even begin the submarine would have to be lowered back to the bottom so that *Vulkan* could be moored directly above her.

It took *Vulkan* an unbelievable eighteen hours to raise *U-3* and it was 3 am the following morning before the conning-tower broke surface. But despite the delay all seemed well and observers saw the periscope move as a signal that the three officers were still alive. Fate, however, was not on their side. There were difficulties in forcing open the upper hatch and by the time the men were dragged out two were already dead. The third died soon after his arrival at Kiel Naval Hospital.

Despite the partial success of the rescue operation, it was clear that specialized equipment was needed to assist individual escape, and, as in Britain, German thoughts turned towards the development of a portable self-contained breathing apparatus compact enough for use in a submarine. The Drager Company of Lubeck was already working on an oxygen breathing-set based on the Fleuss closed circuit principle. Although originally intended for civilian use the small dimensions of the Drager kit made it eminently suitable for submarine escape and in 1912, a year after the *U-3* tragedy, the *Kriegsmarine* placed its first order.

That the Drager Lung, or *Tauchretter*, was well in advance of its time is evidenced by the fact that, with minor modifications, it remained standard U-boat equipment up to and beyond the Second World War. But its issue revealed a strange quirk in German psychology. A U-boat's stock of Drager Lungs never equalled the number of men that made up its crew. Space inside an operational submarine is very much at a premium and no doubt Teutonic logic reasoned that as part of the crew were likely to die before an escape was attempted it was unnecessary to clutter up the interior with apparatus which would never be needed. Logical, perhaps, but it was a gamble no other navy would have dared to take. Except, of course, the Japanese who issued no escape kits at all!

On 2 February, 1912, *A.3* collided with the depot ship *Hazard* off the Isle of Wight and sank with her entire crew of fourteen men. And on 8 June the French *Vendemiaire* was cut in two by the battleship *St Louis* during exercises outside the naval base at Cherbourg.

This latter accident happened during a simulated torpedo attack on a group of 'enemy' warships operating in the notorious Raz Blanchard. *Vendemiaire*'s captain had made his approach underwater and, steering by dead reckoning, planned to rise to periscope depth when 400 yards from his target. But as he passed between Aurigny Island and Cape Hague the treacherous currents in the Race of Alderney swept him off his charted course. When he raised his periscope he was horrified to find the flagship less than 100 yards to starboard. The lookouts on the *St Louis* sighted the stalk of the periscope as it broke surface and, reacting with swift efficiency, the battleship reversed engines. There was nothing the helpless *Vendemiaire* could do but dive in the vain hope of passing beneath the ironclad's keel. But with only twenty seconds separating the two vessels the chances of avoiding a collision were minimal. *St Louis* slammed into the half-submerged submarine and her great ram bow sliced through the thin hull plating as if it was made of paper. *Vendemiaire* was literally cut in two by the impact and twenty-four men perished in the tragedy.

On the night of 4 October Britain's *B.2* was rammed by the Hamburg America Line's *SS Amerika* four miles from Dover in a re-run of the *Pluviose* disaster two years earlier. The submarine was on the surface, probably recharging her batteries, and the liner's lookouts failed to spot her low outline in the darkness. One man was saved but fifteen died and it was clear that a failure of the lookout system on both vessels was responsible for the tragedy. As a final flourish to a disastrous year, the American *F.1* foundered in heavy seas after being torn from her moorings by gale-force winds at Port Watsonville. Two men who were on board at the time were lost.

It seemed likely that 1913 would pass without a major submarine accident, but with only three weeks of the year left to run the Royal Navy's *C.14* came to grief in Plymouth Sound on 10 December. The submarine, under the command of Lieutenant Napper who was to lose his life in *E.24* during the war, was on her way out of Devonport dockyard with the rest of the First Flotilla for a series of diving exercises in the Channel. Visibility was poor, as the boats passed between Drake Island

and Devil's Point, *C.14* collided with the Admiralty Hopper *No 27*. The pressure hull was holed but fortunately the submarine sank fairly slowly and, with their flotilla mates close at hand, the twenty men aboard were able to jump clear and swim to safety.

On 16 January, 1914, *A.7* foundered in Whitesand Bay just a few miles from the scene of *C.14*'s collision a month earlier. The cause of the accident, which cost the lives of all eleven men on board, remains a mystery as, for some reason, the submarine was never salvaged and no one knows what went wrong. But the tragedy evoked considerable sympathy and Grand Admiral Alfred Von Tirpitz conveyed the condolences of the German Navy to the Second Sea Lord, Vice-Admiral Sir John Jellicoe:

'The sad accident of your submarine *A.7* has aroused the deepest sympathy in the whole German Navy. Seeing this effect amongst our naval officers, and the sympathy tendered by the British Navy on the loss of our airship*, I have again been impressed by the natural brotherhood of sailors . . . Since the accident to our submarine *U-3* we have studied seriously the questions tending to lessen the dangers of submarine seafaring. Fortunately we have been able to introduce many valuable improvements.'

Von Tirpitz was being unusually modest, for the safety record of the German U-boat service in peacetime had been, and was to be, exemplary. In the ten years up to the outbreak of war in August, 1914, the Royal Navy lost nine submarines and the French eleven. Germany, in the same decade, lost only *U-3*. And a similar pattern was to emerge in the inter-war years although it is true that during both periods Germany had far fewer submarines in service than her two European rivals. Indeed, from 1919 to 1936 she was prevented from building U-boats under the terms of the Treaty of Versailles.

Perhaps because the class numbered thirteen vessels, or perhaps because familiarity had made the crews over-confident, Britain's A-class boats had a calamitous safety record with six sunk and a seventh, *A.9*. only escaping disaster by the skin of her teeth. Their service history stands in sharp contrast to the Royal Navy's original five *Holland* submarines which, despite their primitive periscopes and notorious unhandiness on the surface, never suffered a serious accident.

---

*The naval Zeppelin *L-2* which caught fire in the air and crashed on 17 October, 1913, with the loss of twenty-eight lives.

Holland No 1 had admittedly given rise to many doubts during construction and Captain Bacon was quite convinced that the drawings supplied under licence by the Electric Boat Company were seriously in error. His suspicions were apparently justified for the submarine nearly capsized on launching and mistakes were subsequently found in the working blue-prints. Although little was said publicly it was official opinion that a Fenian infiltrator had deliberately tampered with the plans before they were delivered to the Admiralty. Bearing in mind the Irish political situation 1900 and Holland's earlier association with the Brotherhood industrial sabotage seems highly likely. But, once the bugs had been ironed out, the little Holland submarines performed remarkably well.

No 1 provided further excitement during her trials in the dock basin of Vickers shipyard. Her commander, Lieutenant D. Arnold-Forster, recalled that the boat 'alarmed the inmates of the sick-bay in the *Hazard* . . . by poking her nose right through the ship's side into their berths'* when she failed to respond to the helm. But although the parent ship, a former gunboat, had to be laid up for repairs the errant submarine sustained no structural damage in the collision.

On another occasion, in December, 1902, Lieutenant Penrose was ordered to take *No 2* to Ryde where he was to give a demonstration of its diving ability to a member of the Royal Family who was visiting the Royal Naval College at Osborne. The submarine continually misbehaved on the outward trip and more than once settled on the sea-bottom without any assistance from her crew. But Penrose finally arrived in the demonstration area without mishap and, at the appointed time, took the boat down to 20 feet and kept her submerged at 4 knots for exactly twelve minutes. Unfortunately, swept off course by the strong flood tide, *No 2* emerged in the wrong place and surfaced directly underneath the keel of an ancient brigantine. 'There was a curious scraping noise overhead, the boat gave a tremor, and she rolled slightly. A startled "What ho, she bumps !" came from the A.B. on his stool forward, and a hollow bump, bump, bump sounded along the hull.'*

The Ways of the Navy by Rear Admiral D. Arnold-Forster, Ward Lock & Co. 1931.

*Arnold-Forster. Ibid.

No 2 ran clear, blew her tanks, and broke surface. The hatchcover was raised and Penrose climbed out on to the sloping deck prepared for the worst. The periscope had been bent to an alarming angle but, to his surprise, the submarine had sustained no other visible damage. The skipper of the dilapidated sailing-vessel was full of apologies. 'We did all we could,' he explained. 'All we saw was a pole coming at us through the water. We all shouted and waved but it took no notice at all.'

It would be pleasant to conclude the chapter on this humorous note but, sadly, in those final months before the Great War three more submarines were lost. Holland suffered her first serious accident on 31 January when *O.5* flooded and sank alongside Scheldt Quay. A mechanical safety device intended to prevent the inner doors and bow caps of the torpedo tubes from both being open at the same time malfunctioned and the sea rushed into the cylinder. One man, trapped in the fore compartment, was drowned but the remaining nineteen men aboard were saved. And in March the Russian *Minoga* sank off Libau when water leaked through an open ventilator. The flooded submarine was raised after ten hours and her twenty-man crew were lucky to escape with their lives.

On 7 July, 1914, nine days after the fuse of war had been lit by the assassination of Crown Prince Franz Ferdinand at Sarajevo, two French submarines were carrying out joint surface exercises off Cape Lardier. Suddenly, as the result of a damaged rudder, *Calypso* lost control of her helm and veered into the path of the fast-moving *Circe*. There was a violent collision and, with the sea pouring through the wound in her side, *Calypso* went swiftly to the bottom. Three men died with her but twenty-three of their shipmates were dragged out of the water by their comrades in the other submarine.

It had been France's eleventh peacetime disaster. And *Circe* herself was to become a victim of the war that now hung over Central Europe. On 20 September, 1918, when the end of the bloody conflict was at last in sight, she was torpedoed and sunk by an Austrian U-boat in the Adriatic. She was fated to be just one amongst many hundreds of other submarines that would be lost by enemy action in the four horrendous years that followed August, 1914.

—FIVE—

'Overdue and presumed lost'

The stresses and strains of war inevitably lead to a higher frequency of accidents. For while in peacetime every precaution is taken to ensure the safety of a submarine's crew similar consideration cannot be guaranteed under combat conditions. But there are other equally important reasons. Experienced personnel find themselves uprooted and scattered piecemeal among a rapidly expanding fleet where their expertise is required in a hundred-and-one departments ashore and afloat and they have to be replaced by recruits whose training, while adequately thorough, cannot make up for years of familiarity with submarine routine.

With all lights extinguished and black-out regulations in force, night movements are suddenly more hazardous, and the deliberate removal of navigational marks, channel buoys and shore lights, can lead to serious errors in fixing the position of a submarine in dangerous coastal waters. Shipping lanes in the approaches to busy ports are congested and overcrowded as convoys assemble and disperse and minor collisions come to be accepted as an unavoidable fact of life, while the constant threat of a sudden enemy attack forces the submarine commander to seek faster and faster diving times.

Finally, men worn out and exhausted by the rigours of extended patrols under war conditions are prone to mistakes, insignificant in detail and trivial in extent, but, for a submarine, almost invariably fatal.

Security and the safeguarding of morale often demand the concealment of accident details, especially when a boat is lost because of an error in identification by friendly forces – the destruction of the *Oxley* by the *Triton* in 1939 being a case in point. And, again, in some instances false information is given in order to mislead the enemy. But there are also many occasions when the authorities have no idea themselves why a particular submarine has failed to return from patrol.

How many of the boats officially listed as 'overdue and presumed lost' actually sank from accidental causes will never be established. For submarine salvage is an impractical luxury in wartime except in very special circumstances, even when the boat can be found. In most cases the precise location of the sunken vessel is as obscure as the reason for its loss.

The first Allied submarine to be sunk in the First World War vanished in just such a manner – without trace and without apparent reason. On 14 September, 1914, the Australian *AE.1*, accompanied by the destroyer *Parramatta*, set off from the newly captured German harbour of Rabaul to patrol the St George's Strait between New Britain and New Ireland in search of the enemy cruiser *Geier* which was thought to be operating in the Bismarck Sea.

During the afternoon *Parramatta* closed *AE.1* and, after an exchange of signals, steered away to the south-eastward. Visual contact with the submarine was lost at about 3.30 pm and the destroyer eventually returned to Rabaul at sunset in accordance with her orders. But *AE.1* was never seen again. Admiral Sir George Patey, the local flag-officer, organized an immediate search but no trace of the submarine could be found and, after three days, the hunt was abandoned.

What could have happened to the missing boat? Destruction by enemy forces was out of the question and there were no minefields in the vicinity. Weather conditions were favourable and in the opinion of Lieutenant-Commander H.G. Stoker, the captain of her sister-ship *AE.2* which was also operating in the St George's Strait, there was no reason for the submarine to submerge. The experts claimed that the mysterious disappearance was due to the boat striking a submerged reef. But the total absence of wreckage makes this an unconvincing explanation and the probable reason for *AE.1*'s loss was an internal explosion of hydrogen gas.

A similar mystery surrounds the loss of many other missing wartime submarines and for this reason and those outlined at the beginning of the chapter the sections covering the war years 1914-1918 and 1939-1945 cannot encompass every disaster. In many instances only the barest details are available and the narrative would quickly degenerate into a repetitious list of names and dates. A comprehensive and definitive summary of all wartime accidents which resulted in the loss of a submarine can, however, be found in the chronological appendices.

Collisions, not surprisingly, account for the majority of wartime accidents, but stranding and running aground stand high in the disaster stakes. In times of peace most submarines that find themselves high and dry on the shore are quickly salvaged and casualties are minimal. In war, however, other factors can lead to the total loss of the beached submarine with heavy loss of life, and on occasions such accidents can have unforeseen and tragic repercussions.

On 30 October, 1915, the French submarine *Turquoise* was forced to abandon her patrol in the Sea of Marmora because of mechanical defects. Heading back to Mudros through the narrows of the Dardanelles she ran foul of the treacherous currents and grounded on the southern shore at Nagara Point. Finding himself under the guns of a Turkish fort, and anxious to avoid unnecessary loss of life, Lieutenant de Vaisseau Ravene surrendered his submarine and crew to the enemy. Unfortunately he did not take the precaution of destroying his confidential papers and, when German naval officers examined their prize, they learned that the British submarine *E.20* was due to rendezvous with the French boat that same evening. A neatly pencilled cross on the Frenchman's chart showed the precise position of their intended meeting-place.

When *E.20* arrived at the appointed spot her companion was nowhere in sight but, lurking at periscope depth 3,000 yards away, was the German submarine *UB-15*. The British boat was a sitting duck and only nine men, including her captain, Lieutenant Warren, survived the subsequent torpedo attack.

A few months earlier another submarine had fallen victim to the powerful currents of the Dardanelles and, like *Turquoise*, found herself stranded in sight of the Turkish shore batteries. But her story had a very different conclusion and demonstrated the impossibility of salvaging a beached submarine on an enemy shore.

On 17 April *E.15* set off up the Dardanelles in an attempt to break through into the Sea of Marmora. She submerged to pass under a line of moored mines near Kephez Point but, caught in the raging undertow, she was swept ashore and ran aground in full view of the guns in Fort Dardanus. The Turks opened fire immediately and as their artillery ranged on the stricken submarine her captain, Lieutenant-Commander T.S. Brodie, tried to free his boat from the mud by running full-speed astern. But although the propellors threshed the water into a froth *E.15* proved to be immovably stuck.

A Turkish torpedo-boat closed in and, as Brodie opened the hatch of the conning-tower, the first shell exploded against the hull killing him instantly. More gunners brought their weapons into action and further hits were obtained – one shot piercing the pressure-hull amidships and exploding in the battery compartment. The sea rushed in through the shattered steel plating and, when it reached the sulphuric acid spilling from the broken batteries, a dense cloud of chlorine gas enveloped the interior of the boat. In the circumstances resistance was impossible and, struggling blindly through the choking yellow fumes, the crew scrambled up on deck and surrendered.

The Turkish torpedo-boat hooked a rope over the submarine's stern and attempted to haul her prize out of the mud but an RNAS seaplane, which had been watching the proceedings, swooped low over the enemy ship and released its bombs. They fell well clear, but were sufficient to frighten off the torpedo-boat which hastily dropped its tow-line and beat a rapid retreat through the Narrows.

From the British viewpoint destruction rather than salvage was now the best course of action and within a few hours the ancient *B.6* was plodding out of Mudros. She successfully closed the stranded *E.15* but her torpedoes missed their intended target. At dusk two destroyers, *Scorpion* and *Grampus*, were ordered to blow the submarine out of the water but the Turkish shore batteries drove them back. The next day three attempts were made to destroy the *E.15* – with torpedoes from *B.11*, bombs from RNAS aircraft and shells from the battleships *Triumph* and *Majestic*. But all failed. As a last resource picket-boats from the two battleships were sent in on an old-fashioned cutting-out operation. The attack was made at night under heavy enemy fire. The first torpedo missed but Lieutenant Claude Godwin, in charge of *Majestic*'s boat, loosed off two more at a range of 200 yards. There was a tremendous explosion and *E.15* seemed to leap off the mud as her hull erupted in flame. Within minutes she was a blackened wreck of no further use to either friend or foe.

Although other incidents in which British submarines ran aground were less spectacular they are, nevertheless, of interest. On the night of 6 January, 1916, *E.17*, patrolling on the surface off the Dutch coast in heavy weather, ran full tilt into a half-submerged mudbank. Stranded on the sandy shingle, she lay helpless as the gale-swept seas pounded and pummelled her with merciless fury. 'Each time the huge rollers came rushing in from astern,' one survivor recalled, 'she was lifted up and then flung down again with a most awful crash'.

Her captain, Lieutenant-Commander J.R.G. Moncrieffe, was washed overboard by the wild seas but, grabbing at the conning-tower rails, he dragged himself back to safety. For the next hour he juggled with the engines and, aided by superb seamanship, he finally managed to ease the submarine off the shoal – only to run smack into another within seconds. This time the raging sea swung *E.17* broadside-on to the wind and sea and, helplessly stranded, she was exposed to the full power of the deepening storm. A torpedo jolted loose from its rack and threatened to blow the boat to smithereens until it was secured, and large amounts of water flooding down through the conning-tower hatch fused the main switchboard and started an electrical fire which the crew had to extinguish in the dim glow of hand-held emergency torches.

Realizing that nothing could be achieved before morning, Moncrieffe ordered the boat to be battened down and, bracing themselves in odd corners of the boat, he and the crew settled down to await daylight as *E.17* rolled and shuddered with the violence of the storm.

The submarine had lost its rudder and the sea had swamped the after-compartments. Both propellor shafts were visibly bent where they had been jolted up and down on their bearings, the electric motors were wet and shorting badly, six or seven of the main ballast tanks were holed, and the hull seams were leaking in a dozen or more places. Anticipating the worst Moncrieffe burned his confidential papers and code books and, with no great optimism, waited to see what the dawn would bring.

Going up on to the bridge at first light the submarine's officers found that *E.17* was only fifty yards from the shore and a few hasty bearings showed that they were stranded on the island of Texel. The storm had now nearly blown itself out and, in view of the improved conditions, Moncrieffe decided to take a chance. The engines were restarted and, steering with infinite care, he guided the submarine through the shoals and headed out towards the open sea. The morning mists had thickened and by the time *E.17* was into deeper water visibility was down to a few hundred yards. But when it began to lift Moncrieffe was horrified to see a cruiser lying some four miles to the south. Hoping they had not been spotted he slipped the boat into a convenient bank of mist and edged slowly westwards. An hour later the cruiser came into sight again, this time less than a mile distant. Her flag was obscured by thick black funnel smoke but her guns were trained towards the submarine.

Moncrieffe had no doubt that the warship was hostile and, ignoring the parlous state of his boat, he gave orders to dive. But with the sea still entering the submarine through the hole left by the absent rudder it was clear that unless *E.17* was taken back to the surface immediately she would go to the bottom and stay there.

The submarine began to rise slowly but when it reached 45 feet the water swilling around the engine-room shorted the main port motor. *E.17* promptly started sinking again and was only saved by the buoyancy of her empty ballast tanks. She steadied for a moment, hung motionless as if suspended in the water, and then returned to the surface in a rush. Expecting to find the enemy cruiser waiting for them, and determined to fight to the last, Moncrieffe ordered the torpedo tubes to be flooded and warned the crews to stand by.

The cruiser was, indeed, waiting for them just a few hundred yards away and a perfect target. But it was not the German warship Moncrieffe had anticipated; it was the Dutch *Noord Brabant*, a neutral vessel that posed no threat to their safety. The last desperate dive that had wrecked any chance of *E.17* making it back to England had not been necessary after all. But it was too late to undo the damage and, having opened the seacocks to scuttle the submarine, Moncrieffe and his crew were taken aboard the warship, given dry clothes and hot drinks, and taken back to Holland where, in accordance with International Law, they were interned for the rest of the war.

Only thirteen days later, on 19 January, another submarine from the Harwich Flotilla, *H.6*, ran aground on the Dutch coast, this time at Schiermonnikoog, only twenty miles from the German island of Borkum. A wireless distress call was transmitted and within a few hours the destroyer *Firedrake* with the Commodore (S) aboard arrived on the scene. Captain Waistell reviewed the situation and decided that the stranded submarine was too close to the German naval bases on the Ems River to permit salvage operations and a motor-boat was sent inshore to take off the confidential books and some of the key ratings. *Firedrake* then departed, leaving the submarine's captain to arrange for the internment of the boat and the rest of the crew with the Dutch authorities. *H.6*, however, survived her ordeal and enjoyed a remarkable career in the years that followed. She was salvaged by the Dutch in February, 1916, and was initially interned, like her crew, at Niewdiep. But some time later she was purchased from the British Government and commissioned into the Royal Netherlands Navy as *O.8*. She was scuttled at Den Helder during the invasion of Holland in 1940 but was again salved, this time by the Germans. After refitting she was put into service with the *Kriegsmarine* as *UD-1* and, as such, patrolled the North Sea under the swastika ensign of the Third Reich. She was finally paid off at Kiel in March, 1943, and scuttled when Germany surrendered two years later. Not many submarines can claim to have sailed under three flags or to have served on opposing sides in two world wars.

E.17 and *H.6* were relatively lucky. Others were not. *E.13*, for example, paid a terrifying price for her ill-omened number. Sent to join the flotilla of British submarines operating in support of the Russians in the Baltic, she ran into trouble while on passage through The Sound when her magnetic compass failed. Unable to steer an accurate course the submarine was soon lost in the maze of narrow channels that separate the Baltic from the North Sea and ultimately stranded herself on the south-eastern edge of the Saltholm flat, a notorious mudbank between Malmo and Copenhagen, *inside Danish territorial waters*.

Under International Law a belligerent warship is only permitted to remain in neutral waters for a maximum of twenty-four hours. If she is still there when the time-limit expires she should be interned. Lieutenant-Commander Geoffrey Layton was well aware of this and the crew worked frantically to lighten the *E.13* sufficiently for her to be floated clear at the next high tide.

The Germans, however, had learned of the mishap and before many hours had passed two enemy destroyers appeared over the horizon. Ignoring the Danish guardship that was anchored nearby to enforce internment when the time came, and disregarding the fact that they were inside Denmark's territorial waters, one of the destroyers fired a torpedo at the stranded submarine. It struck the mud on which *E.13* was resting and, although there was a mighty and spectacular explosion, it did no damage.

Determined not to be foiled of their prey the enemy warships closed to within 300 yards and opened fire with their guns. The submarine stood no chance in the face of such an attack and within minutes she was a flaming twisted wreck. Several members of *E.13*'s crew were killed by the bombardment and, realizing the hopelessness of the position, Layton gave orders to abandon ship.

The survivors, many of them wounded, leapt into the water but the Germans opened fire again and, in all, fifteen died in this brutal attack. Appalled by the slaughter, the Captain of the Danish destroyer courageously placed his own ship between the men in the sea and the German guns and his action undoubtedly saved the lives of the remaining survivors. Sixteen men, including Lieutenant-Commander Layton, were rescued and, like the crews of *E.17* and *H.6*, saw out the rest of the war in an internment camp.*

Collisions involving submarines can, even in times of peace, have tragic consequences, and under war conditions the dangers are multiplied a hundred-fold. Yet not every collision ends in disaster. On 17 November, 1917, the boats of the 12th Submarine Flotilla were ordered to sea with the Grand Fleet for a sweep towards Denmark. It was a routine operation – at least, it should have been. But the 12th Flotilla was made up of nine K-class boats, and, as already noted, these steam dinosaurs were not exactly renowned for their impeccable behaviour.

At 10 pm *Blonde*, the light cruiser leading the flotilla, altered course in accordance with Fleet Orders and *K.1* slowed down as the cruiser swung away. The column bunched up and *K.4* promptly rammed *K.1* which was steaming immediately ahead of her. There was a crunch of torn metal and *K.1* began to sink by the stern as the sea flooded through the damaged plating. The crew's prompt action in closing the watertight doors saved the boat from any

---

*Layton, in fact, escaped from internment and was given command of the *K.6* on his return to England. As Vice-Admiral Sir Geoffrey Layton, he was C-in-C China when Japan invaded Hong Kong and Malaya in December 1941.

immediate danger but it was clear that she was seriously crippled. *Blonde* came alongside and lifted off the crew, but, after taking *K.1* in tow, the weather began to deteriorate and, during the night, the conditions became so bad that the submarine had to be sunk by the cruiser's guns. Exit another of the steam giants.

The crew of *C.12* enjoyed similar good fortune when their boat sank in the Humber. The submarine had been making its way down river when the main electric motors failed. There was a strong ebb-tide flowing and before any emergency measures could be taken she was swept across the river where she smashed against the destroyers lying alongside the Eastern Jetty at Immingham. The submarine was badly holed by the impact and her skipper, Lieutenant N. Manley, who was on the conning-tower bridge when the accident happened, ordered all hands on deck. As they hurried up the ladder only one man, the First Officer, Lieutenant G.H.S. Sullivan, remained below to close off the watertight doors and make a quick assessment of the extent of the damage.

As soon as the men were safely on deck Manley swung himself into the hatchway and, closing the upper hatch cover, began climbing down the ladder into the sinking submarine. *C.12* actually struck the bottom while he was still descending the ladder, but, ignoring the danger, he joined Sullivan and, wading knee-deep in water, the two officers examined every inch of the boat.

Chlorine gas was rising from the batteries as the sea-water penetrated the cell casings and intermingled with the acid but Manley and his Number One made no attempt to escape until they were satisfied that nothing could be done to save the submarine. Then they re-entered the conning-tower, closed the lower hatch and flooded the compartment until the internal and external pressures equalized. They then pushed back the upper hatch and calmly swam back to the surface. The information they had gleaned during their hazardous exploration of the sunken submarine enabled the salvage team to raise the boat a few days later. Men have certainly won medals for less!

C.12's sister-ship, *C.16*, was less fortunate and her collision with the *Melampus* on 16 April, 1917, while exercising with *C.25* ended in tragedy. The weather was good and only a slight breeze ruffled the surface as both submarines made a series of successful dummy attacks on the destroyer. As *Melampus* reversed course and steamed down the range the officers on her bridge saw *C.25* surfacing safely some 500 yards to port and Lieutenant-

Commander Lawrence Bignell, the destroyer's captain, warned his lookouts to be on the alert for *C.16* which was presumably moving in for her next attack.

Suddenly, just ahead of the port bow and less than twenty-five yards away, the tip of the submarine's periscope was seen emerging from the water. Bignell immediately pushed the bridge telegraph to *Full Astern* and ordered the helmsman to go hard a'starboard. But it was impossible to avoid a collision in the few seconds available and the men on the destroyer's bridge felt a slight bump as the submarine struck the *Melampus* near the stern.

Bignell buoyed the position where the submarine had gone down and remained in the vicinity for a considerable time searching for survivors. *C.16* was lying in only forty-five feet of water and escape, while difficult, was certainly not impossible. But, sadly, none of the submarine's crew appeared on the surface and *Melampus*, her hull leaking as a result of the collision, reluctantly returned to harbour leaving her sentinel role in the hands of a minesweeper.

An expert examination of the submarine after she had been raised revealed the terrible secrets of the hours that followed the accident. The impact of the crash had apparently stopped the main motors and had also wrenched the lid of the upper conning-tower hatch partially open. There was evidence that the crew had used the electric pumps in an attempt to reduce the flooding but the water penetrated the circuits and shorted them out. They had then manned the manual pumps to keep the sea at bay and an attempt had been made to blow the main ballast tanks but external damage allowed most of the compressed air to disperse through a broken pipe leading to the boat's whistle with the result that very little pressure reached the tanks.

The degree of organization and discipline demonstrated by these discoveries indicates that *C.16*'s crew had not only survived the collision but had exerted every possible effort to save the boat rather than themselves.

Having failed to vent the ballast tanks and restore buoyancy, it seems that the submarine's captain, Lieutenant Harold Boase, decided on a more direct approach. Mindful of Ensign Whiting's experiments in the *USS Porpoise*, he explained his scheme to the other officers. Exactly what passed between them during the ensuing discussion will never be known but it is apparent that the First Officer, Lieutenant Anderson, agreed to enter a torpedo tube so that he could be blown to the surface with written salvage instructions. There seemed no reason why the plan should not work for, now that the tanks had been partially vented, the bows had risen to within sixteen feet of the surface and everyone was optimistic of success. A note was hastily scribbled and, after sealing it inside a small watertight bag, it was tied to Anderson's wrist. It was still there when the salvage men removed the Lieutenant's body some days later.

> 'We are in 16 feet of water. The way to get us out is to lift the bows by the spectacle and haul us out of the boat through the tubes'
>
> H.Boase

Unfortunately, and for reasons which are not clear, Anderson's brave attempt to help his trapped shipmates failed and, with the poisoned air building up to a dangerous level inside the submarine, Boase decided they could not afford to sit around waiting for rescue. The crew were ordered to don their life-jackets and told to assemble under the fore-hatch. The watertight door to the bow compartment was dogged and clipped and then the inner door of the starboard torpedo tube was cautiously unclamped. It was obviously Boase's intention to emulate Wilhelm Bauer's method of escape from *Der Brandtaucher* by slowly flooding the sealed compartment until there was sufficient pressure of air to blow the waiting men to the surface when the hatch was opened. The plan should have worked, but Fate was to decree otherwise.

When the hatch was raised one of the submarine's cork fenders, which had been torn off in the collision, jammed it against the upper casing and it refused to open more than ten inches or so. It was an unexpected setback but, although disappointing, they still had an alternative chance of survival. There was plenty of air inside the boat and if they closed and clipped the hatch they could afford to wait for the arrival of the salvage vessels and lifting gear which were by now presumably on their way. But *C.16*'s crew were denied even this forlorn hope of survival. When they tried to lower the hatch the fender became so entangled in the mechanism that it refused to close the final two inches. The compressed air screamed out through the narrow opening and, with the air-lock destroyed, the sea poured in and drowned the men below.

It was a tragic disaster. Both attempts to escape were based on methods that had worked successfully in the past and were to work again in the future. But on this occasion, their efforts were in vain.

C.16 had joined the growing roll of submarines lost with all hands. It is particularly sad to note that, had the boat been equipped with the Hall-Rees escape apparatus, it is probable that every man would have survived.

All belligerent navies had their share of wartime submarine disasters. Germany lost *UB-25* on 19 March, 1917, following an encounter with the destroyer *V.26* at Kiel and towards the end of the same year, on 7 December, *UB-84* went down as the result of a collision in the Baltic. Russia suffered several similar losses – *No 1* being sunk at Murmansk when she was rammed by her fellow-submarine *Delfin* and, as noted earlier, *Som* went to the bottom after an accident in the Aaland Strait. France, too, had her tragedies. *Prarial* was run down by a merchant ship off Le Havre on the night of 28 April, 1918, and *Floreal* sank in another collision near Salonika on 2 August of the same year.

Neither did neutrality afford submarines immunity from the threat of disaster. On 9 October, 1916, the Danish *Dykkeren* was exercising in the Skagerrak under the eye of a watchful escort vessel. During one of the submerged trials the submarine's captain, Lieutenant Christaansen, misjudged his depth and suddenly found himself running blind as the periscope dipped beneath the surface. In normal circumstances the submarine would have been in no danger from such a mishap but, unfortunately, there was another ship in the area, and, ignoring the warning flags hoisted by *Dykkeren*'s escort, the Norwegian merchantman *Vesla* steamed into the diving zone. Moments later her bluff steel bows smashed into the submerged submarine which plunged to the bottom with an enormous gash in her pressure hull.

Having closed the watertight doors to confine the flooding to the stern compartments, the crew gathered in the torpedo-room for a council-of-war. It was agreed that, initially, three men should endeavour to escape through the conning-tower hatch. Lieutenant Christaansen climbed into the hollow steel tower followed by the three seamen selected to make the first ascent. His task was to supervise the escape procedures and to close the upper hatch after the men had swum clear. Everything went like clockwork. The lower hatch was shut, the tower flooded, and the upper hatch swung open freely as soon as the pressure had been equalized. A large bubble of air rose to the surface and a few moments later the three men were scooped out of the sea by the crew of the escort ship.

Although the conning-tower was now completely full of water Christaansen was equipped with breathing apparatus and he was in no danger. After closing the upper hatch he signalled the men in the control room to drain down the conning-tower in readiness for the next escape. Once the tower was clear of water the lower hatch could be opened and the procedure repeated.

But Lieutenant Christaansen had overlooked one vital scientific fact. When air enters an enclosed space which is completely flooded with water the pressure drops at a rate which the human body is unable to tolerate and death follows with swift inevitability. The submarine commander was to pay a cruel price for his lack of knowledge. When the lower hatch was opened after completion of the draining-down routine the crew found his lifeless body huddled in a heap on the floor of the tower with the breathing apparatus still in place. Something had obviously gone wrong but the men trapped inside the submarine did not know what. One thing, however, they *did* know. No one else was going to try escaping through the conning-tower hatch.

The sudden appearance of the three survivors was the first real evidence of *Dykkeren*'s fate and the escort ship morsed an urgent message to a nearby lightship which had a telephone landline link to the shore. Within an hour a civilian salvage vessel, *Kattegat*, had arrived on the scene, a feather in the cap of private enterprise when one considers the precious hours lost through delays in despatching naval salvage ships in other accidents. In fact the Danish Navy showed greater efficiency than many of the larger fleets by getting two lifting pontoons under tow inside sixty minutes.

Divers from the *Kattegat* descended at 3.30 pm and 'hammered messages of good cheer in morse code on the side of the sunken boat, to which the prisoners promptly responded.' The salvage men, however, soon encountered problems, for the divers found that the special lifting 'eyes' with which the *Dykkeren* had been fitted were so placed that it was impossible to shackle on the largest cable they needed to employ. And while they waited the arrival of the lifting pontoons *Odin* and *Thor* the men aboard the salvage vessel busied themselves making a special splice in the main wire so that it could be placed around the submarine's bows. Aware, also, that conditions inside the *Dykkeren* must be worsening with every hour, a diver was sent down to fasten a pressure hose to a valve in the submarine's hull to ensure that the trapped men had sufficient air to breathe. This additional precaution undoubtedly saved the

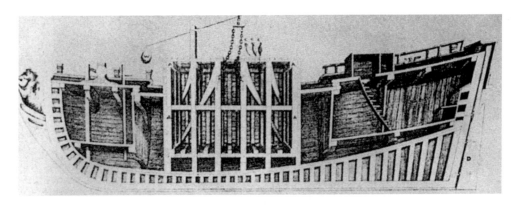

1. The 50-ton sloop *Maria* in which John Day submerged in 1774. His death was the first recorded fatality in submarine history.

2. Despite many accounts to the contrary no lives were lost when Garrett's steam-powered *Resurgam* foundered in 1880. The picture shows from left to right: Engineer George Price, Rev George Garrett, his year old son John William and Captain Jackson.

3. The French *Lutin* in which 14 men died during a diving exercise that went terribly wrong in 1906.

4. The *Bonite* was more fortunate. She collided with the battleship *Suffren* in the same year but was saved from disaster by the action of her quick-witted captain.

5. The accidental loss of the French *Turquoise* in October, 1915, led to the ambush and sinking of the British *E.20* by Heimburg's *UB-15*.

6. No lives were lost when the *Anguille*, a member of the notorious *Perle*-class, was badly damaged by a battery explosion in 1906.

11. The submarine-monitor *M 1* sank with all hands off the coast of south Devon after being rammed by the *SS Vidar* on 12 November, 1925.

12. Was the giant *M 2* a victim of muddled orders or did she sink as the result of a hydraulic failure? Whatever the reason, sixty men died.

13. The American submarine *F 1* sank after colliding with her sister *F 3* in fog on 17 December, 1917, with the loss of 19 lives. This underwater photograph, taken over fifty years later in 1975, shows the wreck of the submarine still lying on the ocean bottom. (*US Navy photo*)

14. *E 13* ran aground on Saltholm Flat in 1915 following a compass failure. German destroyers opened fire on the stranded submarine killing 15 men. The shell-holes in the conning-tower testify to the ferocity of the attack.

15. Britain's *E 15* is inspected by Turkish officers after she had run aground near Kephez Point in 1915.

16. *L 9* – victim of the typhoon that struck the city of Hong Kong in 1923.

17. Rammed and sunk by an American freighter with the loss of 159 lives during the Second World War, the French *Surcouf* remains the world's greatest submarine disaster.

18. The scene off the Isles of Shoals during the rescue operation that saved the lives of the 33 men trapped inside the *USS Squalus* in May, 1939. (*US Navy photo*)

19. *S 4* was lost with all hands after a collision with the Coast Guard cutter *Paulding* off Cape Cod in 1927. This picture shows the salvaged submarine being used for experimental work a year after the disaster. (*US Navy photo*)

20. *Thetis* beached in Moelfre Bay, Anglesey, after being raised and towed inshore in September, 1939. The submarine was subsequently recommissioned as *HMS Thunderbolt*. (*Royal Navy Submarine Museum*)

21. The photograph that shocked the world. The stern of the *Thetis* stands out above the surface of the sea after her fatal dive. But the Royal Navy's rescue attempts all failed and the 99 men trapped inside the submarine's hull died. (*Liverpool Daily Post & Echo*)

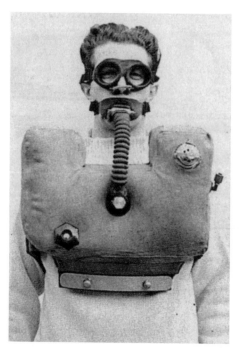

22. (top left) The British preferred individual escape techniques. The system worked when *Poseidon* sank in 1931 but failed when the *Truculent* was lost in 1950. This picture shows the 1948 version of the Davis Submerged Escape Apparatus (DSEA) (*Courtesy of Siebe Gorman Ltd*)

23. (top right) Rescue American style — the US Navy put its faith in the McCann Rescue Chamber. Although successful in saving the men trapped in the *Squalus*, it could not cope with the difficult conditions in the Dardanelles when the Turkish *Dumlupinar* sank in 1953. (*US Navy photo*)

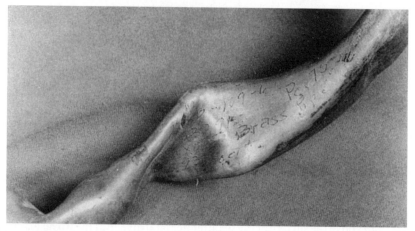

24. The figures 593 scratched on the surface of this piece of pipe dredged up by the bathyscaphe *Trieste* provided the vital proof that the wreckage was from the lost nuclear submarine *Thresher* (SSN-593). (*US Navy photo*)

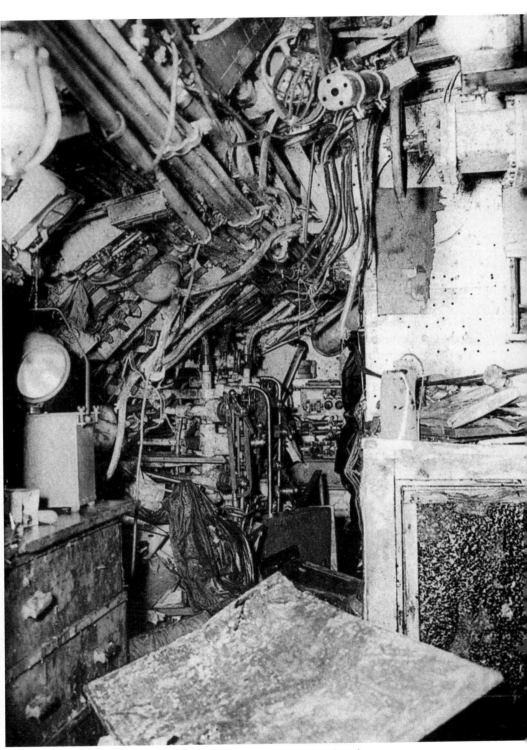

25. The devastated interior of *HMS Sidon* following the spontaneous
detonation of an experimental hydrogen-peroxide torpedo in June, 1953.
Thirteen men were killed by the explosion. (*Royal Navy Submarine Museum*)

26. The disastrous end of America's *Scorpion* in an area known as 'The Limbo of the Lost' gave rise to many ridiculous theories. It was recently revealed that she fell victim to one of her own torpedoes. (*US Navy photo*)

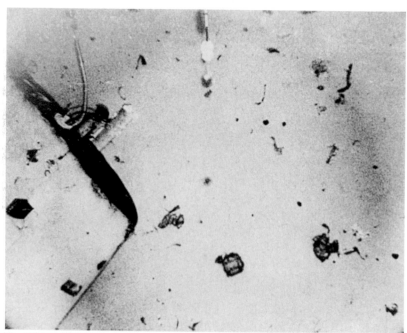

27. This underwater photograph was taken at a depth of 10,000 feet. The conning-tower, or sail, of the ill-fated *Scorpion* is clearly visible in the left-hand corner of the picture. (*US Navy photo*)

28. *HMS Artemis* — the accident that should have never happened. The upper part of the submarine's conning-tower shows above water after she had foundered alongside a quay at Fort Blockhouse. *HMS Ocelot* stands by in the background. (*Royal Navy Submarine Museum*)

29. Rescue operations continued throughout the night to save the three men trapped inside the flooded submarine. (*Royal Navy Submarine Museum*)

30. *Mystic* (DSRV-1) straddles the stern of the *USS Pintado* during exercises off San Diego. The DSRV concept has never been tested in a real disaster situation. (*US Navy photo*)

31. Britain's latest contribution to submarine rescue. The new manned submersible *LR5* is owned by Cable & Wireless Marine, crewed by civilians, and operated by the Royal Navy. (*Crown Copyright*)

lives of the five entombed men for many hours were to pass before it proved possible to release them.

Although *Odin* and *Thor* had now joined the circle of rescue ships, it was decided that *Kattegat* should try to raise the submarine with her own cranes. But the salvage men had miscalculated. Although the lift itself was successfully accomplished the derricks proved to be fractionally too short with the result that *Dykkeren's* fore-hatch, the only escape route, remained twelve inches below the surface. Fortunately the *Kattegat's* skipper was an old hand at salvage and he still had a few tricks up his sleeve. He carefully trimmed the ship's ballast so that the bows sank deeper into the water and the stern, like the opposite end of a see-saw, rose higher to provide the necessary extra few inches of lift. This drastic expedient brought the hatch level with the surface but waves were beginning to break over the submarine as the sea grew steeper and the wind increased in force. Dusk deepened into night, forcing the salvage men to work with searchlights and with weather conditions steadily deteriorating their initial optimism was fading. The sea was now washing continually over the hatch and it was clearly too dangerous to open the cover in case an unexpected wave surged over the lip of the coaming and swamped the submarine.

With the worsening weather any further delay would certainly prove fatal, and so, using fenders, strakes of timber and sacks filled with sawdust, the salvage men built a temporary dam around the vulnerable hatchway to try and hold the sea at bay. This time their efforts were successful and at 11.30 pm, nine and a half hours after *Dykkeren* had gone down, the hatch was opened and the five exhausted survivors clambered to safety. Their release came not a moment too soon. Minutes later the lifting wires snapped under the strain and the submarine slid back to the bottom of the Skagerrak.

The rescue operation was a tribute to Danish resourcefulness and her age-old tradition of Viking seamanship. While the bureaucratic regulations of the larger navies had so often led only to disaster the Norsemen had proved that the essential ingredient for success was instant response and plain commonsense.

Dykkeren's survivors owed their lives to the team-work of the rescuers on the surface. But there were other occasions when the resolute efforts of a single individual achieved an equally dramatic success. On 15 August, 1916, three months before the loss of the Danish submarine, a solitary British seaman, Stoker Petty Officer

William Brown, demonstrated man's extraordinary ability to wrest survival from the most unpromising situation.

E.4 and *E.41* were exercising outside Harwich harbour some two and a half miles from the Cork lightship when the accident occurred. *E.41* was running on the surface and acting as the target ship while the other boat carried out a series of submerged torpedo attacks. A helm error by *E.4*, however, brought the submarines onto converging courses and, before avoiding action could be taken, the two boats collided.

E.4's conning-tower was crushed by the impact and she sank immediately with the loss of all hands. *E.41*, with a twelve-foot gash in her pressure-hull, was similarly doomed but fortunately she remained afloat long enough for most of her crew to escape. When she finally went down, however, there were still seven men trapped inside her.

Lieutenant Voysey called the survivors into *E.41*'s control room and positioned them under the conning-tower hatch. Then, as the sea crept slowly up their legs, he quietly explained that the rising water was compressing the air inside the submarine and that, in time, the hatch would be forced open by the pressure and they would be swept to the surface. The water was already lapping their necks before Voysey was proved correct, but, finally, as predicted, the hatch burst open and the Lieutenant and three ratings shot to the surface where they were picked up by the destroyer *Firedrake*.

This left three men still trapped inside the boat – Brown, a stoker and an engine-room artificer. A glimmer of daylight was visible through the open hatch and, diving into the water that had now filled half of the submarine, they swam towards it. Two of the men succeeded in dragging themselves out through the narrow opening, but, as Brown prepared to follow them, the pressure inside and outside *E.41* equalized and the heavy hatch cover swung back and sealed the exit.

'The midships compartment was in darkness and partly flooded,' Brown wrote later. 'Chlorine gas began to come through. I closed the engine-room door and began to unscrew the clips of the torpedo-hatch above me. At this juncture the engine-room was in complete darkness with the exception of the port pilot-light which was burning through "earth". The water was slowly rising in the engine-room (and was flooding in) through the voice-pipes which I had left open to relieve the pressure on the bulkhead door.'

Brown's only hope of escape depended on compressing the air

inside the engine-room until sufficient pressure had been built-up to blow the hatch open and shoot him to the surface. Aided by his intimate knowledge of the submarine's interior, he began to free the clips and gearing of the hatch so that it would open freely when the compressed air was ready to do its job.

It was a nightmare task. Everything was pitch black. The air was acrid with chlorine gas, the oil-polluted seawater was up to his waist, and vivid blue sparks flickered continuously from the fuses and electrical connections as the water short-circuited the current.

'The heat at this time was excessive and I rested a while to consider the best way of flooding the engine-room. I eventually came to the conclusion that the best way was to flood through the stern (torpedo) tube or the weed-trap of the circulating system, or by dropping the exhaust and induction valves and opening the muffler-valve. I tried the stern tube first but could neither open the stern-cap nor rear door. Then I came forward again. While passing the switchboards I received several shocks. I tried to open the weed-trap of the circulating inlet, but it was in an awkward position, and with water coming over on top of me, I could not ease back the butterfly-nuts.'

Brown proceeded to open the muffler and exhaust valves after which 'I climbed on top of the engines underneath the torpedo hatch and unshipped the strongback, drawing the pin out of the link with a spanner that I had with me.' But the compression was insufficient and although he managed to lift the hatch three times, it would not raise sufficiently for him to get out. He had earlier dropped the hatch clips on to the deck and they now lay under several feet of water. It was, however, essential to recover them for unless the hatch was tightly secured the precious compressed air would seep through the crevice and escape.

Diving down into the cold oily water, Brown found the missing clips and climbed back on top of the engines to refasten the hatch. When this was done he set off into the submarine and opened the scuttle of the engine-room bulkhead to admit more water into the compartment. Then he settled down and waited for the pressure to build up.

At what he judged to be the right moment he struck the clips free and raised the heavy steel door. It lifted a few inches and then slammed down, trapping his left hand. Gritting his teeth against the pain he used his shoulder to lever it open, release his hand and wait once more for the right moment. Finally, after an hour and a half inside the submarine, Brown succeeded in raising the hatch and he, too, was swept safely to the surface.

His escape had been an epic of human endurance and determination. Yet before being taken away for medical treatment he insisted on giving the salvage officers a detailed account of the damage, methodically listing which valves were open and which bulkhead doors closed. Then, and only then, did he agree to go below to see the ship's surgeon. Thanks to the accuracy of his report *E.41* was raised seven weeks later and resumed operational duties shortly afterwards.

—SIX—

'When in doubt – dive !'

The classic story of the Royal Navy's notorious K-class steam submarines features a young and very inexperienced First Lieutenant. Isolated at his control position in the stern, he called the captain urgently on the internal telephone.

'I say, sir,' he stammered excitedly. 'My end's diving. What's your end doing?'

It was a question that probably passed through the minds of many First Officers on the night of 1 February, 1918. For under the shadow of May Island in the Firth of Forth no fewer than *nine* of the lumbering monsters found themselves entangled in the most spectacular series of collisions ever recorded in the annals of submarine history.

The K-boats were now organized into two flotillas – the 12th, under Captain Charles Little in the cruiser *Fearless*, comprising *K.3*, *K.4*, *K.6*, and *K.7*; and the ominously numbered 13th, commanded by Captain Ernest Leir in the destroyer-leader *Ithuriel*, made up of *K.11*, *K.12*, *K.14*, *K.17*, and *K.22*. They left Rosyth in the late afternoon to take part in Operation E.C.1., a full-scale exercise involving most of the Grand Fleet. The light-battlecruiser *Courageous*, flying the flag of Sir Hugh Evan-Thomas, headed the long line of ships as they passed under the Forth Bridge. She was followed by Leir's flotilla, four battlecruisers, the 12th Flotilla, three battleships of the 5th Battle Squadron, fourteen light cruisers and several flotillas of destroyers.

It was dark by the time they reached the mouth of the estuary and a light mist added to the difficulties of night navigation and station-keeping. Leir's boats were travelling at nineteen knots, running nose to tail, each following the shaded blue stern light of the submarine ahead. Suddenly a group of minesweepers, ignorant of the fleet operation in progress, swept across the line of approach.

K.11 cut speed and turned to port. *K.17* followed suit, but *K.14*, the third submarine in the line, continued straight ahead although she, too, reduced speed. Realizing that he was getting too close to the boats in front, Thomas Harbottle, *K.14*'s skipper, ordered full right rudder. But at that vital moment the K-boat hoodoo jammed the helm and she swung away in a wide circle, while *K.12*, immediately astern, continued on course, unaware of her flotilla-mate's antics.

By now the line-ahead formation was in shambles and *K.22*, bringing up the rear, suddenly found another submarine lying broadside across her path. Her captain, Charles de Burgh, saw the glow of a red navigation light two hundred yards ahead and ordered the helm hard a'starboard. But the boat reacted sluggishly and, still moving at nineteen knots, her bows cut deep into the port side of *K.14* just abaft the forward torpedo compartment. Prompt action in shutting the watertight doors saved the two submarines from immediate disaster but the bow section of each boat was flooded and their wireless operators tapped out urgent collision signals.

'What the hell have we hit?' de Burgh demanded. In the circumstances it was a not unreasonable question, but no one could be sure of the answer. On de Burgh's orders *K.22*'s crew rigged emergency lights behind the conning-tower to warn the battlecruisers of her presence and the first three passed clear, although they were close enough for their wash to rock the two crippled submarines violently. But the fourth, *Inflexible*, struck *K.22* a glancing blow which peeled back thirty feet of high-tensile steel plating, ripped off the starboard ballast tank, and almost rolled the submarine on to her beam ends. Leaning forward over the bridge rails de Burgh had the last angry word:

'What the hell do you think you're doing?' he bellowed at the fast departing battlecruiser. But no one bothered to reply.

Leir, by this time, had finally learned of the collisions and, reversing course, he led *Ithuriel* and the three remaining submarines back towards the scene with the intention of sorting out the mess. Realizing the danger of unexpectedly back-tracking, he switched on the destroyer's full navigation lights to warn the other ships of his approach.

The battlecruiser *Australia*, steaming at high speed, suddenly appeared out of the mist, narrowly missed the little group and only avoided a head-on collision with *K.12* by a miracle. Leir's boats then encountered a flotilla of fast-moving destroyers and there was a noisy confusion of helm orders, lurid curses, and shouted warnings as the two groups jinked and twisted to avoid running each other down.

'Tiny' Little, leading the 12th Flotilla, had also picked up news of the original collision and he breathed a sigh of relief as his group passed clear to the east of May Island. If the wireless reports were accurate the danger area was now safely astern. He was, of course, unaware that Leir and the 13th Flotilla had reversed course and were now steering towards him. Suddenly both groups loomed out of the mists and met head-on.

Fearless, leading the 12th Flotilla at all of twenty-one knots, smashed into *K.17* just forward of the conning-tower and the submarine, twisting clear, reeled away into the darkness sinking fast. True to the traditions of the Service her crew remained at their stations calmly carrying out their emergency drill and securing the watertight doors. But the submarine was flooding freely and chlorine gas was already rising from the shattered batteries. Realizing there was no chance of saving her, Lieutenant-Commander Henry Hearn gave the order to abandon ship. The men took to the sea optimistically convinced that they would soon be picked up by one of the many vessels in the vicinity.

K.17 sank only eight minutes after *Fearless* ran her down and by then the rear of the line was in utter confusion. *K.3* nearly rammed *K.4* and a further disaster was only avoided by Herbert Shove's prompt order to port *K.3*'s helm. *K.6* and *K.12* narrowly escaped a head-on collision and, in the excitement, the men on *K.6*'s bridge lost sight of their next-in-line, *K.3*. Spotting a white light ahead Lieutenant Sandford, *K.6*'s Officer-of-the-Watch, assumed it to be *K.3* and brought his own submarine around to take station, as he thought, on its stern. When Geoffrey Layton arrived on the bridge a few moments later he made the same error of identification. But his experienced eye realized that the mystery submarine was, in fact, lying broadside across *K.6*'s path and not end-on as Sandford had supposed. Layton had already demonstrated his courage in the *E.13* tragedy. Now he proved that he had an equally cool head.

'Slow both,' he ordered. 'Stop both.'

K.6 was travelling at eighteen knots and her inertial weight of 1800 tons took a lot of stopping. Layton could see that a collision was unavoidable and he tried to minimise the force of impact.

'Full speed astern. Hard a'port. Sound full astern on the siren. Navigation lights on – searchlight on astern!'

K.6's bows sliced into the motionless submarine and almost cut it in half. The two boats were so entangled that not even the power of *K.6*'s 10,500 hp engines could pull them apart. They remained locked in their deathly embrace for a full thirty seconds before *K.6* finally broke free. Layton stopped engines, sent Sandford below to check the damage, and turned *K.6*'s searchlight astern to warn *K.7* to steer clear. In those few brief seconds *K.4* disappeared, sinking so rapidly that *K.7* only scraped her keel on the wreck as she passed over the spot.

Layton, not fully appreciating the true situation, reported that he had sunk *K.3*. But when Herbert Shove blinked his recognition signal to show that *K.3* was still afloat Layton concluded that he must have collided with the crippled *K.17*. It was certainly a night of total confusion.

K.7 stopped to search for survivors while *K.6* pumped out the water flooding her fore compartment. Searchlight beams circled a number of men swimming in the water and Leir, watching the scene from *Fearless* – which had lost most of her bow section when she rammed *K.17* and was now lying stopped – ordered Gravener, *K.7*'s captain, to pick them up.

The ships of the 5th Battle Squadron, although warned of the collisions by wireless, were unaware that both submarine flotillas were milling around in a macabre dance of death directly ahead and as *K.7* moved in to rescue the survivors the three dreadnoughts swept onto the scene at twenty-one knots. What followed was probably the most ghastly tragedy of that terrible February night.

The escorting destroyers ploughed straight through the struggling pack of helpless men. Limbs were smashed and skulls crushed by the plunging bows, strong swimmers were sucked under by the undertow of the swirling wash and drowned, and those that survived these first two hazards were cut to pieces by the propellors. All fifty-six members of *K.17*'s crew had escaped when the submarine went down, but by the time the destroyers had passed only nine men remained on the surface and one of these died shortly after he had been picked up by *K.7*.

It was, mercifully, the final curtain to a night that every man who was there would remember with horror for the rest of his life. Led by *Fearless*, steaming stern-first to ease the strain on her damaged bows, the remaining submarines of the 12th and 13th Flotillas formed up into a mournful procession for their return to Rosyth. As they steamed slowly through the night the men of the K-boats counted the cost of the disaster. Not a single man had escaped from *K.4* and forty-eight had died in *K.17*. Two boats were lost and three more seriously damaged. Yet, ironically, one of the boats to have survived was *K.22*, the former *K.13* which had been raised, refitted and recommissioned after sinking in Gareloch almost exactly a year earlier.

Such was the price paid by the Submarine Service for the stupidity of those who had insisted on fitting steam engines in submarines. It was also a damning indictment of the ill-conceived policy of operating submarine flotillas as integral units of the surface fleet.

The Court of Inquiry held five days later placed the blame squarely on the shoulders of the K-boat captains and their officers. It was an injustice which even today remains difficult to forgive. But the captains themselves accepted the verdict with unquenchable humour. When Layton handed over command of *K.6* to William Crowther, who had himself been on board the submarine during the tragic events of that February night, he told his successor that the disasters he had witnessed had been excellent experience. They were, he added, 'a bloody good introduction to K-boats'.

* * *

America did not enter the war until March, 1917, but the United States Navy also suffered more than its share of submarine accidents in the 1914-18 period, though none were as disastrous as the Battle of May Island.

F.4 (the former *USS Skate*), a Holland-type boat of 330 tons launched in 1912, was engaged on diving practice one and a half miles from Honolulu on the afternoon of 25 March, 1915, when she literally vanished. Salvage ships were rushed to the scene and after an extensive search the boat was located in 304 feet of water. The Navy Department was anxious to determine the cause of the disaster and, despite the enormous depth involved, it was an essential part of the salvage operation for a diver to go down to supervise the lift. The plan was to pass sweep cables under the keel of the sunken submarine so that she could be raised sufficiently to be towed into shallower water for examination. The diver was needed to ensure that the cables were positioned correctly.

The proposed operation caused a great deal of interest in maritime circles for, until that time, no diver had descended below 200 feet, and only a few months previously a man had been crushed to death while working at 33 fathoms. Several men volunteered for the task and the selected diver was only permitted to remain on the bottom for ten minutes. Fortunately he made his record-breaking descent without coming to any harm and had sufficient time to see that the lifting cables were placed correctly. *F.4* was raised successfully and towed to dry-dock for inspection.

The official cause of the loss, which cost the lives of all twenty-one men aboard, was given as corrosion of the lead linings of the battery tank which had allowed the sea to seep into the compartment. This had upset the trim of the boat and she had gone to the bottom out of control.

In January, 1916, *E.2* (the former *USS Sturgeon*) sank in dock at the Brooklyn Navy Yard as the result of an internal explosion, although she was salvaged and returned to service within a few months. In the same year, on 15 December, *H.3* ran aground near Eureka although on this occasion the mishap did not lead to the loss of the boat.

America's next submarine casualties happened in the Philippines. *A.5*, one of the original eight Holland boats ordered in 1900, was cruising off Cavite when she was sunk by an explosion which killed several crewmen and injured many others. Petrol vapour or hydrogen gas was the probable culprit but the cause was never established even though the boat was salved and recommissioned. Three months later, on 24 July, her sister-ship *A.7* lost her entire crew when she suffered a similar fate. There can be little doubt that the early Holland submarines were particularly vulnerable to this type of internal explosion.

On 14 September *D.2* foundered alongside a jetty at New London and on 17 December *F.1* was sunk following a collision with *F.3* in thick fog off Point Lama on the Californian coast. Five men managed to scramble clear but nineteen died. It had been a disastrous year and the submarine branch of the US Navy must have been mightily relieved when 1917 finally took its bow and passed into history.

Accidents such as these had nothing to do with the war and were merely typical of the hazards that submariners faced every time they went to sea. But there is *one* class of disaster that can *only* happen in times of war, and it is without question the most tragic fate that can befall any ship – to be sunk in error by friendly forces.

For obvious reasons the facts concerning such incidents are rarely revealed officially and information is accordingly sparse. Nevertheless they deserve recognition even though very little detail is available to the historian.

The earliest recorded loss of this nature was that of the German *U-7* which, on 21 June, 1915, was torpedoed in error by the *U-22* under the mistaken impression that she was attacking a British submarine, but the majority of such incidents occurred in the final years of the war – a coincidence that may have been due to the increased vigilance engendered by months of operational duties; the inexperience of the young men conscripted for service to replace the terrible casualties of the earlier years; or merely the fatalistic exuberance of men who no longer took life seriously.

On 10 March, 1917, the Italian submarine *Guglielmotti* was rammed by the British sloop *Cyclamen* off Capraia Island. Apparently unaware that she was attacking a friendly vessel, *Cyclamen* turned her guns on the crippled boat and shelled her until she sank. *Guglielmotti* was not the only Italian submarine to fall victim to the Royal Navy. During a night patrol in the southern Adriatic on 16 April, 1918, the British *H.1* spent several hours stalking an Austrian U-boat on the surface. She finally found herself in an ideal attacking position and loosed off her bow torpedoes. There was a violent explosion and *H.1* rushed to the spot to pick up survivors only to discover that the men they dragged out of the sea were speaking Italian and not Austrian. Despite having had the submarine in sight for a considerable period, *H.1* had made a terrible mistake. Her victim was the Italian *H.5*, and, bearing in mind that she was a class-sister of the British submarine, it is difficult to understand how the error could have occurred. But in the stress of war the eye often sees what the brain wants it to see. And if *H.1* was hunting Austrian submarines, any submarine sighted *must* be of that nationality.

On occasions a genuine mistake can be made in the heat of the moment and the loss of the British *J.6* was a typical example of such error. The submarine was surfaced in fog when she was surprised by a Q-ship. Something, a piece of cloth or a coil of rope, was hanging down the side of the conning-tower partially obscuring the boat's identification mark and the captain mistook the *J* for a *U*. The guns opened fire and the submarine reeled under a deluge of high-explosive shells. A large white table-cloth was waved from the after hatch and a morse-lamp on the conning-tower repeatedly flashed *H-E-L-P . . . H-E-L-P*. But the concealed guns of the Q-ship pounded their victim with merciless accuracy until the unfortunate submarine drifted off into the fog sinking rapidly, her pressure hull punched full of holes. It was only when the fifteen survivors, less than half of *J.6*'s thirty-four man crew, were picked up by the decoy ship that her commander realized he had sunk a British submarine.

A Court of Inquiry was convened and the fifteen survivors were called as witnesses. Having heard the evidence the Court cleared the Q-ship captain of all blame for the mistake, and the submarine men came to attention and saluted the acquitted officer as he left the room.

There were, of course, other occasions when a submarine, coming under attack by friendly forces, managed to survive by outwitting its hunters. *G.6*, for example, was returning to Devonport on 18 December, 1917, when a group of American destroyers mistook her for a U-boat and turned towards the boat with their guns blazing. There was no time for an exchange of recognition signals and Lieutenant Coltart took the submarine deep in anticipation of a depth-charge attack. He was not disappointed. Moments later the destroyers thundered overhead and the depth-charges tumbled from the stern racks. As they exploded *G.6* was thrown about like a cork by the concussion. But Coltart's skilful handling brought the submarine safely through her ordeal. Convinced that he had scored a 'kill', the Senior American Captain broke off the attack and returned in triumph to Plymouth.

Some hours later, in the bar of the wardroom, he was telling his cronies how he had sunk a U-boat when Coltart butted in and introduced himself as the commander of the submarine the Captain *hadn't* sunk!

Another boat of the G-class was less fortunate, and in this instance had only herself to blame for what happened. *G.9* was patrolling off the Norwegian coast on 16 September, 1917, when she sighted a warship in the distance. The submarine dived and steered into an attacking position and a torpedo shot from the starboard bow tube as the target centred in the cross-sights of the periscope. Due to a miscalculation of the deflection angle, it missed, but the line of bubbles denoting its track had been spotted by *HMS Petard*'s lookouts. The attack could only mean that the submarine was hostile and the destroyer captain immediately rang down for full speed. Sighting a periscope, *Petard* rammed the submerged submarine and cut it in two. Of the thirty-one man crew only one rating, a stoker, was rescued. *G.9* had paid the supreme penalty for her error.

Another British submarine, *D.3*, was caught on the surface by a French airship during the afternoon of 12 March, 1918. Unaware that any friendly submarines were operating in the area the airmen concluded that *D.3* was an enemy U-boat and, keeping the sun behind them to blind the lookouts, they carefully stalked their prey. The submarine, however, had spotted the airship and her captain, Lieutenant-Commander Maitland-Douglas, fired off his recognition flares. But the airmen thought they were being attacked with rockets and four 52-kilo bombs whistled down to explode close alongside the British boat. *D.3* rolled violently and started to dive. Seconds later she tried to regain the surface. The near misses had apparently opened her hull seams and, with the sea pouring in through a dozen holes, she sank to the bottom with oil leaking from her ruptured fuel tanks.

Four men were seen in the water shortly after she vanished but, with dusk gathering and no ships near at hand, it was impossible to rescue them and the unfortunate *D.3* was lost with all hands. In the circumstances it was an excusable error, for one submarine looks much like another when viewed from the air. But it is ironic that this was to be the only occasion in history when an airship sank a submarine.

The Russians lost one of their boats on 19 May, 1917, when the *Bars* was rammed and sunk by a friendly destroyer north of Dago in the Baltic. But the British submarine *L.2* managed to escape the same fate when she was attacked by no fewer than *three* US destroyers in February, 1918. The submarine had been misbehaving and despite Lieutenant-Commander Ackworth's attempts to control the trim she porpoised continuously. On one of her playful leaps above the surface she was spotted by lookouts on the destroyers *Paulding*, *Davis* and *Trippe* and the trio of 742-ton four-stackers immediately turned towards the exposed conning-tower. Ackworth watched their approach through the periscope and, following the old submarine maxim 'When in doubt – dive', he took *L.2* down in record time. What happened next is best told in the words of his official report:

'. . . I lowered the periscope and dived to 90 feet. Gunshots being heard, I proceeded at full speed to 200 feet at which depth the first heavy depth-charges exploded, and at the same time the after hydroplanes jammed hard-up. We now took a tremendous inclination by the stern, the tail touching the bottom at 300 feet.

'Four more very heavy explosions shook the boat. Bright flashes were seen (as the switchboard shorted) and she was at an angle of 45°, bow up. We were unable to correct this trim with the forward hydroplanes, so I gave the order to blow Nos 5 and 6. This order was promptly obeyed and the boat slowly commenced to rise, but at a tremendous angle. On breaking surface three destroyers opened a hot fire on us at a range of 1,000 yards – one shot striking the pressure hull just abaft the conning-tower. Recognition signals were made and a White Ensign waved and firing ceased.'

It was an incident that reflected well on all concerned. Ackworth had undoubtedly saved the submarine by his prompt emergency dive and the three destroyers had not only reacted instantly to the original sighting but had also carried out a devastating attack with depth-charges and scored a vital hit with their guns. Finally, the submarine's recognition signal had been seen and acted upon immediately. Official reaction to the encounter also reflected a similar appreciation of the American Navy's efficiency. Having absolved the destroyer commanders from any blame the report ended: 'In view of the small amount of conning-tower exposed and the distance at which it was sighted, it is submitted that these vessels made a most remarkably efficient attack.'

There were other disasters which may have been partially caused by the stress and strain of combat conditions but which could not be blamed entirely on the war itself, accidents which could have occurred just as easily in peacetime. On 29 October, 1917, for example, *U-52* was sunk by an accidental explosion in Kiel dockyard. The U-boat had enjoyed a long run of successes while operating under the command of *Kapitanleutnant* Walter Hans. On 19 August, 1916, she had sunk the 5,440-ton British light cruiser *Nottingham* in the North Sea and had remained on the scene to make a further, though unsuccessful, attack on the *Dublin*. Moving south she torpedoed and sank the French battleship *Suffren* with all hands off Lisbon. Joining the Cattaro flotilla, *U-52* had ranged the Mediterranean and added the Italian liner *Ravenna* to her growing list of victims. Hans then returned to northern waters and on 21 July, 1917, sent the British submarine *C.34* to the bottom with a single shot while on patrol in the Shetlands area. With such a glowing service history it is not surprising that *U-52* was salved and repaired after her mishap and returned to service. It is thought that the explosion was caused by a Schwartzkopf torpedo sliding forward in its tube and detonating when the contact pistol struck the outer door. If such was the case there must have been something wrong with its safety mechanism.

A collision with *U-96* off Barfleur spelled the end of *UC-69*'s promising career on 6 December, 1917, and a similar accident sent the British minelayer *E.36* to the bottom near Harwich when she collided with *E.43* while returning from patrol. It is highly probable that exhaustion and fatigue caused by prolonged and difficult patrols in enemy waters were important contributory factors in both accidents.

German submarine minelayers fell victim to their own deadly cargoes on more than one occasion. *UC-32* was blown up on her own mines off Sunderland on 23 February, 1917, and *UC-42* suffered the same fate south of Cork on 10 September of the same year. On 16 March, 1916, the Austrian minelayer *U-24* blew up near Taranto when her cargo detonated. She was, however, later salved and repaired by the enemy and went into service with the Italian Navy as *X.1*.

Not all submarine minelayers were lost by self-immolation. *UC-5* ran aground on the Shipwash Shoal following an exciting chase by British destroyers and, as she still had her cargo of mines on board, salvage was impossible until they had been removed or rendered harmless. The problem was solved when Lieutenant Patterson, a torpedo officer with the 8th Flotilla at Harwich, entered the half-submerged submarine and, at great personal risk, unscrewed and removed the detonator plugs.

UC-5 proved to be an important capture and after she had been dragged off the mudbank and placed in dry-dock British experts spent hours examining the secrets of her mine-laying apparatus. Many of the lessons learned were incorporated into the Royal Navy's own minelaying boats. Having served her purpose she was put on show in London, moored alongside the Thames Embankment, while thousands clambered over her. Some time later *UC-5* was shipped to the United States where she was exhibited on the streets of New York to promote the sales of Liberty Bonds. She was probably the first submarine to be dragged through the city since that day in 1878 when John Phillip Holland trundled his experimental *Holland II* down to the Upper Passiac River.

Perhaps the strangest of all underwater accidents was that suffered by a Russian submarine, believed to be the *Igor* (or *Ugor*), in the tumultuous days following the October Revolution. On leaving harbour the boat had carried out a practice dive and the after hatch should, of course, have been closed and secured as soon as the preparatory diving order was given by the captain. It remained open, however, because the man responsible for carrying out the task was having his stand-easy at that moment and considered it 'unconstitutional' to get up and close the hatch while he was resting. According to one account of the incident: 'He was near the hatch himself but he just sat there and watched the Baltic pour in as the boat went under. If ever a man died for his principles that man did.'

The Captain and First Officer managed to escape before the submarine sank and a few weeks later they were brought before a Court Martial and charged with responsibility for losing the boat. The trial and the subsequent verdict proved as farcical as the original cause of the disaster. The devious logic of the Court's Comrade President resulted in the two officers being found guilty of 'negligently hazarding the submarine' and both were exiled to Siberia.

The Comrade President defended his bizarre decision by announcing that 'the order to shut down (for diving) was illegal and harsh, in that certain of the crew were taking their rest and could not be expected to obey the order.'

It is hardly surprising that the Red Navy remained a negligible fighting force for the twenty years that immediately followed the Worker's Revolution.

—SEVEN—

'A trifling mistake ...'

Armistice Day, 11 November, 1918, marked the cessation of hostilities although the war itself did not officially end until the signing of the Peace Treaty in June of the following year, and in the very month that the fighting stopped two more submarines were lost in accidents. The ex-German *U-165* sank in the Weser as the result of a collision, while the British *G.11* was wrecked on the island of Howick off the Northumberland coast with the loss of two lives. It was apparent that the sea recognized neither armistice terms nor peace treaties.

Between August, 1914, and November, 1918, a total of sixty-nine submarines were lost by accident, including those sunk in error by friendly forces or blown up by the premature detonation of their own mines and neutral boats not involved in the hostilities. During the same period enemy action sent no fewer than 227 submarines to the bottom, while capture, deliberate scuttling and saboteur-inspired founderings en route to surrender, accounted for a further forty-two.* The grand total was 338 submarines lost in fifty-two months – three boats every fortnight. But the U-boats of the Kaiser's Navy had almost brought Britain to her knees in 1917, and the toll of surface warships lost as a result of underwater attack, including eleven battleships**, was a terrible testament to the destructive power of the submarine.

*See Appendix 4.

**(British) *Brittania, Triumph, Cornwallis, Formidable, Majestic*; (French) *Danton, Suffren, Gaulois*; (Italian) *Amalfi*; (Turkish) *Barbarossa, Mesudieh*.

Britain, not surprisingly, wanted all submarines banned when she attended the Washington Conference on naval disarmament in 1921. And in December, following an earlier British proposal that submarine tonnage should be severely limited, Lord Lee offered to scrap 'the largest, most modern and most efficient submarine fleet in the world and to disband our personnel ... if the other Powers will do the same and desist from further building.'

Admiral Beatty, Britain's First Sea Lord and professional head of the Royal Navy, had a more realistic outlook and minuted this piece of pie-in-the-sky verbiage: 'It is certainly not to be expected that the submarine will be totally abolished'. His view, however, stood in sharp contrast to those of King George V, himself a former career officer in the Navy, who urged in a private conversation: 'We should press strongly for the total abolition of submarines.'*

The British attitude was, in fact, little changed from 1900 when Admiral 'Tug' Wilson tried to persuade the First Lord to include a statement in the Naval Estimates that: 'HM Government considers it would be to the advantage of all Maritime nations of the world if the use of the submarine-boat for attack could be prohibited.' And when this softly-softly approach failed Wilson nailed his true colours to the mast and suggested that Britain should 'treat all submariners as pirates in wartime ... and *hang all the crews.*' The same Admiral Wilson dubbed the submarine 'a damned un-English weapon'.

The United States Government disagreed with the British proposals and stated publicly that they regarded the submarine as 'an effective and legitimate weapon of warfare', although they agreed that 'unlimited submarine warfare should be outlawed', a view that was quickly reversed in 1941 when US submarines were given carte-blanche to sink any and all Japanese ships without warning. Neither proposal proved acceptable to France, the country that had first developed the submarine as a weapon of war, who opposed every suggestion and, finally, refused to ratify the Treaty if *any* restrictions were placed upon the operational employment of the submarine. Britain's pious and self-interested proposal to abolish submarines was quietly shelved.

Six years later, during the run-up to the Geneva Conference in 1927, the British Admiralty was still pushing for a complete ban on submarines – urged on by the King who continued to hold strong

*Royal Archives. GV 2030/1.

views on the matter. But, once again, the proposal was lost in a welter of resolutions and counter-resolutions and nothing came of it. And although at one point a tentative agreement was reached on the limitation of total submarine tonnage the Conference, in fact, broke up in disarray with the Treaty unsigned.

While the world's statesmen and senior admirals were considering its merits and demerits, the submarine continued to claim more victims. It is a sad fact that between 1904 and 1930 not a single year passed without at least one submarine disaster occurring somewhere in the world.

Sir William White, whom we last met at Tilbury in 1887 when he was trapped in the *Nautilus*, had a clear perception of the main danger that faced the submarine, and, as Chief Constructor of the Royal Navy and the most influential naval architect of his day, his views are worthy of note. Eighty years of submarine disasters have provided no evidence to alter or modify his conclusions. 'The human element must always count for much and even with crews thoroughly trained and disciplined mistakes will occasionally be made,' he wrote in 1900. 'Moreover the necessarily small reserve of buoyancy retained in the diving condition makes a trifling mistake, or a small entry of water, a possible cause of serious danger.' The validity of White's warning was amply illustrated when the Chilean submarine *Rucumilla* sank on 2 June, 1919.

It was the first major disaster to be suffered by a South American republic since the submarine came of age in 1900, and by a strange coincidence the accident happened less than 250 miles from the spot where Herr Flach's experimental vessel had been lost in 1866.

Rucumilla was engaged on training exercises in the Bay of Talcahuano, near Concepcion, when the accident happened. The submarine was manned by an inexperienced crew and when the captain gave the order to dive the battery ventilation exhaust valves were mistakenly opened instead of closed – due, it was said later, to the fact that they were, unusually, fitted with a left-hand thread. The sea poured in through the ventilator exhausts and the captain, Lieutenant-Commander Aristides del Solar, ordered the main ballast tanks to be blown. Compressed air hissed through the air-lines and the boat rose sufficiently to thrust her bows up above the surface for a few seconds. Then, with her buoyancy destroyed by the inrush of water, she sank back.

By an incredible stroke of luck *Rucumilla*'s death throes had been witnessed by a passing merchant ship and, realizing that something was seriously wrong, her skipper passed an urgent radio message back to the shore. The Chilean naval authorities reacted swiftly and three heavy cranes were hurried out to the Bay together with salvage and diving vessels. Divers went down to locate the submarine and, less than two hours after she had sunk, the first lifting slings had been secured around her hull. The entire operation proceeded without a hitch and, with the minimum of delay, the *Rucumilla* was raised to the surface. But as had occurred on many similar occasions in the past one of the chains broke under the strain. If a second chain was to snap the submarine and her crew were in danger of being irretrievably lost and, to avoid total disaster, the salvage men quickly lowered the boat back to the bottom.

Conditions for the twenty-five men inside were rapidly deteriorating. Salt water had entered the batteries and chlorine gas was seeping into the engine-room. Electrical circuits shorted and smouldered into flame and there were a series of minor but frightening explosions. To make matters worse the boat was in complete darkness and the crew were knee-deep in water. But del Solar kept up their flagging spirits as he led the frightened trainees into the forward torpedo compartment, the section of the boat that seemed likely to offer the best chance of survival. The watertight door was dogged and clipped to prevent further flooding and when breathing became difficult del Solar carefully bled small quantities of compressed-air into the poisoned atmosphere.

The rescuers continued their efforts and before long the divers had secured further wire slings around the boat. The third and largest of the cranes was now brought into service and the salvage men watched anxiously as the wire cables tautened and vibrated under the load. If anything went wrong this time it would be the end, for storm clouds were darkening the seaward horizon and the wind was already rising.

Inch by inch the massive steel cables wound around the drums of the steam winches as the crane operators maintained a slow and steady lift to minimise the strain on the wires. Finally, seven hours after she had vanished, *Rucumilla*'s conning-tower broke surface. But there was still much to do and the lift continued until the deck and the torpedo-loading hatch were safely clear of the water. As the clatter of the winches died away a group of rescuers jumped down on to the bow casing and hammered on the hatch cover. Moments later the first of the twenty-five exhausted survivors clambered to safety. According to contemporary press reports there were cheers and shouts of '*Viva Chile*' as each member of the submarine's crew was hauled up on to the deck of the salvage ship.

The successful rescue was yet one more example of the apparent ability of the smaller navies to snatch triumph from potential disaster. Denmark had already demonstrated, with the *Dykkeren*, that speed was the key factor in submarine salvage, and now Chile's prompt response had reinforced the point.

Exactly a month after the *Rucumilla* incident the US Navy suffered its first post-war submarine disaster when, on 2 July, *G.2* foundered in Long Island Sound after an unexpected sea washed over the deck and entered the engine-room hatch which had been left open for ventilation while the boat was surfaced. Three men were lost and one was saved, which suggests that the submarine was under tow at the time, but unfortunately no details of the rescue operations and subsequent salvage are on record. There is even some doubt as to exact date of the sinking which various sources quote as being the 2nd, 27th and 30th of July.

A unique combination of circumstances was responsible for the loss of the Royal Navy's *H.41* later the same year. The submarine, commanded by Lieutenant-Commander N.R. Peploe and of similar design to the *Rucumilla*, was moored in a dock basin at Blythe a few yards distant from the 6,620 ton depot ship *Vulcan*. The ex-cruiser was in harbour for repairs to her main engines and during the afternoon she built up a head of steam and began to carry out a slow-speed trial. In the restricted waters of the dock basin the suction from the depot-ship's propellers drew the submarine towards her and, despite the efforts of both crews to keep the two boats apart, *Vulcan*'s screws struck the stern of the submarine, cut through her outer casing and sliced open the pressure hull. *H.41* sank quickly as the sea rushed in and the crew were lucky to escape. The fact that they were all on deck trying to fend off the depot ship undoubtedly helped.

The American *C.5* was also lost in dock at around the same time, but in her case the cause of the accident was the carelessness of the workers responsible for her maintenance. *C.5* was tied up alongside a pier at Coco Solo naval base in the Panama Canal Zone while a dockyard gang watered her batteries, a topping-up procedure familiar to all motorists. In the hurry to get home when the whistle blew at the end of the day they forgot to turn off the valve of the water-line they had been using, and in the ensuing hours the boat slowly flooded and sank. Fortunately no lives were lost. As Sir William White had observed: 'A trifling mistake ... (can be) a possible cause of serious danger'.

1920 saw two more accidents involving American submarines. On 12 March *H.1* ran aground in Magdalena Bay on the coast of California. Salvage operations were put in hand to refloat her but, when she was finally dragged free twelve days later, the damage she had sustained proved fatal and she foundered under the eyes of the salvage team. Four lives were lost, the major part of the crew survived.

The escape of the men trapped in *S.5* when she went down off Cape May, New Jersey, on 1 September, was as dramatic as any incident so far encountered. The submarine, under the command of Lieutenant-Commander Charles W. Cooke, Jr., had just begun to dive when a five-inch pipe in the forward torpedo-room burst and a solid jet of water streamed into the boat. The bow section was speedily evacuated and the crew secured the watertight door to prevent further flooding, while the captain tried to get the boat back to the surface. But the weight of water in the fore-ends defeated all his efforts and, with the typical logic of a highly-trained submarine officer, Cooke decided to exploit the uneven trim to his advantage.

S.5 was 231 feet long and, according to the depth-gauges and the chart, she was marooned in 183 feet of water. Cooke therefore reasoned that if he could literally stand the submarine on its head the fantail would stick out above the surface where it was sure to be noticed by a passing ship. He managed to raise the stern clear of the water and a small hole was cut through the hull; a white shirt was then fastened to a length of steel piping which could be thrust up through the opening and waved should a vessel come close.

Thirty hours later an old freighter, the *Atlantis*, ambled onto the scene but, without cutting gear, there was not much she could do to help. After a few more hours the Swedish *General Goethals* hove into sight. She spotted what appeared to be an uncharted rock projecting from the sea and steamed to investigate. Instead she found the stern of *S.5* poking above the surface. Having learned from *Atlantis* that the crew was still alive she beamed an urgent radio signal the the nearest US Navy base.

Realizing that the Navy salvage team could not be on the spot for several hours and that the delay could be fatal the Chief Engineer of the *Goethals*, William G. Grace, climbed on to the exposed section of the submarine's casing and, equipped only with a cold chisel, a hammer, a crowbar and a hacksaw, he set to work to enlarge the hole made by the crew so that they could crawl out to safety. He finally succeeded and one by one the trapped submariners pulled themselves out. Their incarceration had lasted thirty-five hours.

This amateur rescue attempt stands deservedly high in the annals of submarine history and it demonstrated once again that the major navies were still not geared for a rapid response to disaster. Certainly in this instance it is relevant to question the effectiveness of the US Navy's submarine rescue organization. Someone in authority must have had *some* idea where the *S.5* had gone down. Yet despite the fact that the submarine's stern had been sticking up out of the water for more than thirty hours the Navy failed to find her. Admittedly the failure occurred over sixty years ago. But even in those days air-search facilities and radio communications were well established. It seems incredible that the *S.5* remained undiscovered for so long.

Just how much the submarine's crew owed to William Grace became apparent when the official salvage team finally arrived. When they attempted to lift and tow the submarine into shallower water *S.5* fell into a hole in the seabed. The lifting wires snapped and she sank into the ocean for ever. Had it not been for the efforts of Chief Engineer Grace it is highly probable that her crew would have suffered the same fate.

1921 saw no fewer than five major accidents, one of which was to cost the lives of an entire crew. Not surprisingly, two of the disasters involved the Royal Navy's steam-driven K-class submarines.

K.5 had fully lived up to the reputation of the K-boats in the course of her brief and inglorious career. Although she was not present at the disaster off May Island in 1918 she had made up for the omission in no uncertain manner. During exercises in Largo Bay, in the Firth of Forth, in June, 1920, she had dived out of control and spent ten minutes trapped in the mud at a depth of 120 feet with her stern jutting out of the water. A month later, at Milford Haven, she had rammed an obsolete destroyer while it was being towed behind a tug. No serious damage resulted but *K.5*'s captain, Lieutenant-Commander John Gaimes, had to patch the bows with paint and canvas to hide the scars from the eyes of the Commander-in-Chief. The ruse worked well until the improvised edifice collapsed the first time the submarine went to sea. It was fortunate for Gaimes that the Commander-in-Chief had a sense of humour.

January, 1921, found *K.5* involved in fleet exercises. The weather was atrocious and the flotilla's departure from Tor Bay had to be delayed for more than twenty-four hours. But finally *K.5*, with her flotilla companions *K.9*, *K.15*, *K.22*, and *K8*, followed the cruiser *Inconstant* out to sea en route to the exercise area off the Spanish coast. The submarine misbehaved with monotonous regularity on the outward voyage and, while running at night, she lost suction and was nearly rammed by her next-in-line *K.9*. The latter boat also had her share of troubles for, when the exercise got under way, she stubbornly refused to dive. The fault was finally traced to two safety levers which had been inadvertently locked in position. Fresh danger loomed when the seaman operating the bow vents made a serious mistake and only the prompt intervention of the submarine's First Officer prevented a major disaster.

K.22, the former *K.13*, met with the opposite problem. She dived when ordered but took on such an alarming bow-down angle that her skipper, Commander Allan Poland, promptly threw the motors into reverse and blew all tanks at full pressure to get her back to the surface as quickly as possible. Despite these various trials and tribulations the K-boats completed their parts in the exercise and, one by one, radioed their positions to *Inconstant* as they returned to the surface. All, that is, except *K5*.

A search was instituted immediately the boat was confirmed as overdue but with the constant changes of speed and course during the exercise the chances of finding the missing submarine were extremely remote. Yet, despite the difficulties involved, the lost boat was discovered just before dusk – an achievement that reflected very creditably on the skills of the flotilla's navigation officers. A large oil slick some 120 miles WSW of the Scilly Isles marked the spot where the submarine had sunk, and, as further evidence of the disaster, baulks of painted timber, identified as coming from the decking over *K.5*'s battery compartment, were fished out of the sea. The next day a seaman's ditty box was found floating on the surface. These pathetic pieces of flotsam were all that remained of the submarine and her fifty-seven-man crew.

Many theories have been advanced to account for the cause of the disaster but the most likely reason for *K.5*'s loss was the inclination of the K-boats to run out of control while submerging. The Atlantic Ocean was 3,000 feet deep in the vicinity of the accident and it is probable that the submarine, heading for the bottom in an uncontrollable dive, broke up under the crushing pressure of the sea when she exceeded her safety depth.

There was a public outcry after the tragedy but the jinx-ridden K-boats remained in service. The Navy itself was equally concerned by the appalling accident record of the steam submarines and the former Flag Officer (Submarines), Rear Admiral S.S. Hall, was constrained to write a long letter to *The Times* on the subject in which he observed: 'The accident is deplorable in the loss of so many gallant officers and men, and it is not clear why the K-class should be taken for cruises in the Atlantic in the winter. The vessels may with accuracy be described as 'freak' submarines built entirely for the peculiar conditions of the last war.'

Admiral Hall had undoubtedly made a valid point. With only one exception all the K-boat disasters took place between November and February – in those self-same months which he considered to be unsuitable for their operational use.

The exception, in fact, occurred in that same year, 1921, when *K.15* sank in Portsmouth harbour on 25 June. Like her sisters she had had a chequered career. In May, 1918, while on patrol in heavy weather, she had shipped water down her funnel intakes which had extinguished her boiler fires. Four minutes later she sank by the stern and remained on the bottom for eight hours before her captain, Lieutenant-Commander Vaughan Jones, succeeded in persuading her back to the surface. In 1919 she had twice dived out of control while exercising in the North Sea.

Her end, however, came relatively peacefully. It was an unusually hot summer and a blistering sun had been beating down on the submarine all day as she lay moored alongside the light cruiser *Canterbury* in the dockyard's tidal basin. By the early evening most of the crew were ashore and the few duty-men who remained behind were dozing in cool corners. Suddenly the Officer-of-the-Watch realized that *K.15* was sinking. Water was steadily rising up the sides of the external ballast tanks and was already lapping over the stern. The Lieutenant, only too aware of the K-boat's evil reputation, did not waste time in reasoning why. Climbing down the conning-tower ladder he raised the alarm and the crew hurried on deck where they made their way across to the cruiser. The prompt reaction of the Watch Officer undoubtedly saved their lives. For within minutes of their arrival on board *Canterbury* the submarine dipped beneath the water and settled on the harbour bottom.

The experts who examined the boat after she had been salvaged placed the blame on the weather. The oil in the hydraulic system which kept the vents shut had expanded and overflowed in the intense heat and, as the temperature cooled in the evening, the fluid had contracted. The fall in pressure caused by the oil losses during the day allowed the vents to open slightly and some of the air inside the ballast tanks subsequently escaped. The volume of air lost was replaced by the same amount of water and the tanks slowly filled until the submarine lost buoyancy and sank. It was an accident attributable entirely to the freak weather conditions and it could have happened to *any* submarine. But of course, being a K-boat, it *had* to happen to *K.15*.

1921 was undoubtedly a year of unusual accidents and before it was over two more boats were lost at their moorings. On 26 September the American *R.6* sank alongside the tender *Camden* in San Pedro harbour when someone foolishly unfastened the inner door of a torpedo tube while the bow-cap was still open. The water rushed into the forward compartments and before the watertight doors could be slammed shut *R.6* flooded from stem to stern and went down like a stone. Eighteen men managed to scramble clear but two men, working in the bow-ends, were lost.

An identical human error had been responsible for the sinking of the Dutch *0.5* in 1914, and it is an odd coincidence that in the month immediately following the *R.6* accident *0.5*'s sister-ship, *0.8*, also sank at her moorings in Dan Helder harbour when one of the submarine's sea-cocks was left open. On this occasion the crew escaped before the boat foundered and there were no casualties.

The final weeks of 1921 witnessed one more near-disaster when *S.48* plunged to the bottom of Long Island Sound on 7 December. She was carrying out her builder's trials at the time and the forty-one men aboard included a number of workmen from the Lake Torpedo Boat Company. Before leaving the yards someone had failed to replace a manhole cover on the stern ballast tank with the result that, when the submarine submerged for her first test dive, the sea poured into the tank and flooded the three after compartments. The watertight doors were closed to prevent the rest of the boat from suffering the same fate and, by blowing the for'ard tanks at full pressure, the commander raised the bows above the surface and the men made a hasty exit through the torpedo tubes. It is a pity that a more detailed account of this particular incident cannot be traced.

S.48 was salvaged and, after further trials, was accepted into service with the US Navy. Among her new intake of officers was a certain young Lieutenant Hyman George Rickover – later to gain fame as Admiral Rickover, the man responsible for the nuclear-powered submarine. But in 1921 Rickover, as a newly-promoted Lieutenant, was quite happy in his appointment as *S.48*'s Engineer Officer.

One night, a few months after Rickover had joined the submarine, *S.48* was cruising in Long Island Sound when a serious battery fire broke out. Fearing an explosion of hydrogen gas the captain ordered all hands topsides and the men huddled together on the narrow sea-swept deck while the brass decided what to do next. Holding the opinion that anything connected with the engines and motors was his personal responsibility, Rickover volunteered to go below and extinguish the fire. He had no clear idea how he was going to do so as fire-fighting had never been a matter of much consequence at the Annapolis Naval Academy but, putting on a gasmask, he opened the conning-tower hatch, and descended into the smoke and fumes. Tearing up the decking with his bare hands he located the seat of the blaze and, afraid that use of a chemical extinguisher might result in an explosion, he stifled the flames with a blanket.

On 29 January, 1925, the *S.48* was in trouble again when she ran aground off Portsmouth, New Hampshire. She was refloated none the worse for her experience and remained in service throughout the Second World War as a training boat. She was finally sold for scrap on 22 January, 1946. For a submarine that had survived three major accidents she had enjoyed a surprisingly long and honourable career.

Although history had already shown that attempts to operate surface and underwater craft together was a one-way ticket to trouble the Royal Navy doggedly persevered with the idea of working its submarines in tactical conjunction with the main fleet, and the disasters that followed were the sadly inevitable result of this mistaken policy.

During exercises with the Atlantic Fleet off Europa Point,

Gibraltar, on 23 March, 1922, *H.42* was rammed by the destroyer *Versatile* while she was running submerged. The steel bows of the surface ship smashed an enormous hole in the submarine's pressure hull and she went to the bottom within seconds. Boats and cutters were immediately launched by the ships closest at hand but it was a futile gesture. In the circumstances there could be no possibility of survivors. Twenty-six brave men had gone to their deaths in support of an outmoded theory.

H.24 was luckier. She was struck by the destroyer *Vancouver* later the same year while carrying out submerged exercises with the Fleet. The main casualty in the collision was the submarine's conning-tower, but the pressure hull was undamaged. *H.24* struggled to the surface and was able to return to base without assistance. Had the submarine been trimmed just a few feet nearer the surface the destroyer's bows would have sliced through the main hull and she would have suffered the same fate as her sister *H.42*.

The methods which submarine commanders employ to get their boats off the bottom seem to be as varied as the nature of the accidents they suffer. For the skilled submarine skipper there are always new ways of skinning the proverbial cat, and Lieutenant Charles Momsen certainly found one.

0.15 was his first command and, in an attempt to set a new diving record, he drove her down into the Atlantic under full power in an effort to clip a few seconds off the flotilla's fastest submergence time. Unfortunately, when he gave the order to level off, the hydroplanes jammed in the 'dive' position and *0.15* arrowed for the bottom at a phenomenal rate. She arrived at her unintended destination with a resounding thump and it was lucky that the bottom of the ocean at that particular point was made of soft and very deep mud. Nevertheless with the impetus of her full-power dive *0.15* took some time to stop. And when she finally came to a halt thirty feet of her bows were impaled in the mud.

Momsen considered the problem sitting quietly at the chart table in the control room. Suddenly he threw down his pencil and stood up.

'Open all bow-caps,' he ordered. The message was passed to the forward torpedo-room and the servo motors whined softly as the power came on.

'Bow-caps open, sir. 1 – 2 – 3 – 4. Standing by.'

Momsen hadn't been sure whether the caps would open against

the pressure of the mud, but they had. The first stage of his calculated gamble had come off. Now for Stage Two.

'Check tubes flooded.'

The senior enlisted man in the torpedo-room tried each test-cock in turn and watched for the tell-tale trickle of water.

'All tubes flooded, sir.' he reported as he closed the cock to No 4 tube.

'Stand by ... blow No 1!'

Had the submarine been shipping torpedoes in her tubes Momsen would have been unable to test his theory, and *0.15* might have remained on the bottom for ever. But luck was on his side.

The water was blasted out of the tube as the compressed-air valve was opened but the jet effect of the discharge seemed to have no effect on the trapped boat. Momsen ordered No 2 tube to be blown. Again nothing happened. But the blast of water from the third tube was more effective and the bows of the submarine shifted slightly. Keeping his fingers crossed, the Lieutenant gave instructions to blow No 4 tube. This time the plan worked perfectly. *0.15*'s bows reversed clear of the mud and she came on to an even keel. The main ballast tanks were blown and she rose serenely back to the surface.

Momsen had used a technique which in today's parlance would be termed 'reversed thrust'. He had employed the water inside the flooded torpedo tubes as a form of jet propulsion. It was a nice piece of thinking for a young man not long out of Naval Academy. Not surprisingly, 'Swede' Momsen will be encountered again. For in the years that lay ahead many more submarine crews were to owe their lives to the dedicated determination of *0.15*'s unconventional skipper.

The next accidental sinking occurred in the freezing waters of Anchorage Bay in Alaska. The date was 17 July, 1923, and the submarine *S.38* was moored alongside a tender to carry out routine maintenance work. One of the tasks required the removal of the cover from a sea valve in the motor-room so that some minor adjustments could be made. It was unfortunate that the inlet of this particular valve was situated below the waterline. It was even more unfortunate that a negligent seaman forgot to replace the cover when he had completed his work. As a result water slowly flooded the motor-room and *S.38* settled by th stern until she was completely submerged. Fortunately the crew had time to climb up through the conning-tower and clamber on board the tender and

115

no lives were lost. But, once again, a 'trifling mistake' had sunk a submarine.

On the other side of the Pacific freak weather conditions caused the destruction of the second British submarine in fourteen months when *L.9* was lost in a typhoon.

Hong Kong had received a meteorological warning early on the morning of 17 August, 1923, and the various harbour and naval authorities took immediate steps to ensure that all the ships in their charge were secure. Lieutenant Cresswell was responsible for the submarines of the Reserve Flotilla and the boats not in dry-dock were quickly moored to buoys with strong wires at stem and stern in accordance with established procedures. *L.9*, one of the submarines belonging to the flotilla, was tied up to No 13 Buoy and four men were left on board to keep an eye on things with strict instructions to let go an anchor and fire warning flares should anything go amiss. As there was no commissioned officer available Petty Officer Gordon was left in charge as Watchkeeper.

The typhoon struck Hong Kong at mid-morning the following day. Whipped by the 123 mph winds, the sea smashed across the harbour with terrifying ferocity. Caught in the middle of the maelstrom, the four men on *L.9* did what they could to save their boat but their heroic efforts seemed futile in the face of the thundering seas and shrieking winds that threatened to sweep them overboard whenever they ventured out from the lee of the conning-tower. The cable securing the submarine to its ominously numbered buoy broke under the strain while Gordon and his men were struggling to drop the starboard anchor. Lifting the 890-ton submarine like an empty matchbox, the sea hurled her against the harbour wall. Her bows smashed against the solid granite and then, having been sucked away by the surging undertow, the next wave threw her back again, this time stern first.

As if this was not enough, the engine-room stoker had been unable to close the watertight doors and water was swilling knee-deep in the interior of the boat where the sea had swept down the conning-tower hatch. Realizing that there was no possibility of saving the submarine Petty Officer Gordon gave orders to abandon ship and, as the waves drove *L.9* towards the jetty again, the four men managed to leap to safety. They were bruised, breathless and drenched to the skin, but they were alive.

A short while later Lieutenant T.H. Dickson, one of the officers of the Reserve Flotilla, came along the harbour wall and, thinking that the crew were still on the boat, jumped down on to the heaving deck. Finding the submarine deserted, Dickson made a brave attempt to save the vessel by securing a life-line and throwing it up to a group of dockyard workers on the jetty. But the line broke twice and the mountainous seas threw the submarine against the Japanese steamer *Ginyo Maru* which was anchored nearby. *L.9*'s propellors became entangled in the steamer's mooring cables and the two boats were violently smashed together by the sea. Finally one of the submarine's bulkheads collapsed and she began to sink by the stern.

Dickson, who had already suffered two duckings in his attempt to save the submarine, now tried to climb up the cable which held the rolling *Ginyo Maru* to the buoy. But the mooring wire snapped and he dropped into the sea and disappeared from sight. But, suddenly, his head bobbed to the surface and he struck out for the buoy. It seemed impossible for anyone to survive such a savage sea but, after nearly thirty minutes fighting the shrieking winds and pounding waves, Dickson hauled himself onto the buoy.

Then came the most dramatic moment of that calamitous night. A half-naked figure appeared on the fo'c'sle of the Japanese steamer. Wearing a life-belt and carrying a life-line in his hand he dived over the bows and began swimming to the buoy some forty yards away. The man, later identified as Able Seaman Treagus from *HMS Tamar*, reached the marooned officer and, with the aid of the life-line, the two men were dragged to safety.

Only three days later Japan suffered her first submarine loss since Sakuma's *No 6* went down in 1910 when the *Ro 31* sank during trials off Kobe. She was exercising in Osaka Bay at the time and was swamped when, for some reason, the conning-tower hatch was opened before she was sufficiently surfaced. It was the worst disaster to date and, in fact, in terms of lives lost, the worst until the sinking of the *Thetis* in June, 1939. Five men were saved from the sea but eighty-eight went down with their boat. On 29 October the Imperial Japanese Navy announced the loss of another submarine, *Ro 52*, which, according to the official statement, sank alongside the cruiser *Yahagi* in Kure harbour while undergoing repairs. It was the old familiar story. A torpedo tube was opened in error and the boat was flooded. Fortunately no lives were lost.*

Only a day previously the American *0.5* had come to grief in Limon Bay, Christobel, in the Panama Canal Zone when she was

*Some sources list this submarine as *Ro 55*.

rammed and sunk by the United Fruit freighter *Abangarez*. The submarine was lying only thirty feet down in crystal clear water and had fortunately sunk close to the maintenance depot at the Atlantic end of the canal. Two large floating-cranes, *Ajax* and *Hercules*, were despatched to the scene without delay and the submarine was lifted off the bottom in record time. One man, Charles Butler, decided not to wait for the salvage men, however. Trapped in the flooded torpedo-room where three of his companions had already died, Butler stripped off his clothes and stood with his head in an air-lock. When the pressure had built-up sufficiently he opened the torpedo loading hatch and was blown to the surface. According to one account he was 'thrown several feet clear of the water by the force of the air.' The remaining seventeen men made a more dignified exit through the conning-tower hatch after the cranes had winched the submarine above the surface.

Although the number of submarines lost through accidents was considerably less than in the war and pre-war years it is a tragic fact that in these first five years of peace no fewer than twenty were sunk as the result of collisions, weather conditions, navigational hazards and human carelessness, and at least 185 men paid with their lives. The only encouraging trend to emerge in this immediate post-war period was that 276 submariners had escaped or otherwise survived, proof that rescue techniques were at last improving. Not least it showed that the authorities had finally woken up to the importance of a rapid response when a submarine was known to have sunk.

But submarines were growing bigger every year and were carrying larger crews. In addition the weight of many boats now coming into service far exceeded the lifting capacities of the cranes and salvage vessels available. They were also capable of diving to greater depths which not only increased the problems of salvage but made free escapes (ie escapes without the aid of breathing apparatus) impossible. Furthermore, despite continual research, no one had yet come up with an acceptably compact and reliable breathing-set which would enable survivors to escape from boats sunk in shallower waters.

But, even with these reservations in mind, the disaster toll in the next sixteen years proved to be far worse than the most pessimistic of forecasts. For in the remaining years before the outbreak of the Second World War another twenty-six submarines were to be lost with a death toll of 1,030 men.

—EIGHT—

'Slow torture as well as death'

1924 was only ten days old when disaster struck. The Royal Navy's *L.24* was exercising with a surface Battle Squadron to the south-west of Portland Bill. The weather was cold and wintry and the submarine's Deck Watch breathed a sigh of relief when the diving klaxon sounded. Descending the conning-tower ladder into the warm of the control room they threw off their heavy oilskins and sea boots and headed for a cup of tea in the forward mess space as the upper and lower hatches were shut and clipped. *L.24* angled down in an unhurried dive, levelled off at periscope depth, and steered for the line of battleships fleetingly visible through the mists.

The greyness of the sea and the spindrift of the waves made it difficult to spot a periscope and the lookouts on the 31,250-ton *Resolution* had no idea that a submarine was in their vicinity until it suddenly rose to the surface directly under their bows. There was no time to take avoiding action and the battleship smashed into *L.24* a fraction of a second later. The pressure hull of the submarine was crushed like an egg-shell and she sank to the bottom of the Channel.

Although there was no possibility of survivors a marker-buoy was dropped and destroyers circled the spot until darkness forced them to call off the search. Attempts were later made to salvage the submarine which was located in 180 feet of water and a team of German divers, equipped with a new design of underwater-dress, spent many days on the task. But the deep water and wintry conditions forced them to abandon the operation after several weeks of unavailing hard work and *L.24* still remains on the bottom of the Channel, an eternal tomb for the forty-three men who made up her crew.

Leaving aside the grounding of the *S.19* off Nauset, Massachusetts, on 13 January, 1925, the next four accidents all involved collisions with surface ships and each resulted in heavy loss of life. And, as if to maintain an even balance, the disasters struck at four different navies - Japanese, Italian, American and British.

Japan, still recovering from the shock of losing *Ro 31* and *Ro 55* within two months of each other in 1923, was jolted by a further tragedy on 19 March, 1924 when *Ro 25* collided with the cruiser *Tatsuta* off the southern naval base of Sasebo and sank with all hands. Italy, whose last underwater disaster had taken place during the war when *H.5* was torpedoed in error by a British submarine, lost the 762-ton *Sebastiano Veniero* after she was rammed by the *SS Capena* off Cape Passero in Sicily. She, too, went to the bottom with her entire crew of fifty-four men. And on 25 September, 1925, the American *S.51* met a similar fate.

Operating out of New London, the submarine was running on the surface at night when the accident happened. The cargo-liner *City of Rome* suddenly loomed out of the darkness to the east of Block Island and her bows sliced into *S.51*'s port beam just forward of the conning-tower in the vicinity of the battery room. The men on the bridge leapt for their lives as the two vessels crashed together and three were picked up. But the remaining thirty-three crewmen went to the bottom 132 feet down. Realising that there was nothing he could do, the Master of the cargo-liner dropped a marker-buoy and, having transmitted a general distress call over the radio, resumed his interrupted voyage.

The first naval vessel to reach the scene was *S.51*'s division-mate *S.1* under the command of Lieutenant Charles Momsen who we last encountered experimenting with the theory of reversed-thrust in the *O.15*. But, although *S.1* arrived at the marker-buoy shortly after dawn, the sea was completely empty and, having circled the area two or three times, Momsen decided to steer along the *City of Rome*'s known course on the assumption that the unfortunate *S.51* had been carried away from the point of collision impaled on the bows of the cargo vessel. His intuitive guess proved to be correct and, two miles to the north-east of the buoy, he found a large oil slick and an area of tell-tale air bubbles.

'We tried to contact her but there was only silence. Those of us on the bridge of *S.1* simply stared at the water and said nothing at first. No one at that time knew anything about the principles of escape and rescue. We were utterly helpless.'

Momsen saw the horror on the faces of the men standing beside him on the bridge. 'At least it was fast,' he reassured them. 'They probably never realised what happened.'

Sadly, Momsen was wrong. The crew of *S.51* had not died quickly. But he only learned the truth some time later.

The commander of the New London base, Captain King – the redoubtable Fleet Admiral Ernie King who was to become the US Navy's Chief of Operations in the Second World War – was given the task of salving the sunken submarine. Making use of a submerged pontoon and employing the Navy's best divers, King's team struggled to lift the submarine for several weeks before the winter storms forced them to abandon the mission. Work was resumed in the spring of 1926 and by 8 July the *S.51* was safely dry-docked at the New York Navy Yard. Momsen was not present when they opened the hatches to remove the bodies, but he was soon to learn the horrific details of the contorted faces of the trapped men and of their lacerated hands where they had tried to claw through solid steel. Appalled by what had happened, Momsen came to a momentous decision. For the remainder of his service career he would devote all his resources and undoubted talents to the problems of submarine rescue. His decision meant that the thirty-three men who had lost their lives in *S.51* had not died in vain.

The last victim of this tragic quartet was the British *M.1* – a former K-boat re-engined with diesel units, shortened in length, and fitted with an enormous 12-inch gun – the practical use for which seemed to trifle obscure even to its designers. And the Admiralty stood in such awe of this white elephant that when, first commissioned in 1918, orders where given that the monitor submarines were not to be employed in the North Sea in case the enemy copied the idea. Their Lordships obviously did not credit the Germans with much intelligence!

The gun itself weighed sixty tons and could be elevated, aimed, and fired from inside the control room of the boat. To carry out the operation *M.1* rose from periscope depth so that the tip of the barrel just poked above the surface, fired its shell, and then returned to thirty feet for reloading. The whole process took slightly less than a minute to complete.

On 9 November, 1925 *M.1* left for exercises in the Channel. She was painted in a special shade of green to test her visibility from the air – one of the other M-class boats being decked-out in dark blue for the purpose of comparison. A gale forced the submarine to seek shelter in Plymouth Sound on 11 November but, when conditions moderated after midnight, Lieutenant-Commander Carrie took her to sea again and, once in deep water, the submarine secured for diving and slid beneath the surface.

When *M.1* failed to report her position during the morning the authorities showed an astonishing lack of urgency. The exercise area was well patrolled by anti-submarine vessels and, having learned that their listening equipment had failed to detect any untoward sounds from the seabed, no immediate full-scale search was laid on and it was blandly assumed that the submarine had not only sunk with all hands but that *none of her crew were still alive.* The signal sent to the Admiralty by the C-in-C Atlantic Fleet was laconic and positive: '... it is feared that the submarine *M.1* has been lost with all hands.' In the light of other disasters where trapped men were known to have survived for thirty hours or more it seemed an incredibly premature conclusion, particularly as there was not a shred of evidence to support it.

Acting on the C-in-C's report the Admiralty issued an official statement that same evening, only twelve hours after the submarine had gone missing: 'During exercises early this morning the submarine *M.1* was seen to dive in a position about fifteen miles south of Start Point. She has not been seen since. Every effort is being made to locate her and establish communication.' The optimism of the final sentence, and the inference that some of the crew were still alive, hardly accorded with the earlier signal from the C-in-C that *M.1* had been lost with all hands.

Now that it was too late, an intensive search was organized but, although it continued for a long period, no trace of the missing boat could be found. Then, ten days later, the Swedish freighter *Vidar* arrived in Kiel and her Master reported that his ship had struck a submerged object fifteen miles south of Start Point at 7.48 am on the morning that the *M.1* had vanished. He had thought the object was a dummy mine and had not bothered to stop. But when the *Vidar* was examined in dry dock streaks of green paint were discovered on her port side bottom plating and, after laboratory analysis, it was found to match the special paint issued to *M.1* for the aerial visibility tests. As further evidence of a heavy collision *Vidar's* lower bow section was buckled and damaged. The reason for the submarine's sudden disappearance had been finally established.

Although the approximate location of the collision had now been pinpointed, the wreck of the *M.1* was never found.

Not unnaturally this fresh disaster raised another public outcry in the British press. The Chairman of Lloyds denounced the submarine as 'a deadly machine, which treacherously destroys those in charge of it and, it is feared, inflicts slow torture as well as death.' In a sharply worded article *The Engineer*, a respected and influential periodical, commented: 'There is a not unnatural tendency on the part of the public to challenge the need for such a heavy toll of life in time of peace... One hundred and ninety-three officers and ratings, the very pick of the Navy's manhood, have gone to their deaths ... in the four submarine disasters to occur since the war'. In fact as we have seen, there had been *eight* sinkings and 197 men had died, and that did not include the disasters suffered by foreign navies.

But the terrible toll continued unabated. The French *Nereide* caught fire at Toulon following a battery explosion and her Quartermaster died in the flames. On 9 August, 1926, Britain's *H.29* sank in Devonport dockyard. It had been intended to flood the aft tanks so that her torpedo tubes could be raised clear of the water for inspection, but the orders were misunderstood and the stern of the submarine submerged too deeply. Water entered through the open engine-room hatch and six dockyard workers inside the boat were drowned.

The US Navy suffered another major disaster when the *S.4* – a class with a record almost as unlucky as the British K-boats – was rammed by the Coast Guard cutter *Paulding* off Provincetown, Massachusettes, while she was surfacing late in the afternoon of

Saturday 17 December, 1927. *S.4* reeled under the impact and went to the bottom in a cauldron of bubbling air and spreading oil. *Paulding* transmitted an immediate radio signal and, after launching her boats to search for survivors, she limped towards the shore with a large hole in her bows. The Navy responded with admirable speed and within ninety minutes the first salvage boats were on their way.

It was one o'clock in the morning when the depot ship *Bushnell* and the other vessels arrived on the scene, but the weather was rapidly deteriorating and the situation looked far from encouraging. In the meantime a naval officer who had witnessed the collision from the shore had set out in a picket-boat and laid a circle of brightly painted buoys to mark the approximate area in which *S.4* had sunk. Then, moving slowly inside the buoyed zone, he used a grapnel line to discover the precise position of the submarine. After several fruitless attempts he finally hooked his grapnel into the wreck and held on grimly for several hours as the tiny launch bucked and rolled in the rising seas. But the line snapped shortly before *Bushnell* arrived and it was 10-30 the following morning before the grapnel snagged the hull of the sunken vessel again.

The salvage ship *Falcon* arrived at daybreak but the rough seas made it impossible for the Navy divers to work and it was not until two o'clock in the afternoon that the first men could make their descent. By that time *S.4* had been on the bottom for twenty-two hours. Diver Tom Eadie banged on the Submarine's outer casing with his hammer and was answered by a series of taps from inside. By some miracle the men were still alive.

The news added a vital urgency to the rescue operation and, despite the depth and the appalling weather conditions, the divers went down again to fit an air-hose into the external emergency valve. But their efforts were in vain. The air which was being pumped into the boat had no effect on its buoyancy and was apparently escaping through a damaged section of the hull which had not been located.

Three pontoons, each with a lift of eighty tons, had now arrived from New York and the men from the submarine *S.8* were called in to advise the divers on the lay-out and equipment of the sunken S-boat. But the weather was in an unrelenting mood and little progress was possible. Communication was maintained with the entombed crew by means of morse messages tapped on the hull casing, but little in the way of practical assistance could be given.

The final signal from the submarine came just after six o'clock on Tuesday morning, sixty-two hours after the *S.4* had sunk. It was brief but poignant: *P-L-E-A-S-E H-U-R-R-Y*.

But nothing more could be done. The heavy seas and continual storms made it impossible to move the pontoons into position, and even after the divers had reconnected the air-hoses when the weather abated on Wednesday *S.4* remained immovable. In desperation King's salvage team tried to pass lifting chains beneath the hull but the storms returned with redoubled fury and finally, on Christmas Eve, the rescue attempts were abandoned.

Salvage recovery operations recommenced in January and continued intermittently whenever the weather permitted. Finally on 17 March the conning-tower of the submarine thrust itself above the surface. A few hours later *S.4* was back in dock.

The enormous efforts made to rescue the trapped crew and, when these failed, to reclaim the submarine from the seabed, stand in sharp contrast to the half-hearted response of the British Navy when it was confronted by the *M.1.* disaster. After reading the saga of the *S.4* it is impossible not to wonder whether the men of *M.1* remained alive for an equally long period. The Royal Navy, however, was learning by its mistakes, and it could not be blamed for failure when the circumstances of the accident made rescue impossible within the time available. For it must be remembered that the wreck of the submarine was never discovered, despite weeks of searching.

Diver Tom Eadie was awarded the Congressional Medal of Honor and Captain Ernest King received a second DSM to go alongside the original decoration he had won for his salvage of the ill-fated *S.51*. Only Swede Momsen went unrewarded. He was, of course, not directly involved in rescue work but, a few weeks previously, he had completed detailed drawings for a new design of submarine rescue bell. Backed by Captain King, he submitted the plans to Washington, but the Navy shelved the idea and, when pressed for a decision, rejected the design as being 'impractical from the standpoint of seamanship'. If Momsen's rescue bell had been available when *S.4* went down it is highly probable that at least *some* of the trapped men could have been saved.

Both Italy and France suffered major submarine disasters in 1928 when *F.14* and *Ondine* were lost with all hands after collisions at sea. The Italian boat was taking part in exercises west of Brioni Island on 6 August when she surfaced under the bows of the destroyer *Guiseppe Missori*. With a large hole in her stern, *F.14* sank in 20 fathoms.

Her location on the seabed was pin-pointed by seaplanes and salvage pontoons were rushed to the spot. Heavy seas and strong winds hampered the rescue operation and the divers had difficulties working in the depths of up to 140 feet. But an air-hose was connected and the salvage team laboured manfully into the hours of darkness with the aid of searchlights. Tapping sounds from inside the submarine showed that some of her men were still alive, but, ominously, the messages ceased at around midnight and, although *F.14* was successfully raised the next day it was, by then, too late for the twenty-seven men trapped inside her.

An examination of the boat showed that the crew stationed in the stern section had been drowned in the first few minutes and that the survivors, having closed the watertight doors and isolated the flooding, gathered in the forward compartments. According to a contemporary newspaper report: 'the two officers were both at their posts in the conning-tower and the remaining members of the crew must have all fallen dead at their usual stations. There was no visible signs of panic and the survivors, evidently hoping till the last that they would be saved, had then succumbed one by one to the acid (chlorine gas) fumes.'

The circumstances surrounding the sinking of the *Ondine* were an almost exact copy of the *M.1* disaster three years earlier. The boat was operating in the Bay of Biscay and the shore-based station monitoring her radio traffic lost contact after she had transmitted a signal reporting her position as off Cape Finisterre on the afternoon of 3 October. A search of the general area was made when the authorities realized that she was missing but no trace of the vessel could be found and she was officially posted at 'overdue and presumed lost'.

Then, on 12 October, nine days later, the Greek steamer *Ekateriona Goulandris* docked in Rotterdam and her Master reported that he had collided with an unidentified submarine off Vigo at 11 pm on the 3rd. He did not explain why he had failed to notify the collision at the time but claimed that he had remained on the scene for two hours and had only resumed his voyage when no survivors were found. There is little doubt that a rescue operation could have been mounted with some prospect of success had the Greek captain buoyed the spot and transmitted an immediate report of the accident.

After the run of tragedies which it had suffered in the years before 1914 the French Navy had reason to be proud of the fact that *Ondine* was the first submarine to be lost since the war ended.

All collisions occur unexpectedly. A submarine may surface too close to an approaching ship for avoiding action to be taken. Or when running submerged, her periscope may not be spotted by the lookouts until it is too late. But, on occasions, as with the Royal Navy's *H.47*, some collisions occur for totally inexplicable reasons.

This particular accident happened on a bright summer morning in July, 1929. The sea was smooth and there was maximum visibility. Two submarines, *H.47* and *L.12*, were steaming through the St George's Channel off the Pembroke coast of Wales with *H.47* coming up astern of the leading boat. Both submarines maintained course and the possibility of a collision must have been obvious to everyone concerned. There is, however, a time-honoured 'rule of the road' in the Royal Navy whereby a junior ship, in this case *H.47*, is required to seek the approval of the senior vessel before crossing its bows. No doubt the men on the bridge of *L.12* assumed that *H.47* would veer away at the last moment as no request for such permission had been signalled. But, inexplicably, the smaller submarine held its course, the bows of *L.12* struck her on the port beam just abaft the control room bulkhead and at least two feet of the L-boat's bows speared into the bowels of the helpless *H.47*. She sank rapidly and, as she went down, dragged *L.12* with her. But somehow the senior boat pulled clear and *L.12* bounced back to the surface while her flotilla-mate floundered to the bottom fifty-five fathoms below. Even so, *L.12*'s depth gauges showed that she had touched fifty feet before breaking free.

There were some remarkable escapes. Lieutenant-Commander Oram, the captain of *L.12*, who had been on board *K.6* on the night of the May Island disaster in 1918, was thrown into the sea by the force of the collision and was later picked up. Amazingly, three men survived from *H.47*. Her Commanding

Officer, Lieutenant R.J. Gardner, and two men who were on the bridge with him leapt for their lives at the moment of impact but one of them, a telegraphist, drowned before rescue boats could reach him. The third man to escape was a stoker who had come up on deck for a breath of air bare seconds before the accident happened.

A total of twenty-one men were lost in *H.47* and a further three died in *L.12*. It was a major tragedy by any yardstick and it was, indeed, a miracle that the *L*-boat did not join her companion on the bottom. Only the prompt action of her crew in slamming the watertight doors saved her but, even so, her interior was full of chlorine gas by the time she limped into Milford Haven and she was well down by the bows.

The Navy wasted no time in getting a salvage team together but it was clear that the possibility of finding anyone alive was minimal. The following day another *L*-class boat submerged close to the wreck and tried to make contact with her Fessendon underwater signalling apparatus, but there was no response.

The cause of the collision remains shrouded in mystery and the official report on the accident and the subsequent court-martial proceedings will not be made available for public inspection until the year 2004. It is of interest to note that Lieutenant Gardner was found guilty on two charges: of not handling *H.47* in such a manner as to avoid the consequences of the negligent navigation of *L.12*; and of not handling *H.47* in such a manner as to minimize the negligent navigation of *L.12*. He was sentenced to an official reprimand on both counts.

*　　*　　*

In terms of a submarine history 1930 was an *annus mirabilis*. For the first time since 1904 a complete year passed without a single disaster – a respite which both press and public hailed as the end of a tragic era. The experts, however, entertained no such false hopes.

In the United States research into practical methods of escapes followed two distinct paths – a portable breathing apparatus similar to the Hall-Rees and Drager escape kits, and a submarine rescue bell. The latter was developed by Lieutenant - Commander Allen McCann from an original design prepared by the British safety-engineer, R.H. Davis, in 1917. The Bell, with two vertical compartments, could be lowered and secured to a specially modified hatch on the submarine. By using the lower section as an air-lock survivors could climb into the upper chamber and be winched to safety. The McCann escape chamber's uniqueness lay in its system of down-haul cables which, having been secured to the submarine by divers, enabled the bell to descend under complete directional control unlike the more conventional diving bell used in civilian salvage and exploration work.

Having had his own version of the rescue diving bell rejected by the Navy's top brass in 1927, Momsen concentrated on the development of an improved breathing-set and, by 1929, he had produced the 'Momsen Lung' – a portable apparatus based on the Fleuss-Davis principle of closed-circuit breathing. But, instead of using a self-contained oxygen supply as favoured by Davis Momsen's apparatus was designed for connection to a central oxygen manifold inside the submarine and the reservoir bag was only topped up for independent operation in the final moments of the escape.

In Britain Davis continued to develop his own form of individual escape apparatus which finally emerged, also in 1929, as the Davis Submerged Escape Apparatus or DSEA. Also based on the closed-circuit principle, it was a smaller and neater variation of the original Fleuss-Davis breathing kit. A small high-pressure cylinder contained a 30-minute supply of oxygen and the outfit could double as a gas-mask or smoke-helmet for firefighting.

With goggles to protect the eyes and a clip to prevent the escaper from breathing through his nose the DSEA kit gave its wearer a strangely Martian appearance. But it was well thought out and, within the limitations of contemporary scientific knowledge, it was an effective piece of equipment. The wearer inhaled oxygen and exhaled carbon dioxide through the mouthpiece – a valve diverting the exhaled breath into a canister containing a chemical purifying agent before returning it to the breathing-bag. The apparatus also contained its own inflatable buoyancy-bag and incorporated an apron, or drogue, which could be unrolled to slow down the rate of ascent to the surface, thus avoiding the danger of lung damage which could result from a too rapid change of pressure.*

* For a detailed account of this and other breathing apparatus see *Subsunk* by Captain W.O. Shelford, Harrap & Co. 1960.

The British Admiralty and several other European navies adopted the Davis apparatus in preference to Momsen's Lung although, at this stage, escape hatches, collapsible twill trunks and other aids to escape had not been fitted to the submarines themselves. This meant that, even using DSEA sets, survivors still had to escape from a sunken boat by means of standard hatches as in the past. But the new Davis apparatus was rewarded with an early success and the experts who had criticised the amount of valuable storage space taken up inside the submarine by the DSEA kits were quickly silenced.

The respite offered by 1930 did not last for long and there were two major disasters in May, 1931. The Greek submarine *Nereus* sank with all hands off Pyrgos on the 11th as the result of an apparently misunderstood order. Eleven days later, in the Gulf of Finland, 100 miles SE of Helsingfors, the Russian *Rabotchi* failed to surface after an exercise dive. She, too, was lost with all hands. Unfortunately little is known of these two accidents and few details remain of the sinking of the Russian *L.55* which was rammed by the German *SS Grattia* west of Leningrad on 24 October of the same year. But the loss of 126 lives in three disasters was a grim reckoning after the euphoria of 1930.

On 9 June, 1931, the British submarine *Poseidon* was proceeding on the surface in the North China Sea, some twenty-one miles from Wei Hai Wei, when the Japanese-manned Chinese steamer *Yuta* suddenly appeared out of the low-lying mist and smashed into the boat just forward of her conning-tower. *Poseidon* heeled over with the sea flooding through the jagged rent in her side and, realising that the submarine was doomed, her Commanding Officer gave orders to abandon ship. There was no panic and the crew came up the narrow conning-tower ladder in a steady disciplined stream. By the time *Poseidon* sank thirty-one men had taken to the water where they were picked up by the boats which the *Yuta* had launched with commendable speed.

The remaining twenty-four men aboard the submarine went down with their boat – at least sixteen of them already dead from the flooding and gas fumes that followed in the wake of the collision. The eight survivors squeezed into the forward torpedo compartment in the bows of the boat and, as *Poseidon* settled on the bottom in 120 feet of water, Torpedo Gunner's Mate Willis ordered them to shut and clip the watertight doors leading aft. For the moment they were safe. But for how long? Willis's torch showed that the sea was already leaking into their refuge and he knew that unless they escaped very soon they would die.

The eight survivors included Willis himself, three seamen, Nagle, Lovock and Holt, a Chinese steward, Ah Hai, a Chinese boy and two other members of the crew. The Petty Officer took one of the DSEA kits from its storage locker and asked his companions if they knew how to use it. Five nodded but the two Chinese shook their heads and Able Seaman Nagle was told to give them a quick course of basic instruction while Willis and the others checked out the compartment.

A short while later Willis called the men together and, having explained that no escape attempt could be made until the water level inside the compartment was high enough to equalize the pressure of the sea on the hatch, he led them in The Lord's Prayer. After the final amen the Petty Officer smiled confidently. 'Don't worry, lads,' he told them. 'We'll be alright.'

The flooding valves were opened and the eight survivors waited quietly as the water rose. The oxygen in one man's breathing apparatus ran out and when Willis checked his own kit he found that the cylinder was also nearly exhausted. Somehow he managed to persuade the seaman that everything was working properly and, reassured, the long wait was resumed.

After two hours the water had risen to within five feet of the deckhead and, balancing carefully on a wire that had been stretched across the compartment to lift them closer to the hatch, Lovock and Holt tried to raise the heavy cover. But the pressures had not yet equalized sufficiently and Willis warned them not to over-exert themselves. After ten minutes they had another attempt. The hatch lifted a few inches and then slammed shut.

The two seamen waited a further five minutes before renewing their efforts and this time their patience was rewarded. The cover flew open and the compressed-air inside the compartment blew them through the oblong torpedo-loading hatch. But the speed of ascent proved too much for Lovock whose lungs were ruptured by the sudden decrease in pressure.

The hatch had shut again after the two seamen had made their escape and the remaining six survivors waited for a further hour while the pressure built up sufficiently for another attempt. When

Willis judged that conditions were suitable they gathered under the hatch. The young Chinese mess boy had no DSEA kit and the Petty Officer grasped the frightened lad firmly in his arms as he and Nagle pushed up the hatch-cover.

The aircraft carrier *Hermes* had now arrived on the scene and her boats joined those of the *Yuta*. One of the carrier's officers, Martyn Sherwood, himself a former submarine captain, described the scene: 'We rowed around and around that patch of oil. We pulled through it, noting the circular patches of bubbles that were bursting in it, but not a sign of life could we see. We feared the worst, but no one dared to voice his feelings.

'The sea broke in wavelets upon the extremities of the circle which the oil had calmed so effectively. Suddenly there was a parting of the waters in its centre and a round, dark, hairy object bobbed out of the disturbance.

"Good God: a man!"

'We had them all round us. A mere handful, I know, but at least they had escaped the fate of their comrades.'*

Two men in the final group were never seen again and it is uncertain whether they remained behind in the submarine or were drowned while escaping; and one of those who had risen to the surface with Willis also died from internal injuries during the ascent. But it was a tremendous effort and the Petty Officer was awarded the Albert Medal. Although only four men got to the surface alive the DSEA apparatus had proved its worth. It no longer followed that to be trapped on the bottom of the sea in a crippled submarine meant inevitable death.

DSEA kits were immediately ordered in sufficient quantities to equip every submarine in the Royal Navy, and preparations were put in hand to fit collapsible twill trunks on the underside of the hatches which could be pulled down to form an air-lock if escape proved necessary. In addition the design of submarines then under construction was modified to include two special escape chambers – one for'ard and one aft. Training, too, was stepped up to ensure that each man had some practical experience of using a DSEA set and all boats were fitted with fast-flooding valves and emergency buoys which could be released in the event of a disaster.

Having put the whole of its limited financial resources into the

Coston Gun by Martyn Sherwood. Geoffrey Bles. 1946.

concept of individual escape the Admiralty now announced another change in its previous policy. In future there was to be no provision for salvage rescue operations and the external valves which had been used in the past to feed air into a sunken submarine from pumps and compressors on the surface were sealed off. From now on the survivors would have to find their own salvation.

The authorities also tightened up procedures at organizational level to ensure a rapid response to future emergencies. Submarines were required to radio their position before diving and to indicate not only the proposed duration of the dive but their estimated surfacing position. If a boat failed to reappear at the right place at the right time a priority *Subsmash* code signal was to be relayed by Submarine HQ at Fort Blockhouse so that immediate emergency action could be instigated at the base nearest to the submarine's last known position. Time was to modify the details of the system, notably by the inclusion of a preparatory *Submiss* signal one hour after the boat had gone missing, but, in essence, the basis of the 1931 organization still remains valid today. And the *Subsunk* procedure has been adopted by most of the world's navies, including that of the Soviet Union.

It was an important step forward and, in theory at least, the Royal Navy was now well equipped to handle any emergency that might arise, and it was unfortunate that the system was not fully operational when the next disaster struck on 26 January, 1932. It was also ironic that the victim should be another of the converted K-boats – *M.2*.

M.2, stripped of its 12-in gun, now carried a bulky hanger in front of its conning-tower and was equipped with its own small seaplane for scouting duties. The concept of launching aircraft from submarines was not new. The German Navy had experimented with the idea early in the war and, on 9 January, 1915, *U-12* became the world's first submarine aircraft carrier when an *FF-29* seaplane, piloted by *Leutnant* Friedrich von Arnauld de la Perière, a brother of the famous U-boat ace, lifted off her forward deck during the tests at Zeebrugge.

The United States had dabbled with the idea as well; so, too, had the French, the Japanese and even the Norwegians. So, despite press-reports to the contrary, there was nothing really new about the *M.2*'s role as a submersible aircraft carrier.

In accordance with the new safety procedures Lieutenant-Commander Leathes sent a signal at 10.11 am on the morning of 26 January that *M.2* was about to dive in West Bay, near Portland. Nothing more was heard until the Master of the coastal collier *Tynesider* put into Portland that same afternoon and asked casually whether it was normal for a submarine to dive stern-first. On being asked the reason for his question he explained that, while steaming through West Bay a few hours earlier, he had observed a large submarine submerging by the stern with its bows angled upwards. The Portland naval base was immediately alerted and an intensive search operation began to find the missing *M.2* and her sixty-man crew. It was like looking for a needle in a haystack. West Bay was notorious for the number of wrecks it contained and without an accurate diving position to work on it was difficult to know where to start. In fact it took eight days to locate the submarine, and by that time any hope of rescuing survivors had long since passed.

When divers finally went down to examine her remains they reported that *M.2*'s stern was lodged in the sandy bed of the bay at a depth of 106 feet and that her bows were raised at an angle. More significantly her hanger door was open and closer inspection revealed that the hatch leading from the hanger to the interior of the boat was also unfastened. On the basis of this evidence there was little doubt that the submarine had flooded almost instantly. But why?

In normal circumstances it took fifteen minutes to blow *M.2*'s main ballast tanks and it was an accepted procedure to open the hanger doors as soon as they were clear of the sea and to then hold the stern up by means of the hydroplanes until the aft tanks had emptied and the boat was fully buoyant. The purpose of this dangerous short-cut was to get the submarine's little Parnall Peto aircraft into the air more rapidly, and speed was the essence of naval training.

Several theories were advanced to account for the tragedy. The official explanation was simple and plausible. The hanger door had been opened prematurely before *M.2* was sufficiently clear of the water and had been overwhelmed by the sea. However, submarine officers familiar with the methods employed during surfacing advanced an alternative theory. They suggested that there had been a hydroplane failure, probably in the hydraulic system, and that the partially flooded after ballast tanks had dragged the stern beneath the water causing the boat to sink stern-first as witnessed by the collier captain. They also pointed out that, if the Admiralty's conclusions were correct, *M.2* would have probably sunk bow-first.

Yet another and more ingenious explanation was put forward by Commander William King, the brilliant wartime skipper of the submarine *Snapper,* in his book *The Stick and the Stars.* According to King the preparatory order before surfacing was 'Blow tanks three and four'. And he conjectured that, because of its phonetic similarity, the command had been heard as 'Open hanger door'. If such was the case the ill-fated *M.2* had been sunk by human error rather than by over-eagerness or mechanical failure.

M.2 was fully equipped with DSEA sets but the disaster was so quick that there was no opportunity for individual escapes. It seems clear that the boat must have flooded from stem to stern within a minute or so, but the tragedy in no way invalidated the DSEA system. It did, however, underline the correctness of the Admiralty's decision to scrap its salvage-rescue organization for it had taken eight long days to find the missing boat despite an intensive air and sea search and foreknowledge of her approximate position. A further three *years* of effort were expended in trying to raise the submarine. At one point she was actually brought to the surface with lifting-gear but, at the last moment, the chains snapped and she returned to the bottom where the Authorities then allowed her to remain.

Thankfully the jinx of the K-boats had finally exhausted its venom and *M.2* was the last of these unhappy monsters to be lost. Only *M.3* remained and she was scrapped within a few months.

Later the same year the French Navy suffered its second post-war disaster when the *Promethne* sank off Cherbourg after an hydraulic failure of the main ballast tank vents resulted in the boat flooding. Seven men escaped but sixty-six perished with the submarine.

Three years were to pass before the next major disaster but from then onwards the pace increased, due, no doubt, to the naval expansion programmes of the Great Powers in the years immediately preceding the Second World War. Between 1935 and 1939 a further eight submarines were lost. On 23 July, 1935, the Russian *Tovarich* was rammed by the battleship *Marat* while surfacing in the Gulf of Finland and sank with all hands. Although no precise details can be traced there are indications that a Soviet M-type coastal submarine was also lost in November, 1937.

Germany, now building U-boats again in defiance of the Peace Treaty terms, suffered her first peacetime disaster since 1911 when *U-18* collided with the tender *T.156* in the Bight of Lubeck on 20 November, 1936. The two vessels were engaged on torpedo exercises at the time and the tender was able to pick up twelve survivors from the U-boat's crew before she sank. *U-18* was subsequently salved and remained in service throughout the war being finally scuttled at Constanza on 25 August, 1944.

1939 proved to be a fateful year in every respect: not only did it mark the beginning of the Second World War, it also witnessed a further five peacetime submarine disasters all of which resulted in heavy loss of life. On 2 February the Japanese *I.63* collided with her sister-boat *I.60* in the Bungo Channel between Kyushu and Shikoku. The six men in the conning-tower escaped before the submarine went down but the remaining eighty-one men were drowned. Passing over the *Squalus* and the *Thetis*, which were lost in May and June respectively and which will be the subjects of the two following chapters, the next victim was the French *Phenix*.

The submarine was carrying out a series of practice dives off the coast of Indo-China when, on 15 June, she submerged in 300 feet of water some 225 miles north-east of Saigon and never returned to the surface. The French launched an intensive air and sea search but it was several days before the missing boat was located, and by then it was too late to begin rescue operations. *Phenix* was not salvaged and the cause of her loss has never been established.

In the final week before war broke out the Russian *Shch-424* sank after a collision off Murmansk with the loss of thirty-four men, but, like so many other disasters that occur in the Soviet Union, no details of this tragedy were allowed past the censor.

Shch-424 went down on 24 July. Thirty-seven days later Hitler's troops marched eastwards into Poland while Stalin's tanks rumbled westwards to seize the other half of that sad republic. The war that was to destroy more than thirteen hundred and fifty submarines had begun.

Before moving on to consider the accidental sinkings that occurred between 1939 and 1945 two other disasters must be examined in detail if only to illustrate the different rescue techniques adopted by the United States Navy and the Royal Navy. Here, then, are the stories of the *USS Squalus* and *HMS Thetis*.

—NINE—

'Hi, fellas. Here we are.'
(USS Squalus)

I was just before one o'clock when the telephone rang on
Charles Momsen's desk in the Experimental Diving Unit at the
Washington Navy Yard. The Lieutenant-Commander picked up
the handpiece.

'Momsen speaking.'

'Swede – this is Lockwood.* The *Squalus* is down off
Portsmouth. We need your help.'

'How deep?'

'We don't know for sure – but I guess somewhere between 200
and 400 feet. She went down near the Isle of Shoals. We're
laying on a plane for you. There'll be room for three more. You
have a free hand to take who you want.'

Momsen put the telephone down and leaned forward across
the desk. He flicked the switch of his intercom.

'Tell Lieutenants Yarbrough and Behnke to get the hell over
here fast. And find McDonald. We'll be leaving from the
Anacostia Air Station in less than an hour. This is an emergency!'

* * *

Squalus left her overnight moorings in the Piscatagua River at
7.30 am on 23 May, 1939, and headed out into the Atlantic to
continue her programme of diving trials. The submarine was
brand new. Built at the Portsmouth Navy Yard, she had only

*Commander Charles A. Lockwood of the Navy Department.

138

been commissioned in March and, after ironing out various minor faults, she had tasted the salt water of the sea for the first time on 12 May.

A member of the *Sargo* class of Fleet submarines, officially designated as the *New S class 2nd Group*, she displaced 1,460 tons and measured 310½ feet from stem to stern, only 28 feet less than the British K-class. She was armed with eight 21-inch torpedo tubes plus a deck-mounted 4-inch gun for surface action. On the morning she set off from Piscatagua River on her last voyage she carried a team of five officers, headed by her skipper Lieutenant Oliver Naquin, fifty-one regular crewmen, and three civilians.

Grey clouds were building up on the seaward horizon as *Squalus* plunged her bows into the rolling Atlantic swell and the large white *192* prominently painted on both sides of her conning-tower gleamed each time the early morning sun peeked through the darkening banks of cumulus. The wind was freshening and flecks of spray whipped from the cresting waves as the falling barometer presaged the approach of a deep low pressure area. But the submarine was riding well and Naquin had no qualms about her sea-worthiness. Built for war, she moved purposefully through the water at a full 16 knots – the acrid smoke from her 5500 hp General Motors diesel units trailing astern from the exhaust trunks like the black pennants of a jousting knight.

At 8.13 am Naquin made a preliminary signal to the Portsmouth Navy Yard detailing the precise location and duration of the first dive. Below in the control room the submarine's Executive Officer, Lieutenant Walter Doyle Jr, began the usual routine safety checks that were always carried out on a new boat before submerging. Just before 8.40 he made his report to Naquin.

'Rigged for diving, sir.'

High up on the conning-tower bridge the Captain acknowledged Doyle's report and ordered full emergency power from the engines. He needed the extra speed to achieve a fast diving time. While the final position signal was being transmitted to Portsmouth, Naquin passed the preparatory diving warning down the bridge telephone. Then his finger hit the button and before the squawk of the alarm klaxon had faded Doyle was rapping out a sequence of orders.

139

'Planes hard a'dive. Main tanks 1 & 2 – open valves ... open vents. Flood bow buoyancy tank. Stand by main tanks 3 & 4.'

Naquin shut and clipped the upper hatch, slid down the ladder into the brightly lit control room and reached up to secure the lower hatch. Then he joined his Executive Officer in front of the main control panel and watched the numbered warning lights go from red to green as the various vents and apertures were sealed off. The last two lamps to change were those indicating the status of the main induction valves high up on the conning-tower – one feeding air into the central ventilation system, the other drawing air down for the diesels. This latter valve had malfunctioned during dock tests and Naquin paid particular attention to it.

As soon as the board showed all green Doyle ordered the vents of main tanks 3 & 4 to be opened and *Squalus* gathered momentum as the extra ballast drove her down hard. Naquin clicked his stop-watch at fifty feet. Sixty-two seconds. The target time was sixty, but it wasn't bad for a first dive. No doubt he could find a way to clip those odd two seconds when they carried out the next test. But all thoughts of diving times and possible improvements in the submarine's submergence routine were abruptly swept from his mind as Yeoman Charles Kuney looked up from the battle-phone.

'The engine room's flooding, sir!'

Naquin glanced at the control panel. It was still showing green across the board.

'Blow all main ballast. Blow bow buoyancy. Planes hard a'rise ... close all watertight doors.'

Compressed-air at a pressure of 3,000 pounds per square inch hissed into the tanks as the valves opened and, almost instantaneously, the bows rose encouragingly. But with the sea flooding through the main induction valves at a rate measured in tons per minute the submarine's precariously balanced buoyancy was quickly overwhelmed by the growing weight of water in the rear compartments. *Squalus* hesitated for a moment and then began to sink rapidly by the stern. The interior lights flickered and went out and there was a moment of darkness before the emergency circuits took over.

Metal tools, fittings, wooden boxes and crockery rattled down the central catwalk as the steep stern-heavy angle spilled all unsecured items of equipment to the floor. Feet slipped on the steel decking. Men overbalanced and fell in sprawling heaps. The submarine took on a steeper inclination and the cursing sailors slid helplessly down the length of the compartment until they crashed against the bulkhead at the far end. Bruised and bleeding, they picked themselves up and struggled back to their diving stations.

In the forward battery room vivid blue flames leapt from terminal to terminal in spluttering arcs of fire and Chief Lawrence Gainor, risking instant electrocution, plunged his arm through the hissing arcs and, having located the main port and starboard switches, pulled them down to cut off the power.

Naquin clung to the base of the periscope tube to keep his footing on the canted deck. His eyes met Doyle and an unspoken question passed between them. *How?* It was a question that few of the crewmen had time to ask themselves, let alone answer. While Gainor and his team in the forward battery room were dousing electrical fires and checking the emergency lighting system their shipmates stationed in the bow torpedo compartment were frantically trying to recapture an errant torpedo that had broken loose and was crashing in all directions.

In the after battery space, immediately abaft the control room, the water was already waist-high and the men tumbled through the forward bulkhead door as if all the hounds of hell were snapping at their heels. Lloyd Maness was responsible for the vital watertight door that divided the control room from the flooded stern compartments and as the procession of bedraggled men came to an end he began to push the heavy door shut. A sudden frantic hammering made him pause and, pulling the door back a few inches, he let the boat's cook squeeze through the narrow opening. Then, in obedience to orders, Maness shut the door for the last time and screwed down the clips. If anyone still remained alive in the stern section his only avenue of escape was now sealed.

Less than five minutes after she had begun to dive *Squalus* was on the bottom in forty fathoms. She was literally divided into two distinct halves. The entire area abaft the control room was flooded and the twenty-six men trapped in the stern were almost certainly already dead. The remaining thirty-three survivors were gathered in the control room and the bow compartments. The emergency lighting had gone out and the only illumination was now by hand-torches. Then a hydraulic relief valve burst and sprayed a film of oil over the control room until someone located the manifold and sealed it off. While the trapped men set to work to clean up the mess Naquin and Doyle held a whispered conference.

Both agreed that the flooding had been caused by a mechanical failure in the main induction valve that fed air to the diesel engines and, for some inexplicable reason, this failure had not been reflected by the warning lights on the diving control panel. They also agreed that, in the absence of any sounds from behind the rear watertight door of the control room, all the men in the stern section had drowned. Having established the general situation Naquin ordered a red smoke flare to be fired and told Lieutenant Nichols to release the for'ard marker buoy and stand by the telephone. He then held a roll-call. Twenty-three of the men who answered to their names were inside the control room. And a further ten were safely shut behind the watertight doors of the bow torpedo room.

Having sent five men forward into the bow section to spread the load more evenly Naquin proceeded to hand out the Momsen Lungs. They were not designed for deep-water escape – and *Squalus* was lying in 240 feet – but they doubled as useful gasmasks and there was an ever-present danger of chlorine gas forming in the forward battery room which was awkwardly situated between the control room and the bow compartments and thus separated the two groups of survivors. The men were instructed to move as little as possible, food was passed around, and soda lime was scattered around the boat to absorb the build-up of carbon dioxide in the atmosphere.

Naquin felt as confident as any man could on finding himself trapped in a sunken submarine in forty fathoms of water. *Squalus* was due to make her surfacing signal at 9.40 and a full-scale alert would soon be under way once the senior officers at Portsmouth realized that she was overdue. As the original message at 8.13 had detailed her precise position there should be no delay in locating her on the seabed. Naquin also knew that the Navy now had five McCann Rescue Chambers in service and that one of these was aboard the *Falcon* at New London, only some 200 miles away to the south. Their chances of rescue were good.

* * *

The first boat to establish contact with the *Squalus* was the submarine *Sculpin*. She had been about to leave for a shake-down cruise to South America when Rear Admiral Cyrus W. Cole, the Commandant at Portsmouth, ordered her skipper, Lieutenant-Commander Wilkin, to work out a new course which would take him through *Squalus*'s diving area.

Naquin had been firing distress flares at intervals throughout the morning and as *Sculpin* beat her way slowly across the search area she sighted the smoke from the rocket that had been released just before one o'clock. Altering course and steering towards the red smudge hanging over the sea she found the submarine's marker-buoy and, anchoring alongside, grappled it aboard. Wilkins picked up the telephone and spoke to Lieutenant Nichols who was manning the other end of the line inside the *Squalus*.

Nichols passed a concise and informative report which Naquin had drafted earlier:

'We are in 240 feet of water; no list but eleven degrees up by the bows; heading 150° true. Crew's compartments and both engine rooms flooded. Main induction open. Suggest diver close main induction and attach air-lines to blow out flooded spaces.'

Having delivered the relevant details Nichols passed the telephone to Naquin.

'Hello, Weary.'

'Hello, Oliver.'

Unfortunately they were the only words the two submarine captains had time to exchange. For at that precise and inopportune moment, the line snapped and *Squalus* was cut off from all contact with the outside world.

Meanwhile ashore the rescue operation was getting underway. Admiral Cole informed the Navy's Bureau of Ships that *Squalus* was missing, ordered his tug *Penacook* to get up steam, and telephoned New London to warn them that *Falcon* would probably be needed. As the news spread through the various departments and offices more calls were made, and one of these, as already noted, was to Swede Momsen the Navy's expert on underwater escape procedures and deep-sea diving routines. Another was to commander Allen R. McCann, the co-designer of the Submarine Rescue Chamber on which the lives of the thirty-three men now depended.

Having set things in motion Cole boarded the *Penacook* and set out for the Isles of Shoals. At 3.13 he transferred to the *Sculpin* to take charge of the operation, and while he sat in the submarine's wardroom discussing the situation with Wilkins *Penacook* quartered the area with a grappling line trying to establish the precise position of the missing boat. But as dusk deepened the resting-place of the *Squalus* continued to elude the searchers.

Falcon had been refitting when the first message was received in New London and her boilers were cold. But, disregarding regulations, Lieutenant Sharp ordered them to be relit and within a few hours the tender was under full steam pressure and ready to leave. And while Cole was transferring to the *Sculpin* the little *Falcon*, the tug *Wandank* from Boston and the cruiser *Brooklyn* were already steaming through rising seas towards the Isles of Shoals, the latter carrying 4,000 feet of additional air-hose.

In Washington Commander Lockwood was setting up a central command headquarters to co-ordinate the various ships and services involved in the operation, while Momsen and McCann were being flown to the scene in separate amphibious aircraft. Momsen was the first to touch down at the Portsmouth Navy Yard and, within minutes, he was speeding to the disaster area in a Coast Guard cutter. He arrived at 10.45 pm and immediately climbed aboard *Sculpin* to report to Rear Admiral Cole. McCann and his team of ten divers however had a more eventful trip and it was 4.15 am before they joined the other rescuers aboard the submarine.

At 7.30 in the evening *Penacook*'s grapnel hooked into the lifelines on the submarine's foredeck and a jubilant radio signal advised the Navy Department that *Squalus* had been found again. But until *Falcon* and her divers reached the area nothing could be done but wait. The tension of enforced inactivity was bad enough for the rescuers on the surface. But for the men trapped on the bottom the delay seemed inexplicable and Naquin distributed blankets to the survivors as the temperature inside the boat fell to a shivering four degrees above freezing.

Wandank had by now established audio contact with the submarine by banging morse-code signals on her hull plating, the resonance of the water carrying the sounds to the seabed where the men in *Squalus* read off the dots and dashes. They replied with almost inaudible taps but even this faint response was sufficient to tell the men on the surface that the submarine's crew were still alive.

Cole, meanwhile, had given Momsen command of the diving operations and had placed all the divers, including those on board the still awaited *Falcon*, under his control. He deputed Commander McCann as his technical adviser and senior aide.

Lieutenant George Sharp had had a difficult voyage. Attempting to cut west of Fishers Island to save sea distance he ran into heavy fog and was forced to retrace his tracks and take the longer, easterly, route. Once into the open Atlantic the little *Falcon* had to fight strong headwinds and heavy seas. But Sharp pressed northwards as fast as conditions would allow, although, on occasions, he had to ease back a few knots to protect the precious Diving Chamber lashed down to the fantail.

The tender finally arrived at 5.25 am and, having transferred her divers to the *Sculpin* for briefing, she began the laborious task of mooring directly above the sunken submarine. It took six hours, a time which experts consider to be a remarkable achievement in the adverse weather conditions. In order to operate the McCann Chamber it was necessary to secure the diving tender along the same fore-and-aft axis as the submarine and, initially, anchors were laid out in four directions to hold the *Falcon* steady above her target. But the heavy seas twice dragged the weather anchor and swung the tender out of position and, in desperation, Sharp brought his ship head to the wind and secured her athwart the submarine. This time the anchors held and, having drawn the mooring lines tight to minimize movement, *Falcon* signalled that she was ready.

Momsen and his diving team transferred to the rescue ship and Swede selected Martin Sibitsky to make the first descent even though he was, in fact, a member of the *Falcon*'s team and not one of the highly-trained men from his own Experimental Deep-diving Unit. But personal considerations never influenced Momsen. In his opinion Sibitsky was the best man available and Sibitsky was picked.

As the diver sat on the fantail waiting for the huge copper helmet to be screwed into place Momsen gave him his final instructions. He would have preferred to use the new helium and oxygen breathing mixture he had recently tested at the Experimental Deep-diving Unit but it was impossible in the circumstances and Sibitsky would have to survive on air only, and at the depth at which he was to operate there was an odds-on risk of nitrogen poisoning with all the attendant problems that this entailed. There was no question about it. Sibitsky was being told to put his life on the line to save the thirty-three men trapped on the seabed below, and Momsen was uncomfortably aware of that fact.

'Just do the job, Skee,' were Momsen's parting words. 'I know you can.'

At 10.14 am, nearly twenty-six hours after *Squalus* had gone to the bottom, the diver was lowered over the side of the tender on his wooden platform.

When the cables passed the 150 feet mark Momsen called down the telephone to ask Sibitsky how he was progressing.

'I'm okay, sir. No problems.'

At 200 feet the diver again confirmed that he was feeling fine and that visibility was better than he had expected. Several minutes passed as the platform was winched lower and then, suddenly, Sibitsky's crackled in the earpiece of the telephone.

'I see the submarine ... I'm on her deck.'

There was a cheer from the deckhands lining the rails but Momsen, aware of the difficulties facing a man at forty fathoms, continued to quietly talk Sibitsky through his task. The diver had touched down on the submarine's foredeck casing close to the windlass and only some ten feet or so from the forward escape hatch – the exact spot over which the base of the rescue chamber would have to settle when it was sent down. The vital down-haul cable was lowered to Sibitsky and, after a minor hitch, the diver secured it to the steel ring in the centre of the hatch. The most important preparatory stage of the operation had been successfully completed and, in response to Sibitsky's signal, the diver was slowly hauled back to the *Falcon* with periodic rests at regular intervals to avoid an onset to the dreaded 'bends', the scourge of all deep-sea divers.

The rescue chamber nestling on *Falcon*'s fantail was nearly spherical in shape and was about ten feet high with a maximum circumference of seven feet. Although attributed to McCann it bore a close resemblance in both design and function to the original diving bell which Momsen had submitted to the Navy in 1929. The feature that distinguished it from other deep-diving chambers, and which it shared with Momsen's design, was its system of guidance cables which enabled the bell to descend directly on to its submerged target without any form of control from the surface. One end of the down-haul cable was attached to the submarine's escape hatch by a diver – the task which Sibitsky had successfully completed – while the other end was fed into a power-operated winch inside the chamber. The bell was thus winched down directly on to the hatch and the problem of location suffered by free-descent diving bells was avoided. There was, in addition, a further advantage. All the work of fixing the cable, equalizing the pressure, and raising the escape hatch, was carried out by men from the surface who were fit and fresh and no assistance was needed from the weakened survivors inside the submarine.

At 11.30 am the McCann chamber was lowered into the water and its two operators, Torpedoman 1st Class John Mihalowski and gunner's mate 1st Class Walter Harmon, climbed into the upper compartment where they were handed extra blankets, hot drinks, sandwiches, and cans of chemical carbon dioxide absorbant for the relief of the men inside *Squalus*. It was originally planned to lift out seven men on each dive leaving the remaining five survivors to be brought up on the final descent – a total of five trips in all. But Momsen was worried about the worsening weather conditions and he persuaded Cole to agree to only four dives, lifting nine men on each of the final two ascents. But to ensure that the chamber could cope with the numbers he suggested he conceded that the first lift should be restricted to seven survivors. The Admiral, however, was concerned about breathing conditions inside *Squalus* for she had now been down for twenty-seven hours. So it was agreed that the diving bell should take down an air hose on the initial descent so that the submarine could be ventilated with compressed air.

Having completed the necessary preparations the upper hatch of the chamber was screwed down and, after a thumb's up signal from Momsen, Harmon started the motor of the down-haul reel. The cable began to wind-in and the spherical rescue bell began its slow descent. Mihalowski opened the valve to flood the lower compartment and, in response to the additional weight of ballast, the chamber began to submerge more quickly. Even so it took the two operators nearly an hour to descend the full forty fathoms.

As the bell drew closer to the submarine Harmon used the brake on the down-haul reel to reduce speed and the chamber settled smoothly over the hatch with no more than the suggestion of a bump. The water was blown out of the lower compartment into a special ballast tank on the side – the ballast had to be retained on board in order to neutralize the bell's positive buoyancy – and the air was carefully vented until the pressure equalized. Having checked the gasket seal to ensure that it was

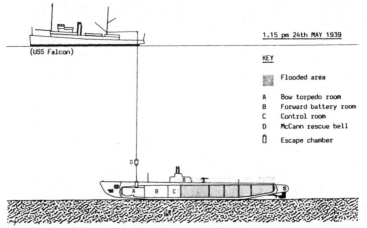

(USS Falcon)

1.15 pm 24th MAY 1939

KEY

Flooded area

A Bow torpedo room
B Forward battery room
C Control room
D McCann rescue bell
0 Escape chamber

watertight, Mihalowski climbed down through the lower section, stood on the submarine's escape hatch, and spun the hand-wheel to release the locking mechanism. Then, stooping down, he pulled back the heavy steel cover. A sea of gaunt white faces peered up at him expectantly as he stood astride the hatchway.

'Hi, fellas,' he said simply. 'Here we are.'

It was a classic understatement. For Mihalowski and Harmon had just made submarine history.

The survivors inside the submarine were in a desparate condition. The temperature was close to freezing and the carbon dioxide content of the air was now up to 3%* Humidity had reached 100% and the internal pressure was double that of the normal atmosphere. But there was no sign of panic or fear in upturned faces. Naquin had told them they'd be rescued and the skipper was always right.

The hot drinks and other items were passed down to the men in the torpedo-room and for the next hour compressed air was pumped into the submarine through a wide-bore flexible hose. Naquin had already drawn up a roster setting out the order in

*A 3% concentration impairs logical thought. 20% is regarded as the lethal saturation level.

which the men were to leave the *Squalus* and, in accordance with the traditions of the sea, his name was the last on the list. As soon as the ventilation had been completed the first seven names were called and, one by one, the men climbed out of the hatch, squeezed through the lower compartment of the rescue bell and entered the circular upper section where Harmon showed them where to sit.

After a final wave Mihalowski closed the hatch, secured the lock, and joined the others in the upper compartment. The ballast was blown clear, the motor of the cable reel started and the ugly steel sphere began its laborious return to the rescue ships that were waiting above.

It proved to be a faultless ascent and the upper dome of the chamber broke surface only fifteen feet away from the *Falcon*. It was exactly 1.42 pm.

One of the seven men brought up on the first trip was Lieutenant Nichols. Despite the young Lieutenant's protests Naquin had insisted that one officer must accompany the initial batch of survivors so that the rescue team could be fully informed about conditions inside the submarine. But in addition to the details he was carrying in his brain Nichols also brought up a sheet of paper which listed the names of the thirty-three men who remained alive. It was the first news of the causalties to reach the surface. The wives and families of the men serving on the *Squalus* knew, from the earlier morse-code signals to the *Wandank*, that twenty-six had died in the disaster. But until Nichols' list was transmitted back to Portsmouth none knew whether their man was dead or alive. Even now no one could be certain as to the ultimate fate of the twenty-six who were still entombed in the sunken boat.

The relatives, in fact, had good cause to worry. For soon after the rescue chamber had left for the surface the chlorine gas contamination in the forward battery compartment had suddenly worsened and Naquin decided to abandon the control room and lead the men through the gas into the bow torpedo room where conditions, although cramped, were clearer.

On the surface Momsen replaced Mihalowski with one of his own men, Chief Machinist's Mate Badders, and the chamber was readied for its next descent. This time, however, there was a minor snag. The clutch of the cable reel jammed and would not engage and the rescue bell had to be hoisted out of the water while mechanics sorted out the problem. It did not take long to rectify and Momsen watched in silence as the steel sphere sank beneath the surface on its next trip.

This time eight passengers crammed into the upper chamber and as it returned to the surface it was clearly riding heavily. Any hope of lifting nine men was out of the question – the McCann rescue bell was obviously on its limit. That meant *five* trips instead of four.

The chamber had already left for its third trip with Badders and Mihalowski at the controls when an officer on Cole's staff suddenly discovered that there had been *nine* and not eight survivors on the previous ascent. He hurried on to the bridge to inform Momsen, and Swede, realizing that he could now evacuate the submarine completely with only two more dives, called Badders on the telephone link and instructed him to lift nine men.

Again everything went smoothly and just over two hours later the white-painted chamber surfaced alongside *Falcon* and nine exhausted and red-eyed submariners clambered up on to the rescue ship's deck from where they were quickly taken below for a medical check-up, dry clothes and hot food. Only Naquin, Doyle and six enlisted men now remained inside *Squalus* and, just before 7 pm, the McCann chamber was ready for its fourth and final descent. Momsen had again rotated the operators and this time Mihalowski was accompanied by Chief Metalsmith McDonald. It was pitch dark when the chamber set out on its final dive and the flickering beams of the searchlights formed a dramatic backdrop to the scene as it slowly vanished beneath the surface on its last forty fathom descent.

At 8.14 pm McDonald reported that the ballast had been blown and the chamber was about to begin its ascent to the surface. He confirmed that Naquin, Doyle and the other six survivors were all safely aboard. But with only 160 feet left to travel the diving bell came to an abrupt halt.

'The wire's jammed on the reel,' McDonald reported calmly. 'We'll soon sort it out.'

The fault was located in the compressed air motor that wound the drum of the cable reel. Worn out by its exertions it had given up the ghost. Mihalowski and McDonald hammered the recalcitrant motor with their fists and then tried kicking it. But nothing would induce it to function. Next they tried to move the chamber by manipulating the braking system. But this, too, proved to be of no avail.

'No good, sir,' McDonald reported. 'We're stuck.'

It was a bitter blow for the rescuers when total success had seemed within their grasp. Momsen tried to overcome the fault by using the retrieving wire, but his efforts had to be aborted when the down-haul cable jammed. Drastic as it seemed there was only one solution. The chamber would have to be returned to the bottom so that a diver could unshackle the tangled down-haul cable. When this had been done the bell could be hoisted to the surface by *Falcon*'s deck winch. Momsen explained the situation to McDonald over the telephone and, having flooded the ballast tank, the operator allowed the sphere to sink down to the seabed.

A few minutes later one of the divers, Walter Squire, was sent down to remove the damaged wire so that the retrieval operation could begin. Squire, like Sibitsky, was seriously affected by nitrogen poisoning but Momsen talked him through the necessary procedures and he succeeded in cutting the down-haul cable. The chamber, with its ten occupants, was now connected to the surface only by the single retrieving wire.

The steam winch spluttered into action and, rising at a steady five feet per minute, the rescue bell began its ascent. But further trouble lay ahead. Unknown to Momsen the retrieving wire had been spliced to obtain the necessary length and, as the chamber neared the surface the strands of the cable started to unravel.

Momsen now ordered McDonald to flood the ballast tank and take the chamber to the bottom again to ease the strain on the wire. Then, after a quick discussion with McCann, he called up another of his divers, Jesse Duncan, and instructed him to go down and fasten a new retrieving cable to the rescue bell. But Duncan fell victim to the perils of the depths and, almost unconscious, he had to be pulled back to the surface and rushed into the *Falcon*'s decompression chamber.

Momsen now faced a moral dilemma. Ten men were trapped at 232 feet and to save them another man would have to risk his life. And if the new diver failed, where would it all end? Could he justify the death or crippling of any more men to save the two operators and eight survivors in the rescue chamber? He decided to try just once more.

Metalsmith 1st Class Edward Clayton was assigned to the

151

task. But he, too, was defeated by the pressure and the nitrogen. And although he remained on the seabed for an incredible thirty-three minutes he was finally forced to admit failure and Momsen ordered him to be brought back to the surface. One fact was now clear. No more divers should be asked to risk their lives.

Despite the dangerous condition of the retrieving cable Momsen and McCann decided that the only chance of recovering the chamber was to haul in the wire by hand – the power winch lacking the essential delicacy of control that would be necessary if a disaster was to be avoided. It was a back-breaking task calling for split-second reactions, for the team was required to slacken the wire each time *Falcon* rose with the swell and then heave in again during the downward roll. While the deck-crew were hauling at the cable McDonald and Mihalowski, crouched over the controls inside the chamber, carefully blew the ballast in brief fifteen-second bursts each time Momsen gave the word. It took just twenty minutes to lift the rescue bell to the surface, but to Momsen, McCann and the ten men inside, it was eternity.

The top of the chamber appeared in the glare of the searchlight beams at 12.23 am and seconds later the hatch opened and the first of the survivors climbed out. Naquin, Doyle and the other six men had spent thirty-six hours marooned in the submarine and a further four hours and nine minutes trapped inside the rescue bell. As Naquin said as he stepped onto *Falcon*'s deck: 'I'm damned glad to be on board'.

* * *

The McCann Rescue Chamber had proved its worth in spectacular manner, but there had been a considerable element of good fortune involved in its success. Firstly, a diving bell had been available within 200 miles of the disaster – a minor miracle in itself – and, secondly, *Squalus* had settled on the bottom in an upright position which had allowed the chamber to be seated on the escape-hatch without undue difficulty.

On the other hand the US Navy had demonstrated a commendable efficiency by its immediate reaction to the submarine's disappearance. As we have seen in previous pages, an instant response is absolutely vital if lives are to be saved. For time is probably the most important element in underwater rescue.

After untold difficulties the submarine was finally raised from her forty-fathom grave in an epic 113 day salvage operation organized and supervised by Momsen himself. She was subsequently recommissioned into the US Navy and, under her new name of *Sailfish*, served throughout the Second World War. Her greatest triumph came on 4 December, 1943, when she torpedoed and sank the 17,830-ton Japanese carrier *Chuyo* off Yokosuka.

By an amazing coincidence among the survivors she dragged from the sea were a number of men from the *Sculpin* who were caged aboard the enemy carrier as prisoners-of-war following the destruction of their submarine by the destroyer *Yamagumo* north-east of Truk the previous month.

Rescuers and rescued had come full circle.

—TEN—

'We couldn't open the hatch!'
(HMS Thetis)

Just seven days after the last *Squalus* survivor climbed out of the rescue chamber, and nearly three thousand miles away on the other side of the Atlantic Ocean, the Royal Navy's newest submarine, *Thetis,* edged her stern into the waters of the Mersey as she left the builder's yards for her first diving trials in Liverpool Bay - the scene of *Resurgam's* disastrous plunge sixty years earlier.

Lieutenant-Commander Guy Bolus was probably unaware of *Resurgam* and its fate. And even if he was familiar with this chapter of submarine history it is unlikely to have worried him. For *Thetis* was hardly comparable with George Garrett's cranky steam-powered contraption. Displacing 1,090 tons in surface trim and capable of taking on 485 tons of water ballast when submerged, she measured 275 feet from stem to stern and packed no fewer than ten 21-inch torpedo tubes into her compact hull - not to mention a 4-inch deck gun and three machine-guns. At 9.40 am precisely on Thursday 1 June, 1939 Bolus backed her away from the fitting-out basin, ordered full starboard helm, and headed down river for the sea.

She was, in fact, already accustomed to the taste of salt water. Her first official sea trials had begun on 30 April but she had encountered serious problems with her steering gear, and her initial diving tests had been abandoned when the hydroplanes jammed. But everything had now been sorted out.

Thetis was the third T-class boat to be completed and had cost the British taxpayer nearly £300,000. Her builders, Cammell

Laird, were already famous for the fine ships they had constructed in the past and their submarines, in particular, were held in high esteem. Her design reflected the latest thinking in underwater technology, and, as befitted her advanced construction, she was equipped with two built-in escape chambers - one forward and one aft. The Admiralty had finally eschewed the freak monster submarines of the early post-war years and the T-class was a logical and conventional development of previous tried and tested designs dating back to the reliable old E-class boats of the First World War.

If 'Sam' Bolus had any doubts in his mind as he took *Thetis* down the busy Mersey it was concerned with overloading. For although the submarine was designed for a crew of five officers and forty-eight men she was carrying no fewer than *fifty* additional passengers. And the ill-fated *K.13* had been similarly overloaded when she went to the bottom of Gareloch during *her* diving trials in January, 1917.

The passengers were a mixture of civilian experts, Admiralty officials, shipyard craftsmen and Royal Navy personnel. Prominent amongst the latter was Captain H.K. Oram, the commander of the flotilla which *Thetis* was to join after acceptance. A seasoned submariner, he had served in *K.6* and, it will be recalled, was swept overboard from *L.2* after her collision with *H 47* in 1929.

Bolus rendezvoused with the escorting tug, *Grebecock,* at noon in the vicinity of the Bar Light Vessel and her skipper, Captain Godfrey, was instructed to follow astern of the submarine to the diving area at a speed of nine knots. The two boats arrived at the pre-arranged position - thirty-eight miles from Liverpool and fifteen miles north of Great Orme Head on the Welsh coast - at 1.30 pm and Godfrey stood-by to take off the surplus passengers before the submarine submerged. He was more than a little surprised when Bolus informed him that everyone was remaining aboard for the dive.

The next signal ordered him to take up station half a mile off the submarine's port quarter and, at the same time, Bolus advised him that the intended course, once *Thetis* had submerged, would be 310 degrees. At 1.40 pm the formal diving signal was made to Submarine Headquarters in accordance with peacetime regulations and it was duly acknowledged by the Admiralty wireless relay station at Plymouth.

From Thetis to Captain S.5 and Admiralty. C-in-C Plymouth ASCB.S.

Important. Diving in position 5335 North 0400 West for 3 hours.

Moving slowly ahead at four knots with the red warning flag flying from one of her periscope standards, *Thetis* steered towards the plotted diving position and Bolus relinquished his station on the conning-tower bridge to descend the ladder into the control room. Both upper and lower hatches were shut and clipped and the Captain ordered the main ballast tanks to be flooded. The First Officer, Lieutenant Chapman, gave executive effect to the command and the sea began to enter the tanks as the valves and vents opened.

Her response was unduly sluggish and, to the onlookers on *Grebecock's* bridge, the submarine seemed to have an excess of buoyancy. Even when the main ballast tanks were fully flooded she continued to loiter on the surface for nearly thirty minutes with a slight bow-down angle. Then, finally, she levelled off and lay in the water with her conning-tower and deck-gun awash and her hull submerged. Once again she remained in the same attitude for several minutes before suddenly disappearing beneath the surface.

Lieutenant R.E. Coltart, who was acting as the naval liasion officer aboard the *Grebecock,* then saw the submarine's bow reappear. 'She just broke surface and I saw a splash of air just for'ard of the bow. She dived horizontally and fairly fast'.

The bubbles which had erupted from the submarine's bow section were puzzling and worrying.

'She went down quickly,' someone observed.

Skipper Godfrey was more positive. 'I think she was in trouble,' he told Coltart.

The young submarine officer was equally concerned, but he felt sure there was a logical reason for what they had seen and he soothed the fears of his companions with a plausible explanation of *Thetis's* strange behaviour. Nevertheless he cancelled the instruction for *Grebecock* to proceed to the estimated surfacing position and ordered Godfrey to keep the tug where she was. It was a sensible decision in the circumstances although it was to have tragic consequences when the hunt for the missing submarine was launched.

Meanwhile the mystery of *Thetis's* antics was deepening. She failed to reappear to check her trim after the initial dive as she should have done, and she did not fire the pre-arranged smoke candles on reaching sixty feet. Coltart's anxiety mounted and at 4.45 he sent a wireless signal to Fort Blockhourse asking the duration of the submarine's dive. The question was intended as a subtle form of alarm for the message to be transmitted *en clair* and he did not want to start off any wild rumours if his inquiry was picked up by some a unauthorized source and passed on to the newspapers. But Coltart's fears were already shared by the Chief-of-Staff at Gosport, Captain Macintyre, who was also feeling a little uneasy over the non-receipt of the submarine's routine surfacing report. Reminding himself that signals were inevitably subject to delay he tried to allay his fears by ordering the Fort Blockhouse radio operators to do their utmost to establish contact with the submarine.

Coltart's inquiry, in fact, had been subject to considerable delay itself for the limited range of *Grebecock*'s transmitter meant that the signal had to be relayed to Gosport via a shore station at Seaforth. And when it finally arrived at Submarine HQ at 6.15 pm Macintyre realized that he had a probable disaster on his hands. Coltart's implied fears and the submarine's failure to radio a surfacing report by 5.05 pm - the latest possible time even allowing for transmission delays - were sufficient to make him raise the alarm. So, in accordance with Admiralty Fleet Order 971/35 the executive signal for emergency operations in response to a submarine accident, *Subsmash*, was flashed to all shore commands and ships at sea.

It was received by the destroyer *Brazen* at 6.22. She was in the Irish Sea steaming south for Plymouth, only fifty-five miles away from the position detailed in the *Subsmash* signal. Her captain, Lieutenant-Commander R.H. Mills, had no idea what type of ship *Thetis* was as she was not yet listed in the official records but a junior rating recalled that she was a submarine. Realizing that the signal probably indicated a disaster *Brazen* immediately altered course eastwards and built up to maximum speed.

Other vessels were also swiftly caught up in the search and rescue operation. Two submarines equipped with underwater signalling equipment were despatched without delay; the deep-diving vessel *Tedworth,* engaged on training exercises in Scottish water, set off for Glasgow to replenish her coal bunkers before steaming south; the eight destroyers of the Sixth Flotilla were ordered north from Portland; and a minesweeping squadron and an anti-submarine flotilla also left for Liverpool Bay. Finally the assistance of the Royal Air Force was requested and a number of twin-engined Avro Anson reconnaissance aircraft took to the skies to add another dimension to the search.

Unlike some previous occasions no one could accuse the Royal Navy of dragging its feet in its response to the *Thetis* emergency.

* * *

Bolus and Chapman had been equally puzzled by the submarine's initial reluctance to dive. All the main ballast tanks were full, the auxiliary tanks had been flooded, and the hydroplanes were at hard a'dive. Any errors in the original trim calculations - figures worked out by an Admiralty official and not by the submarine's own officers – should have been counteracted by the various adjustments carried out by Chapman when *Thetis* first refused to leave the surface. So what could be wrong?

It was clear that the boat was too light for'ard which suggested that she was insufficiently ballasted in the bows. But if the indicators were functioning correctly all the bow tanks were flooded. It was Woods, the Torpedo Officer, who first queried whether the bow tubes should be empty or full. For, as he pointed out, if they were supposed to be flooded but were, in fact, empty this would account for the excessive buoyancy in the fore-ends. Chapman consulted the sheaf of papers he was holding and confirmed that the trim calculations assumed that both No 5 and No 6 tubes were full of water. Woods, convinced that he had pin-pointed the cause of the problem, made his way to the forward torpedo-room to check the condition of the tubes.

He turned the test cocks on both No 5 and No 6 but not a single drop of water emerged. Both tubes were as dry as a bone!

Woods reported his findings to Chapman who ordered him to make a further and more detailed check. This time he was told to open up all six tubes and personally inspect each one. He returned to the forward torpedo compartment to carry out his new orders, but before doing so he carefully checked the arrows of the indicators to ensure that the bow-caps were safely shut. Having satisfied himself on that score, he proceeded with his task.

With the inbred caution of the true submariner he personally checked the test-cock on each tube before ordering Leading Seaman Hambrook to open the loading door. Tubes 1 to 4 proved to be dry and Woods, working methodically, tried the test-cock on No 5 again. When it failed to yield even the smallest drop of water he told the Leading Seaman to open it up for inspection. But as Hambrook pulled down the locking-handle and swung the door open all hell broke loose!

Despite the bow-cap indicator showing 'closed' and the absence of water in the test-cock No 5 tube was wide open to the sea and fully flooded. And the pent-up force of the water that burst from the narrow opening nearly knocked the two men off their feet. As they struggled to close the loading-door Woods shouted a warning back to the control room.

'We're flooding fast through No 5 tube. Blow main ballast!'

Realizing that the door could not be closed against the pressure of the sea, he and Hambrook stumbled through the knee-high water and tried to shut the watertight bulkhead door at the rear of the compartment. But a wing-nut jammed and, abandoning the attempt, they hurried through the torpedo storage room where, with the help of other members of the crew, they succeeded in securing the watertight door of No 2 bulkhead.

Bolus had immediately blown the main ballast tanks and was running the submarine full astern on her electric motors with the hydroplanes hard over in the rise position. But by now the bows were firmly stuck in the mud of the sea bottom and, when he realized that these emergency measures were failing to lift the boat, Bolus belayed his order. The conservation of battery power and compressed-air was of vital importance and there was no point in wasting either in a useless effort to bring *Thetis* to the surface. As the submarine settled on the bottom 160 feet down he ordered the forward indicator buoy to be released and called Chapman, Woods and Captain Oram together for a conference.

It did not take long to establish the reason for their predicament. When the arrows of the six bow-cap indicators were all in the 'shut' position *they did not all point in the same direction*. In fact No 5 pointed to the right and No 6 to the left - an anomaly that no experienced submariner would have ever allowed past the drawing-board. Woods, unaware of this eccentricity, had misread the indicator which, pointing to the left side of the dial, had *correctly* shown the bow-cap as open to the sea. As Sir William White had warned forty years earlier: 'Even with crews thoroughly trained and disciplined mistakes will occasionally be made.'

What the four officers did *not* know, and what was not discovered until *Thetis* was examined after salvage, was that a layer of bitumastic paint, applied before the final coat of white enamel, had sealed the small-bore hole of the test-cock preventing any water from escaping. It was this absence of water that had, not unnaturally, misled Woods when he carried out his initial test. Again, in the words of Sir William White, 'A trifling mistake .... [is] a possible cause of serious disaster.'

The first task was to pump the water out of the two forward compartments so that buoyancy could be restored. But this could not be done until the bow-cap of No 5 torpedo tube was closed. And the operating gear for opening and closing the bow-caps was now under water in the flooded bow torpedo room. So it was agreed that someone would have to go into the fore-ends via the escape chamber and Bolus called for a volunteer. Chapman, the First Officer, was selected and, having donned his DSEA breathing set, he climbed into the chamber. But the flooding-up procedure was inadvertently carried out too quickly and when the needle on the dial reached a pressure of fifty pounds Chapman began making frantic signals to be let out.

The chamber was drained down and the First Officer was in a state of collapse as he was helped through the door. Woods immediately volunteered to take his place but this time Bolus decided that two men should make the attempt so that, if anything happened to one, the other could shut the forward hatch and secure the chamber for draining. Chief Petty Officer Mitchell was chosen to go with him and, having adjusted their DSEA sets, the two men squeezed into the tiny compartment. But, like Chapman, Mitchell could not withstand the rise in pressure during flooding-up and the chamber had to be drained-down for the second time to release him. He was replaced by the Second Coxswain, Smithers. But he, too, fell victim to the pressure and while the two volunteers were being helped out through the hatch Bolus decided to abandon the plan. The time, according to the control-room clock, was 7 pm.

Another conference in the wardroom concluded that the failure to reach the bow-cap operating gear meant that there was no chance of getting *Thetis* back to the surface without outside assistance. Before the flooded compartment could be blown clear with compressed-air supplied from the surface divers would have to secure the forward hatch with a strongback to prevent it from bursting open when the pressure came on. But even this solution was not without difficulties, for, following the Admiralty's decision to seal off the external valves, or in the case of new boats like *Thetis,* to omit them from the design there were only two places to which an air-hose could be connected - the siren on the conning-tower, or the run-out mechanism of the deck gun. In either case there would be a delay while suitable adapters were made.

Although individual escape was perfectly feasible with the aid of the submarine's DSEA sets opinion was hardening against this option. The number of people on board made the time-scale unreasonably long. With two men going up every thirty minutes the complete operation would take at least twelve hours even using both escape hatches. In addition half of the men on board were civilians without experience of, or training in, DSEA drill. And if regular submariners like Chapman, Mitchell and Smithers had trouble dealing with the pressure how could the others cope?

It was therefore agreed that, in the circumstances, external pumping was their best hope of survival. After a further discussion the officers decided that, when *Thetis* had been located by the rescue ships, two men should go up to the surface in their Davis apparatus carrying written instructions for the salvage team.

It was unanimously agreed that Captain Oram and Lieutenant Woods should undertake the mission - Oram because of his vast experience in submarines and his intimate knowledge of the conditions inside *Thetis* and Woods because he had been able to withstand the pressures in the escape-chamber and was therefore physically able to cope with the hazards of the ascent. Bolus, of course, was probably more suitable than either of the men selected but as the Commanding Officer it was his duty to remain with his men. Night had fallen as they sat around the wardroom table working out the details of their contingency plans and, before the meeting broke up, it was decided to postpone the escape attempt until daylight. And dawn was not due until 5 am - in ten hours time.

During the night the trim of the submarine was adjusted to raise the stern closer to the surface. And while the Duty Watch carried out the necessary blowing and venting drill under Chapman's supervision the remainder of the entombed men settled down to snatch a few hours of uneasy sleep. Most felt sure that by dawn an armada of rescue vessels would be standing by ready to pick them up. And with this consoling thought in their minds some of the men managed to doze off.

But as the sun rose just after 5 am the surface of the sea was bare of ships and the escape attempt was postponed. By 7 o'clock, however, conditions inside the submarine had worsened considerably and Bolus realized that unless Oram and Woods set off for the surface fairly soon the poisoned air would make them too weak to operate the escape equipment. Nevertheless he held on for a little longer in the hope that daylight would bring the searching ships into the area. For to reach the surface only to find the sea empty was to merely jump out of the frying-pan into the fire.

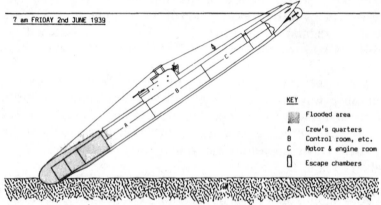

7 am FRIDAY 2nd JUNE 1939

KEY

Flooded area

A   Crew's quarters
B   Control room, etc.
C   Motor & engine room

Escape chambers

One reason for the absence of any ships in the vicinity was an unfortunate, but understandable, error in the position of the *Grebecock* in relation to the *Thetis*. Coltart thought the tug was anchored over the spot where the submarine had submerged. But tidal currents and frequent alterations in course had played havoc with the dead-reckoning track as plotted on the chart and the tug was, in fact, some four miles to the west of the *Thetis's* true resting place. This unintended navigational error was to lead to further delays when the rescue ships finally arrived, and time was fast running out for the 103 men trapped inside the submarine.

When *Brazen* reached the scene at 9 pm the previous evening *Grebecock* suggested that Mills should search to the north-westward of the tug's anchored position. No one was to blame for this incorrect direction as it was completely logical if *Grebecock* had been moored where Coltart *thought* she was. As a result *Brazen* spent the night hours searching the wrong area.

To make matters worse four RAF Anson aircraft from Abbotsinch had actually sighted the *Thetis's* marker buoy before it got dark but had reported an inaccurate fix. It was a doubly tragic error for the first signal from Flight Lieutenant Avent, the Flight Leader, gave the sighting position as 322 degrees and thirteen miles from Orme Head - only one mile SW of the submarine's true position. But to ensure pin-point accuracy Avent had circled the buoy for several minutes while his navigator carefully recalculated the fix. This time he made it 303 degrees and 10½ miles from Orme Head – an error of seven miles in distance and some 20 degrees in bearing. Had the aircrews been less conscientious in their attempts to establish the precise location of the marker-buoy *Thetis* might well have been found before midnight. For *Brazen* was already quartering the area identified by the first report when she was directed away by a radio signal from Fort Blockhouse shortly after receipt of Avent's amended fix.

By 6.30 am the following morning, however, Mills felt convinced that *Brazen* had wasted the entire night searching the wrong area and, altering course north-eastwards, he set off to find *Grebecock* again for fresh instructions. He was about to leave the bridge and go down for breakfast when an excited lookout suddenly shouted and pointed over the starboard bow. Mills raised his glasses and focused carefully on the object. It was the stern of a submarine sticking up out of the water at an angle of some 40 degrees from the horizontal. Moments later the destroyer's radio operator was tapping out the signal:

Have located submarine. Tail out of water. Position follows: 328 degrees distance 14 miles Great Orme Head. TOD: 0754.

With part of the submarine actually above the surface rescue must inevitably follow within a few hours. After all, the US Navy had saved the men from *Squalus* when she had been submerged in forty fathoms, and it was a known fact that the British Navy was superior to everyone else in technical skill and equipment – not to mention seamanship.

Quite by chance, and unaware that the destroyer was approaching, Bolus decided that he dare not postpone the escape any longer. Conditions inside *Thetis* were going from bad to worse and breathing was now extremely difficult. As an experienced submarine captain, Bolus realized that while the breathing problems were physically demoralising the real danger lay in the effect of carbon dioxide poisoning on the brain. Sluggishness, slow reactions, and muddled thinking all flowed from this invisible menace and, if the attempt was not made immediately, a few more hours of delay could make it totally impossible. Accordingly, at just after 8 am, Oram and Woods entered the escape chamber wearing their DSEA breathing-sets and the flooding-up routine began. Both men appeared to cope with the increase in pressure as the water rose and, when it reached their chins, Woods pushed open the hatch and floated upwards followed by Oram. Almost simultaneously the men inside the submarine heard the sharp thump of the explosive charges which *Brazen* dropped to indicate her presence and to signal that she was waiting to pick up survivors as they made their escape. It was a remarkable coincidence.

The crew of the destroyer's whaler sighted Oram and Woods as soon as their heads bobbed above the surface and they bent their backs to the oars with a will. Lifting them gently out of the water, they wrapped them in blankets, and hurried them back to the *Brazen*. Both men were in poor physical shape but Oram had the vital message from Bolus tied to his wrist. And that told the whole story:

'On bottom. Depth 140 feet. Tube space and fore ends flooded. No 5 bow cap and rear door open. Compartments evacuated. HP air required to charge submarine either through gun recuperator connection or whistle connection on bridge. Diver required to tighten down fore hatch so that blow can be put on for'ard compartments without lifting hatch. Strongback required on hatch as soon as possible. Keep constant watch for men escaping through after escape chamber.'

The salvage vessel *Vigilant* had now joined the *Brazen* and the two ships maintained an anxious but patient watch for more survivors. The note had said that further escapes were intended and Oram confirmed that it was planned to send the men up in pairs - a seaman trained in the use of the DSEA equipment, accompanied by one civilian on each ascent. To the men on the waiting ships the situation looked optimistic for the after escape hatch was only some twenty feet below the surface.

There was a similar feeling of optimism inside the submarine as Woods and Oram made their escape, but the next few minutes brought them sharply back to reality. Over-eagerness had led to the door of the escape-chamber being opened before the air-lock was completely drained. The water that remained in the bottom spilled out and ran down the length of the hull. It amounted to no more than a few gallons and it constituted no danger to the stability of the boat. But, coming into contact with some of the electrical wiring, it caused a short-circuit and dense white smoke billowed up from the smouldering cables. Chapman ordered the men to close the watertight doors to isolate the fire and prevent the smoke from spreading and to put on gas-masks or DSEA kits.

The fire was soon extinguished but it had consumed a large quantity of the remaining oxygen and breathing now became painful as well as difficult. Also, despite the original surplus of DSEA kits carried in the submarine, a number had been abandoned in the flooded bow section while others had been exhausted through emergency use. A quick count revealed that there were now insufficient to go around.

Bolus, too, had reached the end of his physical endurance. Although he remained in command, forcing his brain to function by sheer strength of will, he was now forced to lean against the after door of the engine-room with two men holding him upright. So Chapman, acting under his captain's orders, took over responsibility for the escape drill. Realizing that time was fast running out the First Officer decided to send four men up together on the next attempt - two seamen, Kenny and Hole plus two Cammell Laird workmen. The four men squeezed into the chamber - designed strictly for two escapers at a time - and the flooding-up process began. Chapman watched through the glass observation window but it was too dark to see what was happening inside and he was puzzled by the absence of the tell-tale shaft of light which indicated that the hatch open. After twenty minutes he gave orders to drain the chamber.

When the door was opened four bedraggled and inert bodies fell through the hatch and tumbled onto the deck. Three were already dead. The fourth, a civilian, was still just alive.

'It was terrible,' he gasped as the breathing tube was pulled from his mouth. 'We couldn't open the hatch. It's jammed.'

Bolus appeared in the bulkhead door.

'Only in twos next time, sir,' Chapman suggested.

Bolus nodded.

Leading Stoker Walter Arnold and a Cammell Laird fitter, Frank Shaw, agreed to make the next attempt and few moments later the cold seawater was swirling around their legs as the compartment was flooded. When the chamber was nearly full Arnold reached up and pushed at the upper hatch. To his horror he found that it was still stuck. But he remained calm and took stock of the position. He realized that the chamber was not yet fully flooded with the result that the pressure had not equalized sufficiently. He waited a few more minutes and then, signalling Shaw to help him, he pushed at the hatch again.

Suddenly they could see daylight through the shallow water above their heads and the next moment they were shooting to the surface where the ship's boats were waiting to pick them up and whisk them to the *Brazen*. Four men saved out of one hundred and three.

When Arnold and Shaw made their escape at 10 am the submarine had been on the bottom for some twenty hours although the rescue operation itself had only begun two hours previously, at 8 am, when the *Vigilant* arrived. But no time had been wasted and even before Oram and Woods had reached the surface the salvage team had fastened a light line to the submarine's exposed stern to act as a guide-lead for a heavier cable in due course. Captain Hart, the skipper of *Vigilant*, waited to see if any more survivors would come up and when none appeared he instructed the boat's crew handling the wire to hammer a morse message on the hull plating: *C-O-M-E O-U-T*. The signal was repeated no less than ten times but there was no response from *Thetis*.

Hart sent an urgent call to the Mersey Docks & Harbour Board, the owners of the *Vigilant*, requesting burners and burning gear and was obviously considering cutting a hole in the stern of the submarine through which the crew could be brought to safety. But a short while later, after Coltart had transferred across from the *Grebecock* and the message from Bolus which Oram had brought up with him had been passed by boat from the *Brazen*, Hart sent a further signal asking for a portable air compressor, four hundred feet of air hose and, among other items of equipment, a diver and tender.

One of the main problems confronting the salvage men was the tide. As High Water approached most of the exposed portion of the submarine's stern would be submerged. But, because of the strong tidal currents in Liverpool Bay, the only period when a diver could work with safety was just before High Water. Calculations showed that the air supply inside the submarine would only last for some eighteen hours bearing in mind her overloaded state. But the next High Water was not due until noon and by that time *Thetis* would have been down for twenty-two hours.

There were, however, other considerations that must be taken into account when assessing the apparent lack of progress being made by the salvage team. The only senior submarine officer present was Oram, and he was a sick man as a result of carbon dioxide poisoning. Yet Hart never met him face-to-face and was therefore unable to obtain the pertinent data he needed. He did not realize, for example, that the stern of the submarine was lighter than he had supposed and that it would have been perfectly possible to keep it supported clear of the surface by the combined efforts of the *Vigilant* and the destroyer. This is no reflection on the abilities of Captain Hart. He was not a submarine salvage expert and he was, moreover, a civilian. What he needed was experienced technical advice, but there was no one there to give it to him.

The 6th Flotilla of Tribal-class destroyers arrived from Portland at 10.40 am and although neither a submarine man nor a salvage expert the Flotilla Captain, R.S.G. Nicholson, assumed overall control of the operation by virtue of his ranking as the Senior Officer present. His arrival was followed by a further conference of the various experts concerned. The conclusion reached was that the ships should remain clear of the submarine's stern in case any more survivors came to the surface. It was commendable and understandable precaution but any experienced submarine officer - even Leading Stoker Arnold - could have pointed out that in the present physical state of the *Thetis*'s crew further escape attempts were now highly unlikely. The *only* immediate measure that could be taken to save the lives of the trapped men was to connect a supply of compressed-air to the submarine in order to ventilate the fume-filled hull.

Just before High Water, at 11-30 am, the *Vigilant*'s diver went down. His task was to fasten guide-lines to the submarine to assist the next batch of divers - a rather forlorn hope for, by the time the next diving team could descend, the trapped men would be dead. But he carried out his task as instructed, although, being unfamiliar with the submarine's layout, he was unable to locate either the siren or the gun recuperator mentioned in Bolus's note.

There was now no chance of connecting the vital air-hose before the next period of Low Water. And that would not be until 5.30 in the afternoon. By that time the deadline would have long since passed for the men inside the *Thetis*.

Only one possibility remained - to cut a hole in the stern casing. It was a drastic solution but it had worked for the men in both *K.13* and *S.5*. There was only one difficulty. The necessary cutting gear had not yet arrived from Liverpool, and by the time it did there was a strong possibility that the exposed stern of the submarine would have been covered by the tide.

At 1.30 pm an attempt was made to unbolt a manhole cover in the *Thetis*'s stern. But when compressed air began to escape while the bolts were being loosened the salvage men feared that the manhole was in some way connected to the sea and the operation was hastily abandoned. Again, reference to the submarine's drawings would have quickly identified the manhole and indicated whether it was safe or not to open it. But no one seems to have considered making a relayed radio-call to Cammell Laird. And, when the stern of the submarine began to slew with the ebb tide Mr Brock, *Vigilant*'s Wreckmaster, had to jump clear and scramble into the waiting whaler.

The tug from Birkenhead carrying the oxy-acetylene gear finally reached the scene at 2.30 pm and, joined by the *Vigilant*, the two ships went alongside the stern to begin preparations for cutting the hole. Nicholson, however, considered that the submarine should be pulled into a more upright position so that a further securing wire could be passed around the stern and taken back to the salvage vessels. In obedience to his instructions the cable was reeled out and the submarine was slowly hauled into an almost vertical attitude. But the strain on the wire proved to be too great and, at 3.10 pm, it parted with a sharp crack. There was a violent surge of water and *Thetis* disappeared beneath the surface. Only the marker buoy remained to indicate her location but even the wire on this snapped some three hours later the submarine was now totally lost.

The rescue operation had ended in fiasco, due not so much to the failure of any particular individual but to the circumstances of the disaster *and the system*. Admiralty Fleet Order 971/35 had proved to be inadequate, due, in part, to the lack of necessary ships and equipment, but equally to that old bugbear - lack of urgency. The most important vessel, the naval salvage and diving ship *Tedworth*, for example, had been engaged on exercises and was short of coal at the very moment she was most needed. Such situations are, of course, unavoidable when resources are limited. But the lack of urgency showed in other ways.

A team of expert civilian divers had been working in Scapa Flow raising the scuttled German battle-cruiser *Derflinger* when news of the *Thetis* came through. Realizing that speed was vital the Chief Salvage Officer, Tom MacKenzie, acting entirely on his own initiative, pulled his men off the job and rushed them by motor-boat, car and two successive aircraft to Liverpool where they were taken to the scene by a waiting destroyer. By contrast the Navy divers remained on board *Tedworth* while she painstakingly plodded towards Glasgow to replenish her coal bunkers before continuing her journey south. Similarly Captain MacIntyre, the Staff Officer at Fort Blockhouse, was taken north by the duty destroyer which, past her prime, lacked the necessary turn of speed. MacIntyre *could* have been flown to Liverpool in a matter of a few hours and his expert knowledge would have certainly been invaluable to Nicholson.

There is also little doubt that the delay in using the DSEA escape apparatus was a contributory factor in the heavy loss of life for by the time attempts to escape were made the men were too exhausted and befuddled by carbon dioxide poisoning to carry out the necessary procedures with either speed or accuracy. However, both Bolus and Oram realized that help must be close at hand on the surface if the escapers were to survive after they had emerged from the submarine, and they were understandably reluctant to allow any DSEA escapes during the hours of darkness. Their caution proved to be justified some ten years later when the *Truculent* sank in the Thames estuary.

MacKenzie's team, using borrowed diving gear and equipment, went down to the wreck soon after their arrival, but there was no response to their signals, and at 4.10 pm on Saturday, forty-eight hours after she had dived, the Admiralty officially announced that all hope for those on board must be abandoned. The saga of the *Thetis* was over. With ninety-nine men dead it was the world's greatest submarine disaster to date.

There was a not unnatural outcry over the loss of life, especially as part of the submarine's hull had been above water for a considerable period. Not surprisingly, comparisons were made with the success of the American operation to save the men trapped in the *Squalus*. But no two accidents are alike in every detail, and it is impossible to compare one tragedy with another except in the most general terms.

While in no way detracting from the US Navy's magnificient achievement in rescuing the men from the *Squalus* it must be admitted that luck was, to a certain extent, on their side. The location of the boat was discovered quite by chance very early in the search, and the *Falcon*, with its rescue-chamber, was relatively close at hand. The submarine was resting on an even keel, which facilitated the operation of the McCann rescue bell, and there were only thirty-three men to be lifted. Carbon dioxide poisoning was apparently at a much lower level than that in the British boat although this was partially due to the US Navy's use of chemical absorbant powder. Against this, however, *Squalus* was in 240 feet of water and the weather was certainly far worse than in Liverpool Bay.

The *Thetis* was lying at an angle which would have made it impossible to use a rescue bell even had the Royal Navy possessed one, although it is possible that she could have been settled on to a more even keel by selective flooding. There were also unfortunate errors in her position as given by *Grebecock* and the RAF both of which materially contributed to the delay in finding her. And the notorious tidal surges in Liverpool Bay compounded the other difficulties. In addition, because she was grossly overloaded, her air supply lasted for a much shorter period than that of her American sister.

To put it briefly, on the occasion *Squalus* went down the American system of search and rescue worked. When the *Thetis* sank the British system did not.

The Court of Inquiry into the disaster was guarded in both its comment and its attribution of blame, but it made an important series of recommendations which are dealt with in a subsequent chapter. One interesting point, and one which did not emerge during the Inquiry's hearings, was the attitude of submarine commanders and their crews. Not to be sunk was considered to be a far more important objective than escaping after the submarine had gone down. Many commanders even had their Davis Escape Hatches welded down so that there were no weak spots in the boat's hull when she was under attack by enemy depth-charges.

Thetis was subsequently salvaged and, in the process, claimed her one hundredth victim. Petty Officer Henry Perdue complained of the 'bends' while working on the wreck and was quickly brought back to the surface. But while being taken to the decompression chamber in the stern of the salvage ship he collapsed and died from respiratory failure. A post-mortem revealed that Perdue had diseased lungs and a verdict of 'death by misadventure' was recorded by the Coroner's Inquest.

After refitting, the submarine was commissioned into the Royal Navy as *HMS Thunderbolt*, and under her new commanding officer, Lieutenant-Commander Cecil Crouch, she soon made her mark as an efficient and gallant fighting unit. In March 1943, however, she was depth-charged by the Italian sloop *Cicogna* while making a night attack on a North African convoy and she failed to return to her flotilla base at Malta. A few weeks later she was officially posted as 'missing, presumed lost'.

—ELEVEN—

'Here we go for 14 days survivor's leave.'

In the six years between Hitler's invasion of Poland on 1 September, 1939 and the signing of the Japanese surrender on 2 September, 1945 a total of 1280 submarines were destroyed by enemy action or lost by accident. It is ironic that the first submarine to be lost in the Second World War was sunk in error by one of its own kind.

Operating from Dundee, where she was attached to the 2nd Flotilla, *Oxley* was carrying out her first combat patrol off the coast of southern Norway when the tragedy occured. The night of 10 September, 1939, was dark and starless and for some unexplained reason *Oxley* was not on her correct station. In fact she had strayed into the adjacent area allocated to another boat from the 2nd Flotilla, *Triton*. The latter, sighting a submarine on the surface, flashed the challenge three times and, as an added precaution, fired off a recognition grenade. But there was no response from the mysterious stranger and, deciding that it must be hostile, *Triton* fired a torpedo which struck her target amidships and exploded in a brilliant sheet of flame. *Oxley* sank within seconds of being hit and only the two men on the conning-tower bridge at the time of the attack escaped - the Commanding Officer, Lientenant-Commander Harold Bowerman, and a signal rating. *Triton* was unaware of her tragic mistake until the two dazed survivors were dragged out of the sea. The triumph of a successful kill was quickly transformed to numbed horror.

They had sunk a British submarine, and a flotilla mate at that.

Triton's captain was cleared of all blame for the error. He had correctly followed the routine procedure for identifying a strange ship and had he delayed firing the torpedo when faced by what was probably a hostile vessel he would have been courting disaster for his boat, his crew, and himself. The Court of Inquiry also exonerated Bowerman when it learned that *Oxley's* signal lamp and grenade projector had both failed at the critical moment. But, after only seven days of war, it was a shattering mistake and it boded ill for the conflict that lay ahead. As it turned out, only two other British submarines were sunk in error during the ensuing six years. This remarkable record reflects the high standard of training of all those involved in the underwater war.

The other two sinkings both took place in 1942 when the Battle of the Atlantic was at its height and when every nerve was being strained to defeat Hitler's U-boats. The first occured on 21 June when the former American submarine *R.19*, transferred to the Royal Navy and serving as *P.514*, was rammed and sunk by the Canadian minesweeper *Georgian* to the north-west of Cape Breton in Nova Scotia. The second incident happened in the Bay of Biscay on the night of 11 November. Lieutenant D.E.O. Watson had brought *Unbeaten* to the surface to recharge her batteries when an RAF Wellington bomber, fitted with Leigh lights, swooped out of the darkness and sank the submarine with a well-placed stick of bombs. It was a particularly tragic accident for *Unbeaten* had surfaced in an area of the Bay where aircraft were strictly forbidden to attack. But in the heat of war it is not always easy to curb the enthusiasm of air-crews when they sight a target after many months of boring, repetitive and unrewarding ocean patrol.

Fortunately not every encounter ended in tragedy. And despite the dangers involved Britain's submarine captains kept their sense of humour and managed to see the funny side of such incidents. Lieutenant Gregory, the skipper of *Sturgeon*, for example, came under attack by the RAF while returning from a North Sea patrol in the early days of the war and wirelessed his base: 'Expect to arrive 2300 if friendly aircraft will stop bombing me.'

Perhaps the most bizzare incident occurred on 5 September, 1939. A British submarine was running on the surface off the west coast of Scotland when she was surprised by an Avro Anson aircraft from No 223 Squadron. Realizing that there was no time to exchange recognition signals the submarine commander prudently submerged his boat as the plane dived to attack and he survived the incident with little more than ruffled feathers. The aircraft, however, was less lucky. Spurred by over-enthusiasm the Anson swooped to wave-top height before releasing its two 100-pound bombs with the result that they merely skidded across the water and then bounced back into the air. But the impact of striking the surface had activated their time fuses and moments later both missiles exploded beneath the aircraft. Jagged pieces of steel from the casings pierced the Anson's fuel tanks and, with petrol streaming from the wings, the crew was forced to crash-land in St Andrew's Bay and take to their inflatable dinghy. This, surely, must be the only occasion in history where a submarine has destroyed an aircraft without either coming to the surface or firing a single shot!

Britain, of course, was not the only nation to lose submarines as the result of mistaken attacks by friendly forces. Perhaps the most unlucky in this respect was the Italian Navy.

On 8 October, 1940, soon after Mussolini's entry into the war, the *Gemma* was sunk by one of Italy's own submarines, *Trichero*, in the Aegean Sea. The following year, while still an axis-partner of Germany, the *Guglielmo Marconi* was torpedoed by *U-67* in the Atlantic. On 12 September, 1943, only four days after Italy's armistice with the Allies, the *Topazio* was bombed and sunk by RAF aircraft south-east of Sardinia when she failed to make the correct reply to a challenge. Finally, although now an ally of the United States, the *Luigi Settembrini* was depth-charged to destruction by the American destroyer-escort *Frament* in the Atlantic on 15 November, 1944. In the circumstances it is scarcely surprising that the Italian Navy showed a distinct lack of enthusiasm for the war.

The Soviet Union also suffered several losses due to mistaken identity. On 13 October, 1942, the Japanese submarine *I25* sank the Russian *L.16* off the west coast of the United States at a time when the two countries were still at peace with each other. It is a matter of regret that details relating to this unprecedented incident and the diplomatic furore that must have followed in its wake cannot be traced. On 27 July, 1944, RAF aircraft bombed and sank the *B.1* in Arctic waters. This was a puzzling mistake for the *B.1* was the former British submarine *Sunfish* and it should have been readily identifiable by the crew of the attacking aircraft.

The French Navy, like that of the Italians, paid a heavy price for its ambivalent attitude to its erstwhile allies. On 19 December, 1940, several months after the surrender of France, *Sfax* was torpedoed in error by a German U-boat off Cape Juby in the eastern Atlantic. On 8 July, 1944, after France had rejoined the war on the side of the Allies, the *Perle* was mistakenly attacked and sunk by British aircraft.

Neither did the United States emerge unscathed from these fratricidal encounters. The *Dorado* was sunk by American Navy aircraft in the Canal Zone on 12 October, 1943, while the *Seawolf* paid the supreme penalty a year later in October, 1944. This particular incident was especially tragic as it happened in an operationally restricted area off Morotai where, as in the case of the *Unbeaten* in the Bay of Biscay, all attacks on submarines, whether friendly or hostile, were forbidden.

Earlier in the day the destroyer-escort *Shelton* had been torpedoed and sunk by a Japanese submarine and, thirsting for vengeance, her squadron-mates scoured the vicinity seeking a kill. Unfortunately four US submarines happened to be in the same immediate area and these boats, plus the enemy vessel that had carried out the attack on *Shelton*, were all running submerged. As the hunt had to be conducted solely by sonar it was impossible to identify any underwater contacts that were made.

After some hours one of the destroyers, *Rowell*, obtained a sonar echo from a submerged submarine and, in the heat of the chase and unaware that there were American boats in the area, her captain assumed it to be from the elusive Japanese vessel, although he was puzzled by the target's apparent reluctance to escape and by the steady stream of morse signals she was transmitting through her own sonar gear. But, thinking it no more than a typical piece of Japanese cunning, he ordered a depth-charge attack to be carried out. The destroyer-escort made several runs over the invisible target and, after an hour or so, debris shot to the surface followed by a gigantic bubble of air. Sadly, however, her victim was not the Japanese submarine but the *Seawolf*. Lieutenant-Commander A.L. Bontier and his crew had inadvertently been playing the role of decoy while the enemy, taking advantage of the confusion, had made his escape. It was a role that cost them their lives.

Germany seemed more fortunate than other countries and only one U-boat is on record as being sunk in error – the *U-235* which was depth-charged by the torpedo-boat *T.17* in the Kattegat on 14 April, 1945; but a substantial number of U-boats were sunk by collision and it is always possible that many of these incidents were deliberate rammings by friendly ships who were unaware that the submarine was serving under the Swastika ensign.

One very sad example of mistaken identity involved the Polish *Jastrzab*. The submarine was one of the escorts attached to Convoy PQ-15 and she was given the task of attacking any German surface ships which sailed out from their Norwegian bases to threaten the Russian convoy route to Murmansk. The weather had been extremely bad throughout the voyage and it had proved impossible to obtain sun or star sights for nearly a week with the result that, by 2 May, 1942, the submarine was more than one hundred miles adrift from her correct station.

Picked up on Asdic by the destroyer *St Albans* and assumed to be a submerged U-boat shadowing the convoy, *Jastrzab* was immediately attacked with depth-charges by the destroyer and the minesweeper *Seagull*. It was only when the unfortunate vessel was blown to the surface in a sinking condition that the British ships realized their error. But by then it was too late. Happily all but five of the boat's Polish crew were dragged out of the freezing Arctic waters by the two Allied warships, and the gallant exiles who fought under the White Eagle absolved the men of the White Ensign of all blame when the facts of the attack were finally established.

As in the First World War collisions accounted for more submarine losses than any other type of accident. The greatest disaster in human terms was undoubtedly that of the French *Surcouf*. One of the freak monsters that emerged in the pre-war period, she displaced a massive 4,218 tons submerged, mounted two 8-inch guns in a turret for'ard of the conning-tower and carried a hanger and a Besson MB.411 seaplane. She also had a 16-foot boarding launch and space for forty prisoners-of-war. Classified as a corsair submarine, the only one of her kind, she held pride of place for many years as the world's largest submarine.

When France was over-run in 1940 *Surcouf* was refitting at Brest and, as the Panzer divisions struck south, she escaped across the Channel to Plymouth. However, after the surrender, there was a dispute as to whether she should be disarmed and interned, returned to Vichy France or enlisted into the Free French Navy, and in the course of a struggle with Royal Navy personnel who attempted to take over the boat several men were killed. It is of interest that the C-in-C Plymouth who issued the order to seize the *Surcouf* was Admiral Sir Martin Dunbar-Nasmith VC whom we last encountered as the captain of the *A.4* when she sank in Stokes Bay in 1905.

Flying the Cross of Lorraine ensign as a member of the Free French naval forces *Surcouf* carried out several Atlantic patrols before moving to the Caribbean where, it was alleged, she became involved in a number of clandestine operations against various French West Indian islands still controlled by the Vichy Government. Her career ended on the night of 18 February, 1942, when she was rammed by the American freighter *Thomson Lykes* in the Gulf of Mexico while on passage from Bermuda to the Panama Canal and sank with all hands. Her toll of 159 dead remains the worst ever suffered in a submarine disaster.

As already noted, the German Navy suffered a large number of U-boat collisions during the Second World War and there is little doubt that the *Kriegsmarine*'s vigorous training methods accounted for many of these accidents. The main Periscope School for aspiring commanding officers was situated at Kiel and there were numerous training camps and practice diving zones all along the German Baltic coast. An examination of the records shows that at least twenty U-boats were lost as the result of collisions in these training areas, while a further four went down following unspecified diving accidents.

In his book *U-boat 977* Heinz Schaeffer relates that when he took part in one particular fourteen-day tactical exercise in the Baltic two submarines from his training unit were sunk and two others seriously damaged. And Herbert Werner in *Iron Coffins* describes a similar training operation off Danzig in August, 1941, in which more than twenty U-boats were involved. Werner was the Executive Officer of *U-612* and the submarine had a number of trainees on board for experience and instruction. Werner was conducting a training class in the bow torpedo compartment when another U-boat rammed *U-612* while both vessels were running submerged. The other submarine punched a large hole in the stern but *Oberleutnant* Siegmann's rapid response to the accident succeeded in bringing the crippled U-boat to the surface despite serious flooding in the engine-room. He ordered the crew on deck and as the last man stumbled through the conning-tower hatch *U-612* sank under their feet leaving the survivors swimming in the water. Two men died in the tragedy and, although the boat was subsequently raised and returned to service, Admiral Doenitz was deprived of a valuable U-boat for several months.

During the evening of 3 May, 1943, a patrolling *Fw 200* long-range aircraft sighted a Gibraltar-bound convoy in the Atlantic several hundred miles west of Cape Finisterre. A warning call was transmitted on the Kondor's radio and within minutes all U-boats operating in the area were homing on to the target in preparation for a wolf-pack attack. Among the boats hurrying to the scene were *U-439*, a member of the 1st Flotilla under the command of *Oberleutnant* Helmut von Tippelskirch and *U-659*, another Brest-based submarine, skippered by a former *Luftwaffe* officer, *Kapitanleutnant* Hans Stock. Both captains had numerous successes to their credit and were highly regarded by their superiors.

The two U-boats made visual contact with the convoy before midnight and, unknown to each other, were steering similar courses. At 23.55 another member of the gathering wolf-pack engaged one of the convoy's escorting motor gunboats, *MGB 657*, with her 20mm cannon and, setting the British vessel on fire, forced it to turn out of line. The Executive Officer of the *U-439*, notorious for his lazy and easy-going attitude, became so engrossed in the star-shell pyrotechnics of the battle that he neglected to maintain an adequate lookout on the port bow. Had he done so he would have seen *U-659* sweeping past at maximum speed as she closed the convoy.

At this moment, and lacking a warning from his Executive Officer, von Tippelskirch altered course to port. *U-439*'s bow slammed into the overtaking submarine immediately below her conning-tower and, with the sea pouring into her control-room through a gaping hole in her pressure hull, *U-659* was clearly doomed. A large wave swept over her bows and she slipped quietly beneath the water.

Von Tippelskirch ordered the engines full astern within seconds of the impact and as *U-439* backed away from her victim the sea burst through her twisted bow plating and rapidly flooded the forward torpedo compartment. He attempted to compensate for the extra weight by admitting water into the stern ballast tanks but the U-boat settled deeper and a large wave which swept over the conning-tower and entered the hatch hastened her end.

Some two hours later the armed trawler *Coverley* rode over a submerged object and traces of paint found on her keel some days later suggested that she had struck a U-boat, probably *U-439*. A short while afterwards one of the convoy's escorting MGBs encountered a large oil slick and as her captain, Lieutenant-Commander Ashby, slowed to investigate he found himself surrounded by floating corpses and men 'blowing whistles and shouting repeatedly "Don't shoot!".' *MGB 657* stopped engines and dragged twelve survivors aboard - three from *U-659* and nine from *U-439*. Over seventy men had died because the Executive Officer of *U-439* failed to maintain an adequate lookout and two valuable U-boats had been destroyed at a time when Doenitz could ill-afford to lose them. For in that same month Anglo-American forces accounted for a further thirty-nine German submarines. The 'happy time' was over for the *unterseeboots*, and historians agree that in May, 1943, Hitler finally lost the Battle of the Atlantic.

The neutral nations suffered their share of disaster even though they were not involved in the conflict. On 6 March, 1940, shortly before the German army invaded Holland, the Dutch *0.11* was rammed by a naval tug near Dan Helder with the loss of three lives. And on 2 October, 1941, the Japanese *I.61* went down off Iki Island with seventy men aboard after coming into collision with a gunboat. Neutral Sweden lost two submarines during this period through accidental collisions - *Sjoborren* rammed and sunk by the merchant ship *Virginia* on 4 September, 1942, and *Illern* following an encounter with the motor ship *Birkaland* in the Kalmarsund Strait on 12 August, 1943. Fortunately only one man was lost on each occasion. Less lucky, however, was the *Ulven* which sank with the loss of thirty-three men off Marstrand on 14 April, 1943, after striking a mine of unknown origin. Finally, the Turkish *Atilay* failed to surface after submerged trials off Canakkale on 14 July, 1942, and vanished with all hands.

In addition to the three submarines already noted as being sunk in error the Royal Navy lost a further four boats as a result of accidents during the war years. The first, *Unity*, was rammed and sunk by the Norwegian *Atle Jarl* off the entrance to the River Tyne on 29 April, 1940. Two members of her crew, Lieutenant John Low and Able Seaman Henry Miller, gave their lives by remaining behind in the flooded control room so that their shipmates could escape from the sinking vessel.

The next accidental loss, the *Umpire* on 19 July, 1941, was also the result of a collision, but the circumstances were very different. The little 540-ton submarine was built at the Royal Dockyard at Chatham and on completion was posted to join the 3rd Flotilla at Dunoon for sea trials and training. Following established wartime routine, she was instructed to take passage with a north-bound convoy where she would be under the protection of the escort screen. She joined the convoy at Sheerness and the motley collection of ships plodded northwards along the coast throughout the day.

By nightfall the convoy was well into 'E-boat Alley' - a buoyed channel that passed inshore of the east coast minefields where enemy motor torpedo-boats often waited in ambush - when *Umpire* developed engine trouble. Attempts were made to repair the over-heated port diesel unit without losing speed but by midnight it was apparent that the submarine would have to slow down so that the necessary work could be carried out with the port engine shut off.

Shortly before *Umpire* fell astern a south-bound convoy had also entered the buoyed channel and when the two groups met they passed each other starboard to starboard instead of port to port as required by the maritime Rule of the Road. As a result the south-bound convoy was approaching the submarine from almost dead ahead instead of on the anticipated port bearing.

It was a calm night with reasonable visibility but, without running lights, the oncoming ships were little more than a dark ill-defined mass moving on the horizon. Unable to determine the convoy's exact position or course, but aware that it was passing on his starboard side, Wingfield ported *Umpire*'s helm in the hope of steering clear of danger. A few ships were visible to starboard and for a few minutes it seemed that the risk of a collision had been averted. Then, suddenly, the trawler *Peter*

Hendricks loomed out of the darkness. Her bows smashed through the outer casing, penetrated the pressure hull and pierced the forward torpedo storage space.

'You dammed fool! You've sunk a British submarine,' Wingfield shouted as *Umpire* reeled under the impact. His angry accusation was more true than he realized for, moments later, he and his three companions on the conning-tower bridge were swept into the water as the sea surged over the sinking boat.

The men below felt a violent lurch as the two vessels collided. Then the switchboards shorted and the submarine was plunged into darkness. Lieutenant Bannister, the First Officer, was in the wardroom with Sub-Lieutenant Young at the moment of impact and both men leapt to their feet as *Umpire* rolled to port. Bannister ordered all watertight doors to be closed and blew the main ballast at full pressure in an attempt to keep the boat afloat. But with all compartments forward of the control-room flooded there was no possibility of the submarine ever regaining the surface and she settled gently on the sea-bottom in sixty feet of water.

The situation was now extremely dangerous, for although the watertight doors were shut and clipped the sea was slowly flooding the control-room through the ventilation system which had been fractured in the collision. Young quickly found himself knee-deep in water as he searched the wardroom for an emergency torch. When he returned to the control-room he was surprised to find it empty. Looking up, he saw Bannister and two other men squeezed inside the conning-tower. He climbed up to join them and the First Officer explained that once the control-room was completely flooded the pressure would have built up sufficiently for them to open the upper hatch and swim to the surface. He made it sound easy. And his nonchalant attitude helped raise the morale of his companions. The reality, however, was something very different.

Chlorine gas was already rising from the contaminated batteries and the sharp rise in barometric pressure began to hurt their ears. One of the group, a young artificer, was retching from the effects of the gas and the other three were all coughing badly. But there was no alternative and they had to wait for the pressure to build up despite the ever worsening conditions. Finally an air-lock formed and, as the pressure equalized, Bannister pushed the upper hatch open.

'Come on, lads. Here we go for fourteen days survivor's leave!'

The sea rushed in through the opened hatch as the compressed air escaped and the four men had to fight their way clear of the engulfing torrent. Moments later they were floating safely on the surface gulping the cold night air into their lungs. But, alone in the darkness, the little group of men slowly drifted apart despite their efforts to keep together and by the time the rescue boats arrived Bannister and the young artificer had vanished. Only Young and a seaman remained to be picked up. The bridge party who had been thrown into the sea when *Umpire* sank fared even worse. The searching boats found Wingfield floating unconscious in the water but the three men who had been with him were never seen again.

Another group of survivors were trapped inside the engine-room when the watertight doors were closed but, thanks to the determination of Chief ERA Killen, all but four escaped with their lives. As the senior man in the group Killen took charge of the situation and immediately set about organizing the escape drill. A body-count revealed that there were seventeen men in the compartment, but when the DSEA lockers were opened they contained only fourteen sets. Killen was fortunately spared the agony of decision when three members of the group volunteered to make the ascent without escape gear. It is sad to record that not one of these men survived. It is probable that they reached the surface safely but drowned while waiting to be picked up.

Under Killen's direction the flood valves were opened, and keeping close to the engines for warmth, the men waited in the darkness for the pressure to rise. When it had equalized Leading Seaman Band climbed up inside the twill-trunk to open the hatch while Petty Officer Treble checked each man's apparatus. Killen, however, was concerned by the possibility of an obstruction blocking the hatchway and, wearing a DSEA set, he climbed through the hatch and walked about on the outer casing of the sunken submarine while he checked that everything was in order. Then, with incredible bravery, he returned to the hatch and climbed down into the engine-room to supervise the escape of his shipmates.

The trapped men went up through the twill trunk at carefully regulated five-minute intervals until only five remained. It was at this point that Treble realized that Killen was exhausted; he had already spent several hours working on the engines and his examination of the hatch and outer casing had sapped his remaining strength. So, despite the Chief's protests, he insisted that Killen went up next.

Carbon dioxide poisoning nearly claimed the lives of the last four men. Overcome by lassitude and no longer thinking coherently, they put off their own escape and discussed the possibility of remaining in the submarine until daylight. Fortunately Treble could still think clearly and, realizing the danger of the invisible poison, he ordered the other three men to go. Then, having confirmed that no one else remained inside the engine-room, he ducked inside the twill trunk, climbed the ladder to the hatch, and allowed himself to float to the surface where a waiting boat picked him up safely.

Two acts of gallantry deserve particular note. Killen's courage in leaving and then returning to the submarine was recognized by the award of the British Empire Medal - a relatively lowly honour for such a brave deed. But there was no decoration for the unknown hero who shut and clipped the watertight door of the torpedo storage compartment *from the inside* and who, by sacrificing his own life, saved the lives of the men trapped in the after sections.

The third British submarine to be lost was the *Vandal* which disappeared while carrying out working-up exercises in Kilbrannan Sound on 24 February, 1943. She had left the Firth of Forth on the night of the 22nd en route for the practice diving area between the Mull of Kintyre and the Isle of Arran and was last seen leaving Loch Ranza during the afternoon of the 24th. She failed to make a signal to her depot ship at Holy Loch by nightfall, however, and a search was laid on at first light the next morning. But no trace of the missing submarine was found and her final resting place and the reason for her loss remain a complete mystery.

The fourth and final British boat to sink from accidental causes was *Untamed* which went down off Campbelltown on 30 May of the same year. The submarine was acting as an underwater target for an escort group and when she failed to surface at the pre-arranged time an immediate search was started. And within a few minutes the Asdic operator of the yacht *Shemara* obtained a positive echo at a depth of 150 feet. Salvage teams hurried to the spot and twelve underwater charges were detonated - signal denoting: *Rescue is at hand – escape now*. But no survivors appeared and the rescue attempt was called off the following morning.

When *Untamed* was raised six weeks later it proved possible to reconstruct the sequence of events. The problems had originated with the Patent Log which had apparently developed a fault. The designers had envisaged such a contingency and there were provisions for drawing the instrument back into the boat for examination through a special tube. To prevent the sea from entering the submarine while this was being done there was a sluice valve which had to be closed before the inner door of the Inspection shaft was opened. Unfortunately this safeguard failed. The gearing of the sluice-valve had been incorrected assembled and the valve did not shut when the controls were operated. Unaware that the inspection tube was still open to the sea one of the crew had unclipped the inner door and a powerful jet of water shot into the fore-ends at a pressure of thirty pounds per square inch. It was impossible to stem the flooding and the men hurriedly abandoned the compartment and shut the watertight door.

The level of carbon dioxide built up more rapidly than expected and by the time it was decided to pump out the flooded bow compartments most of the officers and men were too befuddled to think coherently. Four vital hours were wasted in trying to lighten the boat and during the final stages the crew were vainly attempting to drain the water out via a 2-inch diameter pipe while the sea was entering the submarine through a 4-inch hole! Such, sadly, is the effect of carbon dioxide.

Having decided to abandon ship the captain led the crew into the engine-room where the after escape-hatch was situated. At this point a second equipment failure occurred. For when the flooding valve was opened no water emerged and inspection revealed that the control handle was incorrectly calibrated. Although the indicator showed 'open' the valve was, in fact, shut. Despite this discovery it still took an unaccountable two hours to flood the compartment, by which time many of the men had succumbed to oxygen poisoning and pressure – the latter having now reached sixty pounds per square inch. Examination after salvage revealed the cause of the delay in flooding-up. When the main valve had failed to operate correctly a small drain-pipe had been opened, possibly inadvertently. This pipe led down to the after bilges and, as a result, much of the water which should have been used to flood the engine-room had, in fact, been channelled into the bilges.

Finally, a Chief Stoker had tried to climb up the twill trunk to open the escape-hatch, but for some reason he failed to reach the top and the remaining survivors were by now so completely overcome by carbon dioxide that they were unable to help either him or themselves. One by one they lapsed into a stupor from which there was no awakening.

The lack of any survivors in the *Untamed* disaster was a brutal disappointment to all those who had put their faith in the DSEA system. Although, outwardly. conditions were perfect for individual escapes the situation inside the boat made it virtually impossible. Certainly the two equipment failures contributed to the tragedy. But it was the delay in beginning a systematic escape operation that ultimately proved fatal - delay due to the time wasted in attempts to drain the flooded compartments. As Captain Ruck-Keene was to point out after the war, submarine crews always tried to save their boat instead of themselves.

* * *

Although details of Soviet submarine losses are difficult to obtain the published memoirs of Admiral Arseni Golovko and Rear Admiral Ivan Kolyshkin have revealed some tantalizing snippets of information concerning Russian accidents during the Second World War. In November, 1940, before the Soviet Union was directly involved, the *D.1* was lost in the Motov Inlet to the north-west of Murmansk during exercises. The submarine, under the command of Captain-Lieutenant Yeltishchev, maintained radio contact with the shore until she was about to dive, and even after she had submerged her periscope remained visible for several minutes. But she failed to reappear at the same time and a search operation was immediately set in motion by the C-in-C of the Northern Fleet. A large oil slick was located the following morning and pieces of cork insulation, splinters of wood and a sailor's cap, were found floating in the water. A salvage vessel belonging to EPRON* was

* EPRON = Special Service for Underwater Salvage Operations.

brought to the scene but despite a search extending for more than a week the rescuers failed to find the missing boat.

It is thought that the submarine had dived too quickly, an inherent fault in this particular class, and had been crushed by the pressure of the sea when she exceeded her safe diving limit. The Official Inquiry into the disaster recommended that, in future, submarines should not dive in waters where the depth of the sea was greater than the safe diving limit of the boat. This nonsensical decision played havoc with the Red Navy's training programmes in the months leading up to the Soviet Union's entry into the war.

In August, 1942, the *Pike*-class submarine *P-402* (or, as classified in some reference books *Sch 402*) suffered a major internal explosion while recharging her batteries on the surface in Tana Fjord. Inadequate ventilation and an accumulation of hydrogen gas was responsible for the disaster in which nineteen men, including the Captain, First Officer, Surgeon, and Political Commissar, were killed. It is an interesting commentary on Soviet naval routine that the first action to be taken by the crew after the watertight doors and vents had been closed was to elect a new Commissar. The honour was bestowed on Warrant Officer Yegorov, the submarine's Party Secretary, and he, in turn, appointed the Engineer, Bolshakov, to take over command as temporary captain. The imagination boggles at the thought of holding a political meeting in such circumstances.

Only when all the necessary new appointments had been completed did the crew begin checking the damaged compartments. The diesel units could not be restarted because of a failure in electric power following the explosion and Bolshakov quickly confirmed that the boat was unsafe for diving. However, by connecting up the batteries they managed to restore life to the main motors and, navigating by means of an unreliable magnetic compass, they finally coaxed the crippled submarine back to her base at Tsyp-Navolok, although, in the process, they nearly made landfall in German-occupied Norway and only realized their mistake at the last moment when they saw an enemy aircraft coming in to land.

P.402's career came to an untimely end on 21 September, 1944, when she was attacked in error by Russian aircraft in the Barents Sea. Although no details appear on record it is believed that four other *Pike*-class submarines were lost by accident during the war years. It is probable that other Russian boats suffered similar fates but, as always, the Red Navy remains silent.

Fortunately for the historian the US Navy does not share the Soviet Union's reticence and the Americans, at least until the advent of the nuclear-powered submarine, have never tried to hide their disasters from public view. Limitations of space, however, makes it impossible to relate details of all the accidents that befell US submarines in the Second World War and, for this reason, a bare summary must suffice.

The United States had not yet entered the war when the first tragedy occured on 20 June, 1941. By a remarkable coincidence, it happened off the Isles of Shoals where, almost exactly two years previously, the *Squalus* had gone down. Sadly *0.9* was less fortunate than her bigger and more modern sister and her entire crew of thirty-three men died when she foundred during a training exercise forty miles south-east of Portsmouth, New Hampshire.

The veteran S-class boats also continued to live up to their evil pre-war reputation. Of the fifty-one submarines that made up the class only one, *S.44*, was destroyed by enemy action, a record comparable with the British K-boats and France's *Perle*-class vessels. Of the remainder no fewer than ten were lost as the results of diving accidents and collisons while one, *S.28*, disappeared off Pearl Harbour in July, 1944 for some undiscovered reason, but which was almost certainly accidental. The ill-fated *Jastrzab* was the former *S.25* before her transfer to the Free Polish Navy.

The S-boats certainly surpassed themselves in 1942. On 20 January *S.36* wrecked herself on the Taka Bakang Reef in the Makassar Straits and suffered such severe damage that she had to be scuttled the following day. Only seventy-two hours later *S.26* collided with the sub-chaser *PC-460* in the Gulf of Panama. She sank in 301 feet of water with both her bow and stern compartments flooded. The survivors gathered in the central section of the boat, but as their only means of escape, the conning-tower hatch, was not modified to accept a McCann Diving Chamber it proved impossible to rescue them and the submarine was lost with all hands.

The crew of *S.27* were more fortunate. Their boat was operating in exceptionally bad weather conditions off Alaska in anticipation of Japanese landing on Kiska, an off-shoot of Yamamoto's grandiose *Operation MI* that had ended in the crushing defeat of the Japanese Navy at the Battle of Midway. Due to unreliable charts *S.27* ran aground on Amchitka Island on 19 June and, pounded by heavy seas as she lay stranded on the shore, she was quickly reduced to a useless wreck. Her crew had to spend the next six days in near-Arctic conditons on the deserted island before being found by US Navy ships. To conclude the S-boat saga of 1942, *S.39* was wrecked on the reefs of Rossel Island during the night of 13/14 August.

* * *

The story of wartime submarine accidents would not be complete without reference to the *USS Tang* and the tragic fate that befell her on the night of 24 October, 1944.

The *Tang* was one of the most successful submarines to operate in the Pacific and, skippered by Commander Richard H. O'Kane, she sank a total of twenty-four Japanese ships grossing 93,184 tons in the course of her brief but dazzling eight-month combat career. Her spectacular and unexpected end came in the Straits of Formosa during her fifth war patrol.

O'Kane made radar contact with a Japanese convoy during the late evening and, adopting the tactics first exploited by Admiral Doenitz in the early stages of the Battle of the Atlantic, he made his attack on the surface. In a similar assault on another enemy convoy the previous night he had destroyed three tankers and two transports but the slaughter had depleted his stock of torpedoes and O'Kane knew that he could not afford to waste any of his remaining weapons as he closed his target.

Picking off his victims one by one with incredible accuracy O'Kane felt proud of his boat and his crew, and was disappointed when the Executive Officer reported that the *Tang* was down to her last torpedo. Scanning the burning and sinking ships of the convoy, he decided to use it on an escort vessel which he had hit and crippled earlier in the attack. He brought the submarine on to a new bearing and passed the deflection angle to the bow compartment on the battle-phone as he crouched behind the torpedo-sight.

'Stand by .... FIRE!'

The torpedo hissed from the tube but, instead of going

straight for the target, it began to wander to port. The deviation became more pronounced and within minutes it had turned a half-circle and was heading back towards the submarine. O'Kane did everything he could to avoid the torpedo but his efforts were to no avail and there was a tremendous explosion as it slammed into *Tang's* after torpedo-room. He just had time to shout an order to close the conning-tower hatch before the boat sank and he found himself in the sea with the eight other men who had been alongside him on the bridge. A few minutes later they were joined by Lieutenant Savadkin who had been inside the conning-tower when the torpedo exploded.

Conditions for the men still trapped inside the submarine were desperate. *Tang* had gone down in 180 feet of water and her three stern compartments were flooded, although, fortunately, the prompt closing of the watertight doors had prevented the sea from encroaching into the other sections of the boat. Several men were seriously injured and there was a fire in the forward battery compartment which, although extinguished, continued to fill the boat with fumes and smoke from the smouldering cables. And, as if this was not enough, the Japanese warships escorting the convoy began a devastating depth-charge attack that was to last four hours.

When the deafening concussion of the underwater explosions finally ceased, the survivors began to make preparations to abandon the submarine. Four men climbed into the escape chamber and an inflatable rubber dinghy was passed through the hatch before the flooding-up routine was begun. After thirty minutes the chamber was drained-down and opened. Three of the men were still inside - half-drowned and barely conscious. Only one of the four had made his escape and even he apparently failed to reach the surface. It was scarcely an encouraging start.

Five men squeezed into the air-lock for the next attempt but when the hatch was opened forty-five minutes later two were still inside and only three had made their escape. To add to their problems the central oxygen supply was now running low and the trapped crewmen were unable to replenish the reservoirs of their Momsen Lungs before entering the chamber. But, under the supervision of an officer, four men took part in the third attempt and this time all safely cleared the hatch although only one survived the ascent to the surface.

The fourth and final group to leave the submarine was led by Lieutenant Flanagan. In his subsequent Report of Proceedings he recalled that the fire in the battery room had flared up again and was so fierce that the paint on the inside of the bulkhead separating the for'ard torpedo-room from the seat of the conflagration was blistering. He also noticed that the rubber gasket forming the seal on the watertight door was beginning to smoulder. In the face of these new dangers there was virtually no chance of survival for those who remained behind after Flanagan and his group made their escape.

So far as can be ascertained thirteen men successfully evacuated the submarine through the forward hatch, although only five were still alive to be picked up by the Japanese the next morning. These five, plus the nine-strong bridge party and Savadkin, were the sole survivors of the tragedy. The remaining seventy-three died with their boat. Of the fifteen men who made their escape only nine were to finally return home when the war ended. Japanese prison-camp brutality had accounted for six of their shipmates.

Happily *Tang's* captain, Commander Richard O'Kane, was one of the nine, and in 1946 he received the Congressional Medal of Honor, America's highest military decoration, from President Truman in recognition of his bravery and as a salute to the men who had sailed with him.

The *Tang* remains an uncharted but hallowed grave for her courageous crew somewhere on the bottom of the Formosa Straits. And despite her successful war record she will always be remembered as 'the submarine that torpedoed itself'.

—TWELVE—

'We are at the north end of Hurd Deep.'

1945 finally brought the Second World War to a victorious end for the Western Allies, and with more than forty years' experience of submarine disasters the Royal Navy now had both the time and the knowledge to consider the whole scenario of underwater escape and survival. Steps were therefore immediately taken to follow up the tentative recommendations of the Nasmith Committee which had been appointed in the wake of the *Thetis* tragedy but which had fallen by the wayside due to the war. Accordingly the Admiralty formed a new committee in 1946 under the chairmanship of Captain Philip Ruck-Keene, who was given a wide-ranging brief to enquire into all aspects of submarine accidents and escape equipment.

Before dealing with the conclusions of the Committee, however, it is necessary to summarize briefly the nature and effect of atmospheric poisoning and air pollution in a sunken submarine. Firstly, as already noted, there is a continual build-up of carbon dioxide from the exhaled breath of the trapped survivors. Under normal pressure the air which a man breathes comprises the following:

	On inhalation	On exhalation
Nitrogen	79%	80%
Oxygen	21%	16%
Carbon dioxide	.03%	4%

But when a confined space is flooded with water the air inside it is compressed, and for every additional atmosphere of pressure the concentration of the exhaled carbon dioxide is doubled. A level of 25% is regarded as lethal and even with much lower concentrations the excessive carbon dioxide affects the normal functions of the brain and can induce unconsciousness.

The absorbtion of nitrogen into the blood also increases in a direct ratio to the rise in pressure, and if a survivor ascends to the surface too rapidly the nitrogen concentration in the blood does not have time to disperse and the victim suffers from the 'Bends'. The use of DSEA apparatus reduces the level of carbon dioxide by chemical absorbtion of the exhaled breath and completely eliminates the nitrogen danger, as the survivor is breathing pure oxygen.

But even pure oxygen is dangerous when breathed under pressure and at sixty feet the user may suffer from convulsions and blackouts. The greater the depth, the higher the pressure, and the more violent the reaction. In addition the onset of oxygen poisoning is accelerated. These, then, are the physiological problems that face the survivors.

As a first step the Committee interviewed twenty-eight survivors - a sample that included men from the United States, German, Danish and Norwegian Navies as well as British personnel. In addition, it made a detailed analysis of thirty-two submarine disasters. One surprising statistic emerged: 86% of the men who were alive when a vessel sank ultimately died with the submarine. It also became clear that the crew directed their energies towards saving the boat rather than their own lives. More surprisingly, only 10% of those who succeeded in escaping died during the ascent to the surface. This number was equally divided between those who were wearing DSEA sets and *those who made the ascent without the aid of any apparatus whatsoever.* The Ruck-Keene Committee's recommendations were wide-ranging in scope and, in some instances, revolutionary in concept. In fact it turned the current theory of submarine escape entirely on its head. For it advised the Royal Navy to adopt the American system of 'free escape' and to only use the Davis breathing apparatus *inside* the submarine during the waiting period before the escape ascent. The Committee also suggested a new type of breathing-set based on a mixture of oxygen and nitrogen as a replacement for the existing DSEA outfits which used pure oxygen.

'Free escape' is based on a simple scientific fact. Air which is inhaled at depth is already compressed and, as a man ascends to the surface, it slowly expands in response to the reduction in pressure. As a result the lungs are being continually exhausted of surplus air throughout the ascent and it is unnecessary to inhale as there is always sufficient air in the breathing organs to keep them full. The man merely opens his mouth and allows the surplus air to escape.

Such techniques clearly demand careful training, if only to convince would-be escapers that the theory works in practice. Ruck-Keene also recommended the installation of a 100-foot training tank for instructional purposes. A similar tank had been in service with the US Navy for some years so there were no constructional or operating problems. The Admiralty accepted the recommendation and built a 100-foot tank at *HMS Dolphin*, the Royal Navy's senior submarine base. The large white tower which now dominates Fort Blockhouse and which is clearly visible from Portsmouth and Southsea, stands as a permanent and tangible memorial to the vision of Captain Ruck-Keene and his fellow Committee members.

Another recommendation, but one not immediately taken up by the Authorities for various specious reasons, was to scrap the existing twill-trunk system and replace it with a one-man escape chamber of special design with smooth interior walls and an ejector-ram.

There were, of course, many other recommendations: the introduction of an immersion suit with built-in buoyancy to keep survivors afloat after reaching the surface; the fitting of a valve in the pressure hull so that oxygen could be pumped into a sunken vessel and the foul air extracted, and the use of indicator buoys fitted with automatic radio transmitters.

Finally, and by no means the least of the recommendations accepted by the Admiralty, was the creation of a standing organization for search and rescue operations. The code signal *Submiss* was to be sent out one hour after a submarine was known to be missing and on receipt of this preliminary signal all available ships and aircraft in the designated area were to be alerted and brought to a state of readiness. One hour later, if the submarine was still missing, the second stage code *Subsunk* was

193

to be transmitted and this signal would trigger a full-scale air and sea search centred on the boat's last known postion and intended course.

Many of Ruck-Keene's recommendations remain valid today and Britain's nuclear-powered Polaris and hunter-killer submarines all carry escape equipment that owes its origin in whole or in part to the findings of the Committee. There can be little dispute that Ruck-Keene achieved a great deal in the field of underwater escape. But it will be apparent in subsquent pages that not even *his* careful foresight could perceive and guard against the unexpected problems that have arisen in some more recent disasters.

*　*　*

It seemed historically appropriate that France should become the victim of the first post-war submarine accident, and the war had only been over for seven weeks when the *Minerve* ran aground near Portland Bill in heavy weather. A far worse disaster, however, was in store for the French Navy when, on 5 December, 1946, the former German *U-2326* was lost in an unspecified accident off Toulon in which twenty-six French sailors died.

The Spanish Navy, which had been singularly free from major submarine disasters despite her long association with underwater warfare, also suffered a tragic accident in the early post-war period. Spain's interest in submarines dated back to 1888 when a young naval Lieutenant, Isaac Peral, designed an all-electric boat that was built at the Royal Dockyard in Cadiz. The propulsion system gave a good deal of trouble but in other respects the *Peral* was a very successful submarine. The Spanish had good cause to regret their failure to develop Peral's ideas when they found themselves at war with the United States six years later. As the American Admiral Dewey commented after his victory over the Spanish fleet at Manila: 'If the Spanish had had two submarines .... I should have been unable to hold the Bay with the squadron I had.'

The story of Spain's *C.4* is quickly told. She was rammed by the destroyer *Lepanto* during exercises off the Balearic Islands on 27 June, 1946, and sank with her entire crew of forty-six men.

Three years later, in August, 1949, the American submarine

Cochino was devastated by an electrical fire and battery explosion while taking part in exercises in Arctic waters off northern Norway. Despite attrocious weather conditions and an accumulation of hydrogen gas inside the boat the crew fought to save the submarine for fourteen hours until a second explosion on the 26th forced them to abandon ship. Only one member of the *Cochino's* crew was lost but, sadly, six men from the submarine *Tusk* died during the rescue operations.

Despite the Admiralty's acceptance of the Ruck-Keene Committee's recommendations the authorities involved showed little urgency in developing and producing the new equipment. This was, of course, the 'austerity' period when Britain was still struggling to convert her war-shattered economy to a peacetime basis, and vast areas of the main industrial cities and ports were still laid waste after Hitler's bombing raids. Foreign currency and investment were at rock bottom and there were shortages of virtually every commodity it was possible to name. The authorities thus had some excuse for their dilatory attitude, although, as the Defence Departments still possessed a modicum of priority for their procurement programmes, there were really no adequate reasons for their failure to implement the recommendations more speedily, and on the night of 12 January, 1950, sixty-four men of the Royal Navy paid with their lives for the delays of the bureaucrats

Truculent had spent the day carrying out trials off the Thames estuary following a long refit at Chatham Dockyard and, as she returned up-river to Sheerness, the off-duty crewmen and the eighteen civilian dockyard officials who had gone to sea to make last-minute adjustments began preparing for a night ashore. *Truculent* was due to leave for Scotland the following day.

The Officer-of-the-Watch, Lieutenant Humphrey-Baker, conned the surfaced submarine past the flashing navigational buoys marking the main channels. Traffic in the river was heavy and the steaming lights of various ships on their way into and out of the Port of London were clearly visible on all sides.

Several miles further to the west the 643-ton tanker *Divina* was making her way down-river from Purfleet en route for Ipswich and then Sweden. She was shipping paraffin and, in accordance with the strictly enforced safety regulations of the Port of London Authority, a bright red light gleamed high up on her foremast to warn other traffic that she was carrying a dangerous cargo. As she cleared the Thames and passed the Nore Light vessel the red lamp was still burning brightly, although now that *Divina* had left the confines of the river and the area controlled by the PLA it no longer had any real meaning.

Shortly after *Truclent*'s escorting destroyer, *Cowdray*, had taken her leave and returned to Chatham, one of the submarine's lookouts detected a strange group of lights ahead of the port bow. Humphrey-Baker picked them up with his binoculars but, unable to make head or tail of them, he reported their presence to the captain. As *Truculent* was in pilotage waters Lieutenant Bowers took over from the Watchkeeper, steadied the helm, and searched ahead of the bows with his powerful night glasses. He found himself sharing Humphrey-Baker's puzzlement and concluded, not unreasonably, that the lights denoted a stationary ship on the northern edge of the channel. The presence of shoaling waters along the right-hand boundary of the fairway meant that the submarine could not pass the obstruction by going to starboard in the approved manner but, satisfied that he was not standing into danger, Bowers ordered the coxswain to steer to port.

But the mysterious vessel was considerably closer than the lights suggested and *Truculent*'s bows had only just begun to swing onto the new course when the Swedish tanker loomed out of the darkness. The horrified men on the submarine's bridge suddenly realized that the two vessels were on a collision course!

Bowers reacted instantly with a string of calm but positive orders: 'Hard a' port helm ... stop engines. Full astern together ... secure all watertight doors'

Captain Hommerberg on the *Divina*'s bridge also responded to the danger but even as he reached up to pull the lanyard of the ship's siren there was a rending screech of torn metal and the tanker shuddered with the impact of the collision. Hommerberg thought he had run down a Thames lighter that had disobeyed the Rule of the Road and crossed his bows and, having rung down for 'Full Astern', he shouted to the *Divina*'s Mate to launch one of the ship's boats.

Truculent heeled sharply to port, came back on to an even keel, and began to sink rapidly by the bows. Within seconds Lieutenant Bowers and the other men on the bridge found themselves struggling in the cold waters of the estuary as the submarine disappeared. The tide carried them swiftly away from the scene of the collision and, although the tanker's boat was lowered without delay, they had already been swallowed up by the night before it reached the spot where they were last seen.

Forty-five minutes later the Dutch *Almdijk* heard shouts for help coming out of the darkness. Although unaware of the accident, she slowed slightly and switched on her searchlight which quickly pin-pointed a group of men in the water. The five survivors from the submarine's bridge-party, including Bowers and Humphrey-Baker, were pulled to safety and taken below. No one realized that they had come from a submarine and it was generally assumed they were from a barge or lighter. It was nearly half an hour before the frozen and exhausted men were coherent enough to explain what had happened. At 8.14 pm *Almdijk*'s dramatic radio signal alerted the Authorities to the tragedy:

SOS. HM Submarine Truculent *sank north west Red Sands Tower between X4 buoy and East Piles buoy. Have picked up five survivors. Believe submarine has been in collision with Swedish ship* Divina. *All ships please keep a lookout.*

The men inside the submarine responded calmly to the emergency as an anonymous voice ordered them to their Collision Stations. In the control-room, directly beneath the bridge, the First Officer, Lieutenant Hindes, ensured that all watertight doors, ventilators and valves were shut. An Electrical Artificer, Buckingham, hurried in from the Petty Officer's mess to secure the still open lower conning-tower hatch while Fry, the submarine's aptly named Petty Officer Cook, closed off the inboard ends of the bridge voice-pipes. The compressed air was still roaring into the ballast tanks as the lights went out and Hindes, accurately weighing up the situation, ordered everyone aft.

The First Officer was familiar with the findings of the Ruck-Keene Committee and, aware that carbon dioxide was already building up rapidly, he decided on an immediate escape. He reasoned that, although there had not been time for the issue of a *Subsunk* alert, the presence of heavy river traffic would ensure that there were plenty of rescue ships on hand when they reached the surface. The engine-room twill trunk was therefore rigged while someone operated the release gear of the indicator buoy and, having carefully appraised the situation again, Hindes decided that there were too many men crowded into the engine-room and he ordered the survivors to split into two parties - one group to escape from the aft section under his personal supervision while the remainder would go through the engine-room hatch in the charge of the Chief ERA, Sam Hine.

In a repeat version of the *Umpire* tragedy, it was quickly discovered that there were not enough DSEA sets to go round despite the fact that *Truculent* was carrying her normal full complement plus the mandatory one-third reserve. But the men agreed that the non-swimmers should have first priority and, while Hine sorted matters out in the engine-room, the flood-valves were opened. It took a long time for the water to fill the compartment but finally Petty Officer Fry ducked inside the trunk and climbed up to open the hatch. The heavy cover hinged back easily and, to Fry's surprise, he found himself being swept up through the hatchway towards the suface by the surge of released pressure.

When Fry failed to reappear there was considerable consternation among the men waiting below and many recalled that the crew of *Untamed* had died in a similar situation when the hatch failed to open. But Hine quickly set their minds to rest by going into the trunk himself to find out what had happened. He emerged a few minutes later, pulled out the mouthpiece of the DSEA set, pushed up his oil-clogged goggles, and grinned widely,

'Cheer up, lads. The hatch is open. Fry's already gone up to get our supper ready.'

One by one the men inside the engine-room responded to his cheery confidence and, some wearing DSEA sets and some not, they stooped to get inside the twill trunk and set off for the surface. Finally only Buckingham and Hine were left. They exchanged a thumb's up signal and Buckingham adjusted his breathing set before joining the others. A few minutes later the Chief followed him up.

In the stern section the escape drill had proceeded with equal calm and self-discipline. Once again there were insufficient DSEA sets to go around and two of the men grabbed large mess tins and announced that they intended to go up with these over their heads instead. The special flood valve failed to operate properly and the breech of the underwater signal gun had to be smashed to admit sufficient water.

Although Hindes took the precaution of telling a young electrician to hold on to his legs when he opened the hatch the rush of compressed air proved too powerful and, like Fry, Hindes, too, was swept to the surface by the sudden surge of pressure. Fortunately his instructions had been so clear that the men remained behind had no difficulty in making their escape. They formed an orderly queue as, one by one, they slipped under the skirt of the twill trunk and rose rapidly to the surface.

In all a total of sixty-seven men made their escape from the sunken *Truculent*, and this figure excludes the bridge party which had been swept into the sea at the time of the collision. This successful exodus was a resounding triumph for both the Davis Escape System and the Royal Navy's training programmes. Yet only ten men survived to be picked up alive. The rest were swept away by the tide and died from either drowning or exposure. What had been a triumph had become a tragedy.

With hindsight it is apparent that the crew made their escape too quickly. but precedent pointed to the necessity of an early evacuation if success was to be achieved, and with half of the submarine flooded and an extra eighteen passengers aboard Lieutenant Hindes was quite correct in being worried about the rapidly rising level of carbon dioxide inside the boat. Further, propellor noises could be heard on the surface and the submarine had sunk in an area normally crowded with traffic, and the fact that there had been a collision presupposed that the alarm would be raised quickly. With all these factors in mind it is difficult to fault the First Officer's decision to waste no time.

Some of the men who died during the ascent were found to have ruptured lungs and this feature still puzzles the experts, for the boat was only forty-two feet from the surface. The speed of ascent, however, is something which can only be controlled by the individual concerned and this facet of the disaster must fall within the category of human error. Nothing can ever completely guard against this.

The most damning aspect of the tragedy was the loss of men through drowning and exposure. Ruck-Keene and his Committee had recommended the adoption of an insulated immersion suit in 1946 and by the end of that same year the first successful prototype had been tested. Yet, three years later, these suits were only in limited production and none were carried by *Truculent*. On this count, then, the Authorities responsible must carry a heavy blame for what happened. There is little doubt that the survivors would have remained afloat long enough to have been picked up had they been wearing immersions suits, and the automatic flashing light fitted to the suit could have enabled them to be spotted as they were swept out to sea.

Ignoring the question of the lack of immersion suits, it is sadly apparent that the tragedy of the *Truculent* was, once again, the result of sheer bad luck. Everyone directly concerned had acted, according to their viewpoint and circumstances, with absolute correctness, and there had been no failure of equipment. Yet sixty-four men had died.

Only fifteen months later the new British submarine *Affray* left Portsmouth for a series of exercises in the Channel in the course of which she was to land a small Royal Marine's raiding party. In addition to the Marines she was also carrying twenty-three officers under instruction plus her own crew - a total of seventy-five men. In view of the strange story which is to follow it is necessary to give a precise account of her known movements that day.

The submarine sailed from Portsmouth at 4.15 pm on 16 April, 1951, steering a course that would take her south of the Isle of Wight. At 9.15 pm she transmitted her diving position, intended course and estimated time of surfacing. According to that signal she was proceeding westwards, in the general direction of Falmouth, at 4½ knots with the intention of resurfacing at 8.30 am the following morning.

But the resurfacing signal was never received and two hours later, in accordance with Standing Orders, the executive *Subsunk* code was flashed from the radio room of Fort Blockhouse for the launch of a full-scale air and sea search. Involving more than twenty surface ships, including two US Navy destroyers, and several dozen aircraft it was the largest rescue operation ever mounted by the Royal Navy, and it was to be substantially enlarged with every passing hour.

Unfortunately the potential search area extended over several thousands of square miles. And, to make matters more difficult, *Affray's* captain had been given very flexible instructions before leaving Portsmouth which made it impossible to predict with any degree of accuracy the precise course that the submarine had taken after diving the previous evening, or, indeed, whether she had remained submerged throughout the night.

It was known, however, that she was to be in a certain position at noon on the 17th to take part in an anti-submarine search exercise for a group of naval aircraft based at Plymouth. But even this position was vague for *Affray*'s captain was only required to be within thirty miles of the designated spot when the exercise began, and that covered an immense amount of sea room.

The hunt for the missing submarine showed the Admiralty organization at its best and on this occasion no one could accuse the authorities of either delay or lack of effort. French and Dutch warships joined the British and American units, every lifeboat on the South Coast was mobilized, and a full salvage team of tugs and lifting vessels including fourteen Royal Navy salvage vessels made for the search area at maximum speed.

One of the most valuable ships in the rescue armada was the Navy's Deep Diving Vessel *Reclaim*. She had been refitting when the *Subsunk* signal was received, but, breaking all regulations, her captain, Lieutenant Commander Bathurst, flashed up the boilers and had her under a full head of steam in an amazingly short space of time. Joined by various tugs, mooring-vessels and another salvage ship, *Salvictor*, the little convoy set out on its mission of mercy hours earlier than anticipated.

Although the search area extended, on its eastern boundary, from the Isle of Wight to the French coast and from Land's End to the Channel Islands at its western limit, the main effort was concentrated on a line from the Isle of Wight to Start Point on the south Devonshire coast, the most likely course to be followed by the submarine according to her final signal. But despite the immense number of ships and aircraft involved no trace of the *Affray* could be found, and on 18 April the Admiralty issued a communique which, after listing the facts and probabilities, concluded: 'In view of the lapse of time the chances of the submarine having misinterpreted her instructions are lessening and the chances of an accident must be regarded as increasingly probable.'

Twenty-four hours passed but there was still no trace of the missing boat and, reluctantly, Admiral Sir Arthur John Power, the C-in-C Portsmouth who had master-minded the search operation with typical drive and determination, authorized the issue of a further statement confirming that the *Affray* must be presumed lost. At the same time Operation *Subsunk* was cancelled. Once again a British submarine had completely disappeared with all hands, and on this occasion the death toll of seventy-five men ranked the disaster second only to that of the *Thetis* in the records of the Royal Navy.

Although the rescue operation had been called off the search for the *Affray* continued. A squadron of frigates backed by two survey ships scoured the seabed with their underwater detection devices while *Reclaim* and her diving team stood by to investigate any contacts that seemed promising. It was a daunting task for the search area was not only extremely large it was also notorious for its number of wrecks. In addition, strong tides and fierce currents made diving a hazardous task. But the Navy pursued its quest with dogged determination and all underwater contacts were reported back to a central search HQ at Portsmouth controlled by one of Britain's leading submarine salvage experts, Captain W.O. Shelford.

By early May the *Affray* had still not been located but Shelford was impressed by the number of letters and telephone calls his HQ was receiving from clairvoyants, mediums, and other sources of psychic and para-normal phenomena, all of whom claimed to know where the submarine was located. Almost in desperation he plotted the various positions on his chart and was surprised to find that they all centred on one specific location and at a point that was outside the main search area. In Shelford's own words:

'I told the Admiral that so much evidence was accumulating in this way that we should send a ship to investigate it. Captain Foster Brown went himself and immediately reported such loud echoes on the Asdic that "they nearly knocked him off the bridge". A fuller investigation revealed absolutely nothing in the area (and) it was in any case some seventy-five miles from the spot where *Affray* was eventually found.'*

No one has ever explained why there should have been such a

---

* *Subsunk* by Captain W.O. Shelford, Harrap, 1960.

powerful sonar echo in that particular location, and the unanimity of the psychic references to the same spot makes it all the more puzzling. But this was only one of the para-normal mysteries that surround the *Affray*.

An even more astonishing story was told by Warren Armstrong in his book *Sea Phantoms*. Some years after the disaster he met the wife of a Rear Admiral who related a strange manifestation she had experienced on the night the submarine was reported missing:

'Quite suddenly, I realized that I was not alone in my room and in the half-light I recognized my visitor. He had been serving as an engineer officer in my husband's ship, a cruiser, at a time when my husband was an Engineer-Commander, and we had often entertained him in our Channel Islands home.

'He approached me and stood still and silent; I was astonished to see him dressed in normal submariner's uniform although I did not recognize this fact until I described his clothing to my husband. Then he spoke quite clearly and said: "Tell your husband we are at the north end of Hurd Deep, nearly seventy miles from the lighthouse at St Catherine's Point. It happened very suddenly and none of us expected it". After that the speaker vanished.'*

The woman immediately telephoned her husband who told her that he had no knowledge of the officer in question being aboard the *Affray* or, indeed, even having transferred to the submarine service, and he pointed out that Hurd Deep was well outside the main search area. He also implied politely that he had no intention of interfering with the search operation on the basis of a ghost story. And there the matter rested.

Admiralty scientists at the Teddington Research Laboratory had recently produced an underwater television camera which could be used to examine wrecks on the seabed and a team of experts under the supervision of Commander Lionel Crabb, who later achieved notoriety as the missing frogman when Bulganin and Khruschev visited Britain in the cruiser *Ordzhonikidze* in 1956, installed the underwater camera equipment in the *Reclaim* shortly before she left to search a new area to the north of the Channel Islands. No one was optimistic as the new location was

* *Sea Phantoms* by Warren Armstrong, Odhams, 1956.

a considerable distance from *Affray*'s probable track. But the navigational experts were satisfied that the submarine *could* have travelled that far to the south-west.

Just before noon *Reclaim* anchored and an observation chamber was lowered to examine a wreck previously located by Asdic. The diver reported that he could see an *unrusted* rail and the television camera was sent down to inspect his discovery. As the search team gathered around the screen they saw the lens pick out the gun-tower of a submarine and then, moving slightly aft, it focused on the nameplate: A-F-F-R-A-Y. The six-week search was over, and, incredibly, *Reclaim was anchored at the northern end of Hurd Deep!*

All that now remained was to discover the cause of *Affray's* loss and, before sending the divers down again, the salvage team made use of their newfound toy - the underwater television camera. The resulting pictures gave them a good deal of information. The submarine was lying in 278 feet of water with her hydroplanes in the *hard a'rise* position and a camera inspection of the bridge telegraphs revealed that her motors were at *Stop*. All hatches were secured, there was no apparent external damage, and her indicator buoys had not been released. All the signs, in fact, of an unexpected and overwhelming calamity.

Divers later found that the submarine's thirty-five-feet-long snort-mast had snapped at deck level and when this was subsequently raised and examined scientists discovered a metallurgical weakness in the tube which had caused it to fracture. But the revelation posed another puzzle. There was an induction valve at the base of the snort where it entered the pressure hull. This should have been closed immediately water began to enter the submarine. But bad weather put an end to the salvage operations before it could be positively ascertained whether this vital valve was open or closed, and for some reason the investigation was never resumed when conditions improved.

In November the First Lord of the Admiralty made a statement in which the loss of the submarine was attributed to the broken snort-mast. But, not content to leave it at that, he added that it was possible there had been an explosion of battery gases early in the morning of the 17th which had split the external battery ventilation trunking thus allowing seawater to flood the batteries. It is impossible to verify this surmise or to know upon what evidence it was based for Shelford states 'there was no external damage' in his account of the salvage operation. It is, however, well-known that the A-class boats had a history of such explosions.

So the mystery of the *Affray* remains. What had caused the large sonar echoes at the spot where the psychics claimed the submarine had sunk? And why did all the para-normal vibrations point to the same place? Was there a battery explosion and what evidence exists to support this explanation of the sinking? And if there is no evidence what persuaded the First Lord to add this rider to his statement? Finally there is the extraordinary story of the Rear Admiral's wife and her ghostly visitor who so accurately identified the place where *Affray* was to be found.

*   *   *

Admiral Sir Max Horton died on 30 July, 1951. As a very young officer he had commanded the *A.1* when it was recommissioned following its tragic loss of Spithead in 1904. He had won a chest-full of medals while captain of *E.9* in the Baltic and became one of the Royal Navy's best-known submarine commanders of the First World War. He was the first Commanding Officer of the *J.6* and he captained the ill-fated *M.1*. In both instances he had moved on to another command before the boat was lost.

Horton rose to become Flag Officer (Submarines) and, as such, controlled all British submarine operations in the early part of the Second World War before his appointment as C-in-C Western Approaches during the crisis years of the Battle of the Atlantic.

The *Affray* sank on 17 April and was located and positively identified on 14 June. Although Horton had been ill for some time his letters show that his brain was still active and lucid and, with his intense interest in submarines, he must have been aware that the mystery of her disappearance had been solved. Yet his last recorded words before he died on 30 July were: 'Any news of the *Affray*?'

In view of the many other strange manifestations connected with the submarine's loss it is impossible not to wonder why the Admiral asked that particular question.

—THIRTEEN—
'Gertrude ... Check K.'

While the British Navy was still recovering from the shock of two major disasters in the space of fifteen months France suffered her third post-war submarine tragedy on 23 September, 1952, when the *Sibylle* vanished between Cannes and the Isle of Porquerolles. *Sibylle* was a British-built boat, the former *HMS Sportsman,* transferred to the French Navy to replace war losses, and had been engaged on routine diving exercises at the time she sank. As she was never salvaged the cause of her disappearance must remain a mystery. The submarine's entire crew of forty-seven died in what proved to be the first of three similar accidents in the same area over the next eighteen years.

The Turkish Navy, which had already lost the *Atilay* in 1942 as the result of a diving accident, was shaken by a second accident in April, 1953, when the *Dumlupinar* was rammed by the Swedish freighter *Naboland* off Nagara Point – the same spot where the French submarines *Saphir* and *Turquoise* had run aground in 1915. The collision occurred at 2.15 in the morning while the boat was surfaced and, although five of the men on the bridge were picked up safely, a total of eighty-one Turkish sailors were trapped inside. Some of them were certainly still alive at this stage for they released an indicator buoy which was sighted by a searching naval launch at 6.40 am.

Dumlupinar was an American *Balao*-class submarine – a sister, in fact, of the *Tang* – supplied to Turkey as one of a batch of eight boats under the Mutual Assistance Program. In common with all American-built vessels her hatches were modified to accept the McCann Rescue Chamber. Some time after the submarines had been delivered the United States gave the Turkish Navy a rescue ship for service with its new underwater flotilla and also supplied them with a rescue diving bell. Her name was *Bluebird* which the Turks changed to *Kurtaran*.

Once the indicator buoy had been found no time was wasted and by 11 am the *Kurtaran* was moored directly above the lost submarine, a very creditable response by the Turks who had had very little experience in handling such disasters. But the situation was hopeless. *Dumlupinar* was lying in 276 feet of water and the tidal currents in the Narrows were fierce and treacherous. Two divers managed to descend to the vessel's deck but the current prevented them from securing the down-haul cable, and without this the McCann Chamber was useless. By the late afternoon the rescuers realized that they were facing an impossible task and the rescue attempt was abandoned, even though many of the entombed men were probably still alive. It was a hard decision but, in the circumstances, there was really no alternative.

While the failure in no way reflected on the skills or determination of the men directly concerned with the rescue operation nor, indeed, on the McCann Chamber itself, it did serve to justify the British Navy's reservations about this particular method of submarine rescue, and it served to emphasise the element of luck that had made the *Squalus* operation so successful.

Ever since a group of British technical experts had examined the high-speed Walther U-boats which the German Navy had been developing in the Second World War the Royal Navy had demonstrated a keen interest in the theory of hydrogen-peroxide as a source of propulsive power, and in the 1950s Britain built two experimental submarines, *Explorer* and *Excalibur,* fitted with High Test hydrogen-peroxide engines. Neither proved to be a success and the experts quickly discovered, as had the *Kriegsmarine,* that this highly volatile mixture was extremely dangerous. Both submarines suffered a series of internal explosions and on one notable occasion the crew had to stand on the outer casing until the fumes had died down. Ultimately the two boats were scrapped but, in the meanwhile, a hydrogen-peroxide torpedo had been developed, and on 16 June, 1955, one of these new weapons exploded and sank the British submarine *Sidon* in Portland harbour with the loss of thirteen lives. Not surprisingly the Royal Navy's enthusiasm for hydrogen-peroxide waned after that and research was switched to less dangerous forms of fuel.

The American *Stickleback* was more fortunate. While exercising south-west of Pearl Harbor on 30 May, 1958, she broached and was rammed by the destroyer *Silverstein*. The bows of the surface vessel penetrated the pressure hull between the control room and the forward battery compartment and it was immediately apparent that the submarine had sustained a fatal wound. The order was given to abandon ship and by the time *Stickleback* took her final plunge to the bottom of the Pacific Ocean every man of her eighty-two-strong crew had scrambled to safety through the hatches. The sea was warm, weather conditions were good, there were plenty of ships around and within minutes of taking to the water all the survivors were picked up. The French *Laubie*, the former German *U-766*, was equally unlucky when she sustained such serious damage in a collision that she had to be scrapped in October, 1961.

1963 opened a new chapter in the history of submarine disasters when the nuclear-powered *USS Thresher* sank some 220 miles east of Boston with the loss of 129 lives. As she was the world's first atomic submarine to be lost her tragic story demands its own special place in this book.

Thresher had experienced a number of equipment and structural problems during her first year of service. Her air-conditioning plant had failed more than once and internal temperatures had soared to a shattering 136°F. There had been trouble, also, with the low-pressure blowing system. This was operated by electro-hydraulic valves but someone had carelessly wired it backwards and when the switch-indicators showed 'closed' the valves were, in fact, open. This type of fault, it will be recalled, had been partially responsible for the *Untamed* disaster during the war. It seems inconceivable that such a serious fault was not discovered by the inspection staff during construction.

Further problems were located in the boat's internal pipe system which was found to be misaligned, and her original skipper, Commander Axene, complained that it was difficult to obtain access to certain vital components and inspection points because, in the interests of appearance, they had been covered over or boxed in by decorative non-functional plastic laminates. In his Report of November, 1962, Axene also drew attention to the possibility of salt-water flooding into the boat at, or near, test depth. The dangers resulting from sea water coming into contact with a submarine's battery system have already been vividly demonstrated on a number of occasions.

After a year in service *Thresher* was returned to the Portsmouth Navy Yard for refitting and modifications, an overhaul that consumed 100,000 man-hours and took three times longer than the original estimate. On 31 March she left dry-dock for a test drive during which, to the consternation of her new Commanding Officer, Wes Harvey, it took a Damage Repair Party twenty minutes to isolate a 'leak' in the after auxiliary sea-water system.

The following day the submarine set out for the Piscatagua River for a four-day series of sonar tests. But the main sea-water suction valve refused to close properly and the trials were aborted for another spell in dry-dock. During this period technicians found that the torpedo door shutters were malfunctioning.

As the prototype of a new class of hunter-killer submarines such teething troubles were not entirely unexpected. But it *did* seem that the *Thresher* was suffering rather more than normal, and several members of the crew were heard to complain that the refitting schedule had been rushed - an opinion, incidentally, not shared by Wes Harvey who expressed his complete satisfaction with the work done.

Thresher, code named *War Club*, left Portsmouth on 9 April in company with the Rescue ship *Skylark* to carry out a series of deep diving trials in the Gulf of Maine east of Boston. Although the log of the *Skylark* has been made available to the public many of the entries are incomprehensible to the general reader. There is a simple reason why this should be so. To avoid passing confidential information to the Russians, who frequently eavesdrop on signal conversations between submarines and surface ships, much ship-to-ship communication is carried out in a special service jargon designed to confuse and mislead the unofficial listener.

For example, in order to protect the all-important secret of the submarine's maximum diving limit, depths are frequently given in terms relative to the Test Depth. Thus if the Test Depth is 500 feet and the submarine reports 'Test Depth plus 200' the signal means that she is actually at 700 feet. Without pre-knowledge of the key Test Depth figure the message would mean little or nothing. It is as well, therefore, to pass over the bulk of the signals exchanged between *War Club (Thresher)* and *Dipper Sierra (Skylark)* and to quote only the final group.

At 0747 *Thresher* reported that she was about to begin her deep dive. *Skylark* acknowledged and at 0752 the surface ship received a further message: '*War Club* to *Dipper Sierra*. At 400 feet and checking for leaks.' This was followed two minutes later by a signal from the submarine advising *Skylark* that all future references to depth would be given relative to Test Depth. And for the next half an hour the signals related only to course changes and depth readings.

According to these reports *Thresher* was descending in a continuous spiral and at 0853 came: '*War Club* to *Dipper Sierra*. Proceeding to Test Depth.' And, again, *Skylark* acknowledged with a laconic: 'Roger - out.' At 09.02 *Thresher* reported another change of course and it was apparent to the captain of *Skylark*, Lieutenant-Commander Stanley M. Hecker, that the submarine intended to continue descending in a spiral pattern so that she remained in close proximity to the surface ship's position. But the voice contact was oddly distorted and Hecker was sufficiently concerned to call *War Club* at 09.12: 'Gertrude Check K.' This was a coded request for the submarine to make contact on UQC - the underwater telephone - with 'K' meaning 'over'. There was no response and the 'K' signal was repeated twice more within a few seconds.

Finally at 09.13 came an indistinct and garbled reply from the *Thresher*: ' ... have positive up-angle. Attempting ...' These are the only words of the message actually recorded in *Skylark's* log, but Hecker later reported that the complete reply was: 'Experiencing minor difficulty. Have positive up-angle. Attempting to blow ...'

At the same time that the message was coming through Hecker and his Number One, Watson, heard the sounds of *Thresher* closing her vents and blowing compressed air into her ballast tanks over the loudspeaker of the UQC link.

It is at this point that an element of mystery, or perhaps secrecy, enters the story. Skylark continued to call the submarine and at 09.17 the log records *Thresher's last signal: '900 N.'* No one in authority has ever explained the meaning of this cryptic code and, at the subsequent Naval Court of Enquiry, it was never mentioned although Hecker told the Court that, just before 09.17, he heard a garbled message that concluded: ' ... test depth'. This message, however, was not noted in *Skylark's* log *unless* it is a translation of the *900 N* code signal. The only alternative is that the code group related to a specific 'condition' - for example 'out of control' or 'below 900 feet' - similar to the numerical system used by police forces and CB radio buffs throughout the world.

Whatever the significance of this last signal, and whether its true meaning is known to the US Navy, nothing more was heard from the *Thresher* other than the noises of a submarine breaking up, which Hecker described as 'a dull muted sound'. *Skylark,* however, remained on the spot repeatedly calling the lost submarine and firing depth grenades. Finally at 11.04 Hecker transmitted a despairing message to COMSUBLANT. (Commander Submarine Force, US Atlantic Fleet.)

'Unable to communicate with *Thresher* since 09.17. Have been calling by UQC voice and CW, QHB. CW every minute. Explosive signals every ten minutes with no success. Last transmission received was garbled. Indicated *Thresher* was approaching Test Depth. My present position 41° 57' west. Conducting expanding search.'

Due to freak reception conditions the signal was not received for more than ninety minutes but finally at 12.45 New London acknowledged and the *Subsunk* code was flashed to all ships, aircraft and shore stations in and near the Gulf of Maine.

The US Navy conducted a massive search operation to find the missing *Thresher* and every conceivable scientific instrument was employed in the hunt - underwater TV cameras, deep-towed magnetometers, side-scanning echo sounders, fathometers, Geiger counters, and a host of other space-age detection devices many of which were still on the secret list. In the later stages of the operation even the bathyscaphe *Trieste* was mobilized to assist the searchers. For not only did the Authorities want to find out what had happened to *Thresher* they were under strong Governmental pressure concerning possible radiation leakage from the submarine's nuclear power unit.

When Rear Admiral Ramage, the Deputy Commander, Submarine Force, US Atlantic Fleet, reached the spot in the destroyer *Blandy* the searchers had already found a large oil slick and various pieces of flotsam and debris which might have come from the missing submarine. By morning more items had been retrieved, notably several pairs of rubber gloves, pieces of cork insulation, and some strips of yellow plastic. All suggested that the submarine had broken up. But no one could be sure for the subsequent laboratory test, while agreeing that the debris *may* have come from the *Thresher*, could not give positive confirmation that they *had* done so.

It was rather like looking for a needle in a haystack with the aid of a small magnet on the end of a string, but within a fortnight a dozen possible contacts had been located by the fathometer inside the ten square mile search area and each was methodically entered on the charts. On 27 May Task Force 89.7, as the search team was officially designated, began the third stage of the hunt and the next day the *Robert Conrad* dredged up fifteen packets of 'O' rings which experts considered *might* have come from the submarine. More finds followed until, finally, on 24 June *Atlantis II* brought up a damaged battery plate which was specifically identified by the Exide representative as coming from the *Thresher*.

It was now certain that the final resting place of the submarine had been located and numerous underwater photographs were taken of the debris while the *Trieste* carried out a series of investigatory dives. And, significantly, while the search operations continued, various Soviet 'trawlers' passed through the area electronically sniffing for information.

Trieste found the remains of the *Thresher* lying on the ocean bottom at a depth of 8,400 feet. Details of what she discovered were given a high security rating and have never been disclosed but it seems that the submarine had been crushed by the enormous pressure of the sea – some 3,700 pounds per square inch – and was scattered in thousands of pieces over a large area. The observers in the Bathyscaphe also saw a large crater which some naval experts thought might contain the main bulk of the submarine, but this theory is still subject of dispute behind the doors of the Pentagon. In the course of her investigations the *Trieste* lifted a small length of piping which bore the *Thresher's* official number, *593,* and this was sufficient evidence to satisfy the Navy. On 5 September, 1963, Secretary Korth released a Press Statement in which he confirmed that the search was now being abandoned and that, officially, was the end of the *Thresher* story.

Three years passed before the next serious accident and this time the location was the coast of East Africa, an area of the world hitherto singularly free from submarine disasters. The British *Rorqual,* patrolling in the vicinity of Mozambique during the Rhodesian UDI crisis in August, 1966, suffered a devastating explosion in her engine-room that left two men dead and several injured. Luckily the pressure hull was undamaged and she limped back to Durban under her own power on 2 September. Only twelve days later, on 14 September, Germany experienced one of her rare peacetime disasters.

The *Hai*, West Germany's first post-war U-boat – it was the war-built *U-2365* which had been salved and refitted after being scuttled in the Skaggerak on 8 May, 1945 - was exercising off the Dogger Bank in the North Sea when a seam in the engine-room split open, the seas flooded through the fault in the welding and *Hai* sank before emergency measures could be taken to stem the inrush of water. Only one member of her twenty-strong crew survived. Seven weeks later, on 4 November, the American submarine *Tiru* ran aground on Frederick Reef although she was more fortunate that the *Hai* and was subsequently salvaged.

1968 proved to be reminiscent of the 1920s when, in the space of six months, no fewer than four submarines were lost with all hands. The year was only twenty-five days old when the Israeli *Dakar* vanished in the Eastern Mediterranean with her entire crew of sixty-nine men. The cause of her loss has never been established. Only two days later, on 27 January, the French *Minerve* disappeared without trace on the opposite, western, side of the Mediterranean with fifty-two aboard. Her ultimate fate also remains a mystery.

There was another inexplicable disaster in May which involved a nuclar-powered submarine carrying a crew of ninety-nine officers and men. The American *Scorpion,* an attack submarine of the *Skipjack* class, was returning to Norfolk, Virginia, from the Mediterranean. And at approximately 0800 on the morning of the 21st, when in a position some 250 miles west of the Azores, she made her routine progress signal to

213

COMSUBLANT, which proved to be her last contact with the living world.

Although the disaster did not receive the massive press coverage afforded to the earlier tragedy, a Thresher-scale operation was mounted by the US Navy and *Scorpion* was finally located five months later 460 miles south-west of the Azores at a depth of 10,000 feet. Underwater photographs were reported to show her hull virtually intact with no visible evidence to indicate why she had sunk, a statement that was to be drastically revised by the authorities some twenty-five years later when the truth finally emerged.

Scorpion, like the *Thresher*, had suffered various minor technical problems during her early service, although she was a successful boat in other respects and, in 1962, broke the record for submerged endurance when she maintained a sealed atmosphere for seventy days. A good deal of nonsense has been written about this disaster, mainly because the submarine sank on the edge of the legendary Sargasso Sea and inside the boundaries of the mythical 'Limbo of the Lost,' an area considerably larger than the original Bermuda Triangle delineated by Charles Berlitz and Victor Gaddis.

But leaving aside the pseudo world of UFOs and para-normal forces, two very puzzling aspects of the *Scorpion* tragedy have emerged from the facts as officially released by the Pentagon. The submarine's last known position was 250 miles west of the Azores, yet she was found 400 miles *south-west* of the islands. This position, if accurate, hardly seems consistent with her intended destination, although there may have been a very good reason for her to steer south of west before settling down to a westerly track. Nevertheless this deviation is significant. For, even if the US Navy was aware of the course change, it had no precise knowledge of the time that the submarine had sunk, or more correctly it has never admitted to such knowledge. Indeed, the Navy performed a minor miracle in finding the vessel at all, bearing in mind that it had taken more than a month to locate *Thresher* in a search area of just *ten* square miles.

One enterprising writer has even suggested that the Russians had tracked the *Scorpion* as part of their routine worldwide surveillance network and that the Soviet Navy had made its records available to the Americans to enable them to pinpoint the position of the lost boat. It seems a far-fetched theory. But is it any more incredible than the fact that the US Navy found the submarine in a search area covering tens of thousands of square miles?

Much has been made of the statement in the official report that *Scorpion*'s hull was virtually intact when the wreck was located. *Thresher*, it will be recalled, was found scattered across the ocean floor in a thousand small pieces, due, it was said, to the crushing pressure of the sea. If the latter boat had been crushed at 8,400 feet why, asked the sceptics, was *Scorpion* still intact – at the greater depth of 10,000 feet? The reason, they argued, could not be due to improved hull design because *Thresher* was the more recent boat. Neither could it be attributed to an explosion because the noises heard by the officers of *Skylark* were described as those of a submarine breaking up and not blowing up. The answer to the 25-year-old mystery was finally revealed in a US Navy report released in 1993.

This blamed the disaster on a faulty torpedo which the crew had jettisoned after its propulsion motor was accidentally started. The weapon, fitted with an active homing device, at first sped away from the submarine but, once fully armed, it 'sought out its nearest target' – the unfortunate *Scorpion*. Circling back, the torpedo struck the conning-tower sail and the detonation of its warhead sent the hapless boat to its grave on the bottom of the Atlantic. The catastrophic nature of the sinking explains why *Scorpion* remained intact. The damage caused by the exploding torpedo allowed the sea to flood the hull and, with the pressure equal both inside and outside the submarine, the crushing power of the ocean depths was neutralized. The *Thresher*, on the other hand, sank as the result of a minor leak which short-circuited the electrical system. This in turn shut down the reactor and deprived the boat of power. With normal atmospheric pressure inside the hull *Thresher* was crushed like an empty eggshell as it nosedived through 1400 fathoms to the seabed.

The story of the Russian *Golf*-class missile submarine that blew up and sank in mid-Pacific in the Spring of the same year boasts all the ingredients of a James Bond 007 movie. But before dealing with the bizarre aftermath of this particular disaster it is perhaps time to turn back the pages of history and recount a series of Russian submarine accidents that have only recently come to light following further searches of archival material during the last ten years. These nine tragedies, dating between 1934 and 1961, are additional to those already covered in the preceding chronological text, and are included at this point to ensure that the Russian navy's long and painful history of underwater diaster is as complete as possible.

Following the loss of the former British submarine *L.55* in October, 1931, to which reference was made in Chapter Eight, there were a spate of accidental sinkings. But information about events in Stalinist Russia, especially concerning disasters that might reflect adversely on communist efficiency, is sparse in quantity and frequently inaccurate in content. Reliable sources suggest, however, that in addition to those incidents already mentioned, the *Proletary* (ex-*Zmeya*, ex-B.5) and the *Metallist* (ex-*AG.22*) both sank in 1934 from accidental causes – the later boat being of particular interest as it had been assembled in Russia in 1916 from parts pre-fabricated in the United States. 1938 witnessed two more tragedies: *M-90* was rammed and sunk by a tug outside Leningrad while her sister, *M-174*, inexplicably failed to surface after diving trials. This latter submarine frequently creates confusion as many references list the boat under its earlier identity, *M-91*. The Russian navy's inclination to renumber and rename its submarines, plus the fact that many boats were salvaged and returned to service under their original names or numbers, has been responsible for various errors in otherwise reliable statistical tables.

Following the loss of the *Dekabrist* (ex-*D.1*) noted in Chapter Eleven, the *Sch-136* disappeared while taking part in diving exercises during the final fateful weeks leading up to Hitler's invasion of Russia in June, 1941. And, although no firm details are available, the *M-20*, *M-51* and *Sch-410* are all known to have been lost in accidents during the Second World War. Apart from the sinking of the *Sazan* (ex-*Sch-201*), which was reported to have been wrecked at Poti in 1956, the Red Navy remained surprisingly free from major underwater accidents from the end of the war until 1961 when an early nuclear-powered missile submarine, the NATO codenamed *Polar Circle*, caught fire in the Atlantic while on her maiden voyage. The problems had begun with a leak of radioactive coolant and the resultant overheating led to a reactor fire. Captain Nikolai Zateev, the submarine's commander, reported that the roof of the reactor glowed violet as the internal temperature soared to several thousand degrees centigrade and repair teams fought valiantly to prevent a meltdown and the threat of an environmental catastrophe. Eight men died in the struggle and a further six succumbed later to the effects of radiation poisoning. After lying on the surface for more than ten hours the crippled boat was located by another Russian submarine and escorted back to its Arctic base. As an indication of the difficulties facing historians it should be pointed out that details of this near-disaster were not made public until December, 1992 – more than thirty years after the event! One cannot help wondering what other forgotten tragedies still lie entombed in Russia's secret naval archives.

The *Golf*-class missile submarine mentioned at the beginning of this chronological digression into previously unrecorded Russian disasters, blew up and sank in mid-Pacific on 11 April, 1968, and its loss set in motion the craziest salvage scramble ever to have taken place outside of a Hollywood scenario.

Both the Soviet Union and the United States track each other's submarines using air and sea surveillance equipment operated from aircraft, ships and satellites, supplemented by static sonar arrays situated on the floors of the world's oceans. On this occasion the Americans tracked the submarine from its base at Vladivostok and followed it to a point some 1000 miles north-west of Hawaii. It was a low-key routine piece of electronic observation similar in pattern and results to many hundreds of previous trackings. Or rather it *was*, until the surveillance officers detected the faint sound of an explosion and it was realized that the engine noises had stopped. There could be no doubt about it. A Russian submarine had blown up somewhere in the central Pacific.

Confirmation of the disaster quickly followed when a fleet of Soviet ships and aircraft descended on the area and combed the sea in search of the missing boat. But the submarine was lying nearly three miles down and the watching Americans noted that when the Russians abandoned their search they left the scene empty-handed.

The *Golf*-class boats were conventional diesel-driven vessels displacing 2,350 tons in surface trim. They carried a crew of eighty-six officers and men and, in addition to torpedo tubes, were equipped with three ballistic missiles armed with nuclear warheads. By American standards they were obsolete and the US Navy had no interest in them except tactically as potential enemies. But for reasons too complex to explain in this volume the American Government – or more precisely Henry Kissinger –

wanted more information on these boats as an aid to his negotiations in the coming round of SALT talks. As it was inopportune to give the job of raising the submarine to the Navy for obvious reasons, the task was passed to the CIA. *Operation Jennifer* – the most fantastic salvage operation in maritime history – was on the launching pad.

In 1969 the CIA offered Howard Hughes $350,000,000 to recover the submarine and Hughes accepted without blinking an eyelid. His company, Global Marine, was given the contract and work was started on two very special and highly secret salvage ships. The *Glomar Explorer*, built in Pennsylvania and described as a deep-sea mining vessel, was 618 feet in length and equipped with a 209-foot derrick with a lifting capacity of 800 tons as well as some other cranes. The second boat was a deep-diving barge some 350 feet long and 160 feet wide. Just to confuse everyone she was constructed at San Diego on the West Coast.

The two vessels were completed by the middle of 1973 and set out for the Pacific early the following year. Their true role remained secret, of course, and the press and public were told that they were engaged on survey and exploratory work for a deep-sea mining venture, a story that was readily accepted as Hughes was known to be involved in underwater prospecting.

Certain 'official' facts have been subsequently released by the CIA while investigative American and British journalists have unearthed other details. But it is impossible to discover the truth of this covert salvage operation and many pressmen suspect that the CIA has deliberately spread disinformation to muddy the waters.

According to the official account the bodies of seventy Russian sailors were recovered and, although the *Glomar Explorer* had been fitted with a special refrigerated mortuary, it was decided to bury the men at sea to avoid diplomatic complications. A Soviet burial manual was used to conduct the last rites and a colour movie was taken of the committal ceremony to prove that the victims were laid to rest in an appropriate and reverent manner should any dispute arise with the Soviet Union about the incident in the future. The account also claimed that the whole submarine was raised off the sea-bed but that when it reached 8,000 feet the stern section containing the missiles broke away and was never recovered. Some leading American journalists claim, however, that the entire submarine was successfully recovered and is now in the possession of the CIA.

218

The story of *Operation Jennifer* makes interesting reading. But certain so-called facts remain extremely suspect. The submarine sank in 16,000 feet of water, almost half as deep again as the *Scorpion* and twice as deep as the *Thresher*. At such depths the hull would probably have been crushed and, if it had been flooded and was still intact, the sheer weight would have been beyond the lifting capacity of the *Glomar Explorer*. By the same token it is improbable that anything recognizable as a human body would have been recoverable.

Nevertheless there is probably a small grain of truth hidden away somewhere in the labyrinth of lies and evasions that surround the incident, and it does, at least, serve to demonstrate the new problems that have arisen with regard to submarine salvage when international politics enter into the equation. All that can be said with any certainty is that a Russian submarine *did* sink off Hawaii in 1968 and that two Global Marine vessels *did* conduct a sea-bed search of the area six years later.

1968 also witnessed the loss of the Soviet navy's first nuclear-powered boat when an unidentified Russian submarine was reported to have been sunk in an estuary close to the Northern Fleet's Arctic base of Severomorsk with the loss of some ninety lives. Although no official details of the disaster were ever made public, leaked information indicates that some members of the unfortunate crew survived inside their iron tomb for a considerable time, for, when the vessel was finally raised and inspected some months later it was found that all the stocks of food on board had been consumed.

A fourth nuclear submarine sank on 16 May, 1969, when the American *Guitarro* foundered in dock at Mare Island Navy Yard while she was under construction. The submarine was in the fitting-out basin and sank in thirty-five feet of water, the damage caused by the consequential flooding costing a staggering $25,000,000 to rectify. The accident, in which fortunately no lives were lost, was attributed to the negligence of dockyard workers. As the Congressional Report of the incident observed, the disaster 'was wholly avoidable'.

Accidents during construction are not unusual. In 1923 a boiler exploded in the British *K.26* scalding two men to death and in recent years the Brazilian *Tonelero* was badly damaged by a fire in her cable system while being built at the Vickers yards in Barrow and she had to have a new sixty-foot midship section fitted before the Brazilian Navy would accept her into service. In January, 1976, the Chilean *Hyatt* suffered a minor explosion while under construction by Scotts of Greenock which delayed her delivery by several months. And on 21 September, 1979, the Danish submarine *Spaekhuggeren* capsized while in dry dock at Copenhagen. While rarely leading to the total loss of the boat concerned, such accidents are not uncommon in the world's shipyards and most remain unreported in the national press.

On 4 March, 1970, France lost her third submarine since the end of the war when the *Eurydice* vanished without trace in the Mediterranean with fifty-seven men aboard. It is believed that the disaster stemmed from an internal explosion, although its origin remains a mystery. A shore laboratory in Toulon recorded a powerful underwater explosion on its instruments in the vicinity of the submarine's estimated position and this independent evidence appears to have satisfied the French naval authorities. There were, however, a number of interested parties who were *not* satisfied. Both *Minerve* and *Eurydice* were members of the commercially successful Daphne class and a number of these vessels had been sold to foreign navies. It is significant that, after this latest disaster, buyers from abroad showed a distinct lack of enthusiasm for the Daphne boats.

There is a certain amount of confusion about the next Russian sinking in April, 1970. One non-Soviet source stated that an unidentified nuclear submarine was scuttled off the Faeroe Islands on the 12th when an internal fire threatened to spread to the reactor. Another equally unofficial source alleged that a November class hunter-killer also sank 75 miles south-west of Land's End 'with considerable loss of life' on an unspecified date in the same year. It is probable that these two reports relate to the same incident – such duplication being not uncommon when details do not tally precisely and the names of the vessels are not known. The only doubtful aspect of this particular accident, assuming that only one and not two submarines were involved, was the exact nature of the disaster. According to the CIA, which released details in 1985, the vessel was scuttled to prevent an internal fire from reaching the reactor. But as the reactor's heavy protective shield would have effectively isolated it from even the fiercest of internal fires it seems more reasonable to assume that, as in the case of the *Polar Circle* in 1968, the fire was in fact *inside* the reactor and that the submarine was scuttled to prevent a meltdown.

Collisions between submarines are rare, but on 20 August, 1970, the South African *Maria van Riebeck* and the French *Galatee* became involved in an accident off Toulon in which the French boat lost four men killed and a further two missing. There were apparently no serious casualties aboard the South African vessel which was still undergoing its sea trials and had only been delivered a month previously. Later the same year a Russian Alpha-class nuke suffered several fatalities amongst its crew members when it developed a radiation leak and was towed home in a crippled condition. And in April, 1971, according to CIA sources, a missile-armed *Yankee*-class vessel survived an unspecified accident while on patrol in the Pacific.

The Royal Navy's *Artemis* sank alongside the jetty at Fort Blockhouse on 1 July, 1971, and France lost the *Sirene* at Lorient in 1972 due to a faulty torpedo tube, but fortunately neither mishap can be considered comparable with the other tragedies charted in this and earlier chapters.

The *Artemis* incident was, however, a good example of an accident that should have never happened and it was, in some respects, reminiscent of many pre-1914 sinkings. The submarine was refuelling and, as a preliminary part of the operation, her bunkers were being flooded with water – a procedure known as 'first filling'. The additional weight increased the boat's draught and reduced her slim margin of buoyancy. She settled progressively deeper in the water until, finally, the sea lapped over her deck casing and entered the opened hatches. Disaster might have been avoided even at this late stage, but, unfortunately, a power cable leading down through the engine-room hatchway from a shore generator made it impossible to close the after hatch and stem the inrush of water.

It was a perfect scenario for tragedy,especially as three young Sea Cadets were on board the submarine at the time. But, risking his life to save the boys, Chief Petty Officer David Guest abandoned the security of the deck where he had been 'enjoying a bit of sunshine' and climbed down into the sinking boat. Having found the three lads and seen them up the ladder to safety Guest then set off through the various compartments to see who else was aboard and unaware of the danger. He discovered two more seamen in the bowels of the boat but it was, by then, too late to escape and the three men shut themselves inside the watertight torpedo stowage space as the *Artemis* sank to the bottom of Haslar Creek. They remained entombed inside the submarine for ten hours before the pressure equalized sufficiently for them to open the hatch and swim back to the surface and the waiting rescue team.

While no fatal casualties were suffered in either the *Artemis* or *Sirene* incidents, the hoodoo of death and disaster continued to pursue the Soviet Union's underwater fleet. March, 1972, saw two incidents. The first appears to have been a relatively minor accident to a *Yankee*-class missile-carrier in mid-Atlantic for which no details are available, and in the second, involving a Hotel II class boat, several crewmen were said to have died as the result of radioactive contamination from the leaking warhead of a nuclear torpedo. Although this incident was not confirmed by official Soviet sources, the vessel is known to have surfaced some 900 miles off Newfoundland and was observed being towed back to Severomorsk by Red Navy warships which had been sent to its assistance.

December, 1972, witnessed another radiation accident aboard a Soviet submarine in the Atlantic but, again, no details were made public by the communist authorities. In September, 1973, one of the new *Echo II*-class boats was involved in a collision in the Caribbean and, on 28 September, 1976, another submarine of the same class collided with the *USS Voe* in the Mediterranean while carrying out covert intelligence surveillance of a NATO exercise. Happily no serious damage or casualties were reported in either incident.

Just a month later, in October, 1976, a reactor fire on board an unnamed Soviet submarine patrolling in the North Atlantic killed three officers, while in November of the same year a conventionally-powered Foxtrot class boat fell victim to an unspecified but apparently minor accident in the Pacific. There were two incidents involving Russian nuclear submarines in 1977 but, as usual, the confirmed facts are sparse. In the first twelve officers were flown back to Russia for urgent medical treatment following a leak of radioactive material. And there were rumours of crew deaths in the second incident when a disabled and unidentified boat was towed back to Vladivostok after yet another reactor fire. The submarines of the ill-starred Echo II class also continued to attract trouble and in 1978 one had to be assisted home after its reactor failed while cruising submerged off Rockall. The year concluded with a collision involving the British submarine *Olympus* and an unknown merchant ship on 6 December. Fortunately there was no loss of life or serious damage.

The Russian hoodoo struck again late in 1979 when an unidentified nuclear submarine was scuttled in mid-Atlantic following an unspecified 'radiation leak'. And in August, 1980, an Echo II class vessel suffered fatal casualties following a reactor fire off Okinawa. Like so many of her sisters she, too, had to suffer the humiliation of being towed home.

Although three less serious accidents were reported during 1981 the Soviet Navy could not claim a complete monopoly of incidents. On 9 April, 1982, the Peruvian *Pisagua* survived a collision with a merchant ship during sea trials and on 24 July of the same year the Royal Navy's *Opossum* was involved in an almost identical mishap. No significant damage was reported by either boat.

But there was another major tragedy in September, 1983, when the Russian navy lost its fourth nuclear-powered submarine, a 4,700-ton Charlie class boat which sank off Kamchatka in the northern Pacific with its entire crew of ninety men. No reason for the disaster has ever been given, but unofficial sources suggest that the vessel concerned was subsequently salvaged. This tragedy was followed in February, 1985, by the sinking of an unidentified North Korean submarine which went down with all hands in 350 feet of water.

Minor accidents and reactor failures involving Russian submarines were now becoming so commonplace that there is little point in recording every incident. And, to be completely fair, submarines of other nations also have their share of mishaps which are not always accorded media coverage. Examples include a collision between the Spanish *Siroco* and the destroyer *Almirante Valdes* in June, 1985; the loss of a propeller by the American *Nathanael Greene* a year earlier; and a nearly fatal 35º uncontrolled nosedive by the British nuke *Repulse* in 1983 which could have easily ended in tragedy.

The fog of secrecy that had enveloped Russian underwater disasters since before the Bolshevik Revolution in 1917 was swept away with the appointment of Mikhail Gorbachev as President of the Union of Soviet Socialist Republics and the new policy of *glasnost* – openess – received its first public test on Friday 3

October, 1986, when an SSN-6 Sawfly missile aboard a Yankee class submarine patrolling submerged north-east of Bermuda exploded spontaneously and triggered a serious internal fire. With three men dead, the missile hatch covers blown open, the outer casing peeled back like a skinned banana and a large hole in the pressure hull, the vessel's captain brought the 8,300-ton monster to the surface in an attempt to clear the smoke from the interior so that the crew could tackle the flames with chemical extinguishers. Details of this latest disaster were disclosed by Moscow within 24 hours – a quite unprecedented response – and, as Soviet surface ships hurried to the scene, American surveillance aircraft circled above the burning vessel monitoring radiation levels.

The Russian merchant ship *Krasnogvardeysk* took the crippled boat in tow, but by Sunday night it was clear that, despite the gallant efforts of the submarine's crew, the fire was now raging out of control and later that night liferafts were observed ferrying survivors from the smoke-shrouded submarine to the waiting rescue ships. Within hours the burning wreck had gone to the bottom of the Atlantic in 18,000 feet of water. Whether she foundered or was scuttled is uncertain, but it is more than probable that the captain ordered her to be sunk when the reactor came under threat from the flames. If so, his resolute decision deserves praise, for subsequent checks by American aircraft and monitoring ships have failed to detect any abnormal increase in levels of radioactivity in the area of the sunken submarine.

A human tragedy more in tune with the pioneering days before the 1914-18 war than with the advanced technology of the closing years of the twentieth century made headlines in August, 1987, when the 2,030-ton Australian submarine *Otama* submerged south-east of Sydney while two of its crew members were still working inside the free-flooding fibreglass fin. With the hatches secured and communication lines shut off for diving the marooned victims were unable to alert the control room or seek safety inside the pressure hull and, despite an intensive air and sea search, neither man was ever seen again.

Peacetime accidents have always been a rare occurrence amongst the submarines of Germany's underwater flotillas but in March, 1988, *U-27* rammed the Norwegian oil rig *Oseberg B* west of Bergen. Fortunately there were no casualties although 320 rig workers had to be evacuated from the platform as a precaution while divers went down to assess the extent of the damage. The submarine itself escaped with superficial scratches to its bows. Immediately after the collision, and with typical teutonic correctness, an officer from the U-boat was sent aboard the rig to deliver his captain's apologies for the mishap. Somewhat surprisingly, given the adverse weather conditions usually encountered in the North Sea, this is the only known occasion of a submarine colliding with an oil or gas rig.

Just a month after the *Oseberg* incident three men were lost and a further twenty-three injured as the result of an explosion aboard the *USS Bonefish* while the submarine was taking part in a submerged training exercise 160 miles from the Florida coast on 25 April. Ironically the 30-year-old diesel-powered veteran was one of only four non-nuclear submarines which still remained in service with the US Navy at the time.

The sinking on 26 August, 1988, of the Peruvian *Pacocha,* a former US submarine of even greater vintage than the *Bonefish,* and the dramatic rescue operation to save the men trapped inside the partially flooded boat caught the attention of the world's media and produced headlines similar to those seen in the 'thirties.

The 1,870-ton submarine had been cruising partially submerged with its conning-tower awash when it was struck in the stern by the 410-ton Japanese tuna fishing boat *Kyowa Maru.* Although the *Pacocha* sank rapidly twenty-two members of her crew managed to climb up through the hatches and jump into the sea before she went down. But the remainder were still trapped inside the submarine when she finally came to rest on the bottom in 100 feet of water.

Although he had leapt clear with the other survivors immediately after the initial impact, *Pacocha*'s captain, Daniel Nieva Rodriguez, bravely went back to secure the opened hatch of the stricken submarine before it vanished beneath the surface – an action that was to save the lives of twenty-three of the men still entombed inside the hull. Sadly, the gallant captain and three crewmen who returned to help him were themselves trapped in the flooded outer casing and died trying to save their comrades.

The US Navy responded promptly to news of the disaster and local rescue operations were postponed by the Peruvians when they were informed that a C-141 cargo jet was being rushed to Lima with a diving bell and other state-of-the-art survival equipment on board. Meanwhile divers had established communication with the trapped men inside the *Pacocha* by tapping morse signals on the hull - as Royal Navy divers had done more than seventy years earlier when *K.13* lay on the bottom of Gareloch. Learning that sea water was beginning to contaminate the batteries and that chlorine gas was slowly filling the submarine, the Peruvian salvage experts decided that an immediate rescue mission would have to be launched if the survivors were to be brought out alive.

Taking a calculated gamble that they could contain the risk of further internal flooding, the divers opened the submarine's escape hatch and painstakingly lowered a diving bell into position. Bringing out two men at a time in an almost exact duplication of the *Squalus* operation in 1939, the bell made a total of twelve descents and saved all twenty-three survivors who had, by now, spent nearly 24 hours trapped inside the crippled vessel. The three remaining members of the crew died in the flooded stern compartment within minutes of it being holed by the *Kyowa Maru*.

It had been a copybook rescue operation that owed much to the lessons of history and which demonstrated once more that the diving-bell, or something similar, remained the most reliable and successful method of saving the crew of a sunken submarine provided the boat was lying on a relatively even keel and the depth of water was not too great. Captain Daniel Nieva's valiant act of self-sacrifice was typical of submariners of every nation who, as we have seen over and over again, have laid down their own lives to help others. As the President of Peru, Allan Garcia, said in a public tribute to the *Pacocha*'s dead commanding officer, 'I want to stress the bravery of [Captain Nieva] who, having left the ship through the hatch, went back to save his shipmates.'

Another major tragedy followed less than a year later when, on 7 April, 1989, fire broke out on Russia's titanium-hulled 6,400-ton nuclear monster *Komsomolets* while it was running submerged in the Barents Sea 118 miles south of Bear Island. The warning klaxon rasped the alarm at 11.02 and the instrument panels in the control room pinpointed a fire – the result of an electrical short circuit – in Compartment Seven. Within minutes the temperature inside the compartment had risen to 160ºC and it was clear that the fire could only be extinguished by releasing freon gas which would smother the flames by depriving them of oxygen. Aware that a young seaman, Nadari Bukhnikasvili, was still on watch in the burning compartment the *Komsomolets'* captain, Yevgeniy Vanin, tried to call him up on the communication system. But the line was dead. Balancing the life of a solitary man against the survival of the submarine and its entire crew, he suppressed his personal feelings and gave the order for the gas valves to be opened.

Captain Vanin, however, was unaware that the heat had already ruptured a critical high-pressure air line and, instead of releasing freon gas, his order resulted in the blazing compartment being filled with pure oxygen. Within seconds the *Komsomolets* shuddered from stem to stern as a violent explosion threatened to blow the submarine apart. The warning instruments in the control room registered 1,000 degrees and the bulkhead began to melt as burning hydraulic fluid added to the chaos. Within moments the submarine's entire electrical system was on fire. 'There were flames everywhere,' an officer reported later. 'Cables and panels were burning . . . the men were trying to rip them out with their bare hands. There were explosions everywhere.'

Faced by the uncontrollable conflagration Vanin gave orders to surface and at 11.16 the submarine emerged into the freezing chill of the Arctic air as the radio operators beamed an urgent SOS to the Soviet admirals in Moscow and Severomorsk.

Conditions inside the *Komsomolets* were worsening by the minute. Sections of the hull were glowing red with heat and the temperature inside the boat resembled a blast furnace. To make matters worse the compressed air supply lines had been damaged and the crewmen fighting the fires were breathing, not lifegiving oxygen, but lethal carbon monoxide. By the time officers had shouted warnings several men were already dead. Portable oxygen masks proved equally ineffective and the rubber facepieces were melting in the intense heat causing terrible burns to the unfortunate firefighters.

Although a Soviet aircraft arrived overhead at 14.40 surface rescue ships were still many miles away. By 15.23 the Compartment Six bulkhead temperature reading had reached 200ºC and an hour later a series of explosions ripped through the boat as the oxygen tanks erupted. At 16.42, as the stern of the submarine began to slip below the surface, Captain Vanin gave the order to abandon ship. But the drama was not over yet.

Although he was aware that the captain and some other men were still inside the burning submarine, a senior officer closed the hatch to prevent the sea from flooding the crippled boat and the survival of the men still trapped inside now rested with a special

227

escape capsule which, uniquely among the world's navies, all Soviet submarines carried in their conning-towers. Five of the six men who were still alive managed to climb into the capsule but the release mechanism failed to work and, locked inside the steel egg, they were dragged to the bottom with the submarine. But another violent explosion miraculously blew the escape capsule free and it raced to the surface like a released cork. Vanin knew it was rising too fast for safety but there was nothing he or the occupants could do to slow its rate of ascent. On reaching the surface the pent-up internal pressure blew off the hatch cover and one man died as he was sucked out through the exit hatch by the blast of released air. Warrant Officer Slyusarenko, the next man out, emerged alive. But as he slid into the water semi-conscious the sea poured into the open hatchway of the capsule and it sank back to the bottom with Captain Vanin and two other crewmen still inside. They were never seen again.

It had been an horrendous disaster fully equal to the worst of those described in previous chapters. And it served to demonstrate that the Russian escape capsule concept was, to say the least, seriously flawed. It showed also that speed of response was vital if rescue was to be successful. But on this occasion the demands of national security brutally overrode humane considerations. Because the titanium-hulled *Komsomolets* was a top-secret design the Russians were determined that NATO ships should be denied any opportunity of getting there first and salvaging the submarine. And by the time their own surface ships reached the scene at 18.20 many of the survivors struggling in the black Arctic water had died from hypothermia or exhaustion. As a Norwegian air-rescue expert observed, 'We could have had a helicopter over the submarine within two hours and it could have lifted as many as twenty men, taken them ashore, and then returned for more. Unfortunately by the time we knew what was happening it was too late.'

The lesson was obvious. If speed was to be the priority requirement and a rapid rescue achieved – the only certain way to save lives – international co-operation was a prime necessity. And, as will be seen in the final chapter, we are perhaps at last on the edge of such a worldwide rescue organization.

—FOURTEEN—

'Don't Lose Hope!'

According to *The Times* newspaper the Greenpeace organization recently claimed that Russian submarines had been involved in 121 accidents during the period 1956 to 1991. But, like all statistics, this is probably a little misleading, for, on occasions, Soviet vessels were the victims rather than the perpetrators of near-disaster. Indeed the public still remains largely unaware of the risks taken by submariners from both East and West in their efforts to gain intelligence information during the Cold War. Operating in close proximity to surface ships has always been a dangerous occupation, as this book has already testified, and more than a few submarines experienced frighteningly close shaves when their opponent unexpectedly decided to take evasive action. On other occasions submarines played hide-and-seek with each other in the black waters of the Arctic, emulating the tactics of fighter pilots circling to get astern of their enemy. Rear-end shunts, to appropriate a motoring term, were not uncommon and it was a miracle that such daredevil incidents did not result in the loss of one or both of the submarines concerned.

Make no mistake about it, the Cold War was a *real* war, although it was a conflict in which no weapons were employed. Nevertheless it tested the skill and determination of the submarine captains and crews who were involved in this battle of nerves. A moment's hesitation or lack of decisive action could result in the death of every man aboard, while the increasingly complex technology of the weapon and electronic surveillance systems added a new dimension to the demands made upon the men who operated them.

Several incidents from the Cold War have been mentioned in the previous chapter and, while this book cannot encompass all the accidents to which Greenpeace referred, the following details will help the reader to understand and measure the strain under which submarine crews on both sides operated during that prolonged period of international tension. The survey will extend up to and beyond the *Kursk* tragedy and cover incidents in which British, French, North Korean and South American submarines, as well as those of the two main protagonists, the United States and Soviet Russia, were involved.

The first accident on record during the period delineated by Greenpeace occurred in September 1957 when the Soviet Union's experimental *M.256*, powered by an unreliable and dangerously temperamental closed-cycle diesel engine, caught fire and sank when the crew's over-enthusiastic attempts to douse the flames ended with the flooded submarine sinking under their feet. So far as can be established there were no casualties.

Two years later, in May 1959, *S.99*, another experiment submarine which was at the time testing a German Walter turbine unit, suffered a violent explosion while running submerged. Despite a large hole in the pressure hull the crew managed to resurface and there was no loss of life. Nevertheless the damage proved so serious that she was never repaired. The cause of the explosion was later traced to a blocked fuel line. Neither of these accidents had any connection with the quasi-combat operations of the Cold War. Nor did *Anchorite*'s unfortunate encounter with an uncharted rock on 3 October 1960 while running submerged in Hauraki Gulf, close to New Zealand's largest city, Auckland, although, fortunately, she was able to return to harbour under her own power.

One of the earliest victims of the Cold War seems to have been the American *Swordfish* which sustained minor damage when a Russian submarine attempted to surface under her keel. The nuclear-powered *Skipjack* also collided with a Soviet destroyer during the 1960s while engaged on an intelligence-gathering mission, although this incident was concealed from the public until 1975. In another sparsely reported episode *USS Barbel*, a conventionally-powered submarine, rammed an unidentified freighter off North Vietnam in March 1966.

While some of these incidents were no more than the accepted hazards of the sea and unconnected with the rivalry between the United States and Soviet navies which was rapidly growing in intensity, accidents involving the two Cold War antagonists were beginning to snowball. In December 1967 the nuclear-powered *George C. Marshall* was grazed by a Russian submarine while engaged on surveillance duties and on 9 October the following year two unidentified American and Soviet boats collided in the Barents Sea, the latter being holed, while the former had to seek emergency docking facilities in Norway to carry out makeshift repairs to her damaged hull. In November 1969 *USS Gato's* tail was struck by an over-inquisitive Russian shadower and on 14 March 1970 the sonar dome of the American nuke *Sturgeon* struck the conning-tower of a Soviet submarine while both boats were engaged in a game of submerged hide-and-seek. None of these incidents resulted in any serious damage and, happily, no one was hurt, which was, at least, an encouraging contrast with similar accidents in the past in which many ended with the loss of one, and sometimes both, of the vessels involved.

* * *

The new decade had opened with the collision between the French *Galatee* and South Africa's *Maria van Riebeck*, mentioned on page 221, and the dangers resulting from human error were demonstrated again in January of the following year when a Russian diesel-powered *Foxtrot*-class submarine collided with a Soviet merchantman in the Mediterranean, although, unlike *Galatee*, it emerged relatively unscathed from the experience.

Apart from a bare three-line item in the *New York Times*, no details have been released about the collision between a Russian and an American submarine in March 1971 and the same wall of silence surrounds a similar incident in the Mediterranean involving *USS Dace* and another unidentified Soviet submarine. At around the same time the American nuke *Puffer*, a sister of *Sturgeon*, referred to earlier, was shunted by its Soviet underwater shadower while diving. To balance the scorecard the blame for the next two incidents appears to rest with American vessels: *Pintado* rammed a Russian submarine near Petropavlovsk in March 1974, while on 3 November of the same year the 7250-ton ballistic missile submarine *James Madison* hit a *Victor*-class hunter-killer in the North Sea. Such incidents, however, were by now becoming so

231

commonplace that they frequently passed unreported, the bored silence of the media being greatly appreciated by the admirals and politicians on both sides of the Iron Curtain who were anxious to prevent the public from knowing just how dangerous these 'war games' were becoming. Without human casualties or the drama of search and rescue operations, these apparently minor escapades lacked the headline value of other disasters and editors quietly relegated them, firstly, to the inside pages and then, ultimately, omitted them altogether. But whether publicized or not the underwater confrontations of the Cold War persisted as each side strove for the upper hand.

Accidents, of course, continued to befall submarines even when they were *not* at sea and some of these have already been reviewed in an earlier chapter. The sorry saga continued with the Dutch *Walrus*-class hunter-killer which became another building-slip casualty when fire broke out in August 1986, although, fortunately, the resulting damage did not prevent its completion on schedule. More recently, on 1 May 1992, Britain's *Turbulent* erupted in flames while berthed at Devonport and the ensuing conflagration left twenty-four injured. But to end this brief digression on a lighter note, there is the salutary story of *HMS Triumph*, the final boat of the Royal Navy's new *Trafalgar*-class of nuclear hunter-killers, which, like most of the earlier incidents, was also set in a shipbuilder's yard, in this instance that of Vickers at Barrow-in-Furness. The submarine had been laid down in 1986 at a projected cost of £240 million, but in April 1988 it was revealed that a cylindrical hull section measuring a not inconsiderable 20ft × 30ft had been welded into place *upside down* and would have to be cut out with acetylene torches and repositioned the right way up. As one of the shipyard's workers observed, 'It's what you might call a classic cock-up.' That was the polite way of putting it.

* * *

The relentless underwater struggle between East and West had, by the 'eighties, become increasingly dangerous. In 1981 Britain's nuclear-powered *Sceptre* rear-ended a Soviet submarine which she had been shadowing. It was revealed in the *Daily Telegraph* as recently as August 2000 in a background article to the *Kursk* disaster that the next-of-kin were informed that she had struck an iceberg. Fortunately *Sceptre* returned safely to base with her outer casing and sail badly damaged, although, by a miracle, the integrity of the pressure hull had not been breached. It was clear even to the untrained eye that the submarine had come within inches of disaster. However, every member of the crew stuck to the official Admiralty line that their boat had struck an iceberg and this was finally accepted as the true reason for the damage.

But was it? Eight days later the same newspaper published a letter in which a crew member of an unidentified submarine alleged that his vessel had run into the stern of a Russian *Echo II*-class boat while trying to photograph it in the Barents Sea. The Soviet submarine lost a propeller, while the British vessel suffered extensive damage to her conning-tower and outer casing. In addition the periscope was inoperative, the steering mechanism ineffective and the radio system out of action. Emergency repairs were carried out at sea and, although delayed by a few days, the somewhat battered submarine finally returned to her Scottish base under her own power. And here comes the point of the letter: according to the writer, 'the official version was that we had hit an iceberg during exercises'. He went on to recall that the incident had occurred in 1968 – a plausible date as he referred to the Russian vessel as 'a then new' *Echo-II* type and the records show that this particular class came into service between 1962 and 1967. In addition he could not have been referring to the *Sceptre* incident, which had been the subject of the report published eight days earlier, for this was known to have taken place in 1981. Moreover, *Sceptre* was not even ordered until 7 September 1971, three years *after* the accident in which he had personally been involved. It can therefore only be concluded that, despite the outward similarities, two separate incidents had been identified. And, significantly, the iceberg euphemism was used in both cases. One wonders what excuse would have been offered had a similar collision taken place in warmer waters. Perhaps the blame would have been laid on a very large whale.

By an odd coincidence the Cold War *did* change location from the arctic ice of the Barents Sea to the more temperate seas fringing the Atlantic coast of South Carolina when, on 31 October 1983, one of the latest *Victor III*-class nuclear hunter-killer submarines managed to get its propeller tangled in the towed sonar array being trailed by *USS McCoy*. This particular type of Soviet submarine had an unusual propeller system made up of two 4-bladed screws set in tandem and co-rotating. Such complex machinery does not take kindly to becoming entangled in foreign objects and, deprived

233

of propulsive power and starkly exposed to the cameras of US Navy aircraft, the submarine wallowed helplessly on the surface for four days before the tug *Aldan* arrived to take her in tow back to Castro's Cuba. Despite possibly losing *McCoy*'s SQR-15 towed sonar array gear to the Russians, senior American officers were said to be 'extremely delighted' with what they regarded as an intelligence coup, namely their stolen pictures of Soviet Russia's latest submarine never before seen by Western eyes.

1984 also witnessed a major collision between the carrier *USS Kitty Hawk* and a *Victor 1*-class submarine in the Sea of Japan on 21 March. The American vessel was closing in on a group of replenishment ships which the Russian captain had been tracking, but as the carrier was approaching from astern the submarine's detectors were probably unable to pick up the sound of her propellers and, denied time to take evasive action, *Kitty Hawk*'s bows struck the Russian's tail causing the submarine to broach. It was a pitch-black night, but the carrier's probing searchlights quickly illuminated the submarine lying stopped on the surface. Little signs of damage were visible to the officers on *Kitty Hawk*'s bridge and, dousing its lights, the 81,123-ton American ship swept past leaving the unfortunate submarine to its fate. Old-fashioned chivalry had no place in the dog-eat-dog climate of the Cold War. It is believed that the Russian vessel survived the collision, although it is not known whether she suffered any casualties.

Details of *Repulse*'s uncontrolled nose-dive in 1985 were given in Chapter 13 and it has now been revealed that one of her class-sisters found itself in trouble during the same year. On 9 June *Resolution* collided with the 40-ton American trawler *Proud Mary* off the coast of Florida while running on the surface at 30 knots on her way to test-fire one of her new Polaris missiles. The submarine incurred no damage, but the little fishing boat, still miraculously afloat, had to be towed back to the shore with three members of her crew suffering from minor injuries caused by the impact.

Repulse had a second brush with disaster on 18 September while she was undergoing a routine refit at Rosyth. A blower-heater failed and the plastic sheeting which encased the vessel began to melt and release toxic fumes. Two civilian dockyard workers owed their lives to the quick response of the submarine's crew who dragged them clear in time. *Repulse* sustained no damage.

Towed sonar arrays played a part in two accidents reported in 1986. *USS Augusta* lost her trailing detectors in October when she struck an unidentified Russian submarine during a risky surveillance operation and on Christmas Eve Britain's *HMS Splendid* had her towed array torn off while playing cat-and-mouse games with another Soviet submarine. This particular incident sparked a political row with questions being asked in the House of Commons about a possible breach of security. It was in many ways a storm in a teacup for the Russian navy already possessed a very similar towed sonar array system and the vital part of the equipment, the computer programme for processing the information produced by the sonar signals, was safely secured *inside* the submarine. The parliamentary repercussions, however, served to illustrate the political aspects of the Cold War and explains why confirmation of so much of the information disclosed in this and the previous chapter is virtually impossible. Two brief quotes from *Hansard* will suffice:

Martin O'Neill MP asked why the submarine was patrolling so provocatively close to the Soviet Union. To which the Ministry of Defence spokesman replied, 'We cannot confirm that *Splendid* has been involved in an incident because we do not discuss operational matters.' A splendidly informative answer if I may be permitted the indulgence of a pun.

A rather different and potentially far more dangerous accident occurred in September of the same year when a dummy intercontinental ballistic missile was fired into Chinese territory by a Russian *Delta*-class submarine submerged in the Barents Sea. The rocket's target was a test range on the Kamchatka peninsula in Soviet Siberia, but it veered seriously off course and crashed just inside the borders of the People's Republic of China. No casualties or damage were reported and, surprisingly, there appear to have been no political consequences.

In February 1987 an unidentified submarine found itself trapped in the trawl nets of the Ulster fishing boat *Summer Morn* while proceeding submerged through the Irish Sea. The skipper of the trawler told reporters that he and his three-man crew had been dragged for 2½ hours over a distance of ten miles before they were able to cut the nets away and break free. A Pentagon official subsequently admitted that the incident had involved a United States vessel. Newspapers used to abound with reports of submarines becoming ensnared in fishing nets, but most incidents can nowadays only be found tucked away on the inside pages of obscure local news-sheets. One such story related how the 34-ton Brixham trawler *Joanna C* was towed backwards in a series of circles after her nets snagged an unidentified submarine while she was night-fishing off Berry Head. Her skipper adamantly insisted that it was of Russian origin, although the vessel never showed itself on the surface. However, as the episode was located fairly close to the Royal Navy's 2nd Submarine Squadron's base at Devonport, it is equally possible that the culprit was a British boat.

Two months earlier a Russian *Whisky*-class submarine was trapped for three hours in Norwegian waters after getting enmeshed in a net and was forced to surface and ask the local coastguards to help free the boat from its embrace. A similar incident featuring another diesel-powered Soviet submarine occurred in November 1989. Most of these incidents were trivial by nature and of little consequence. But, by the laws of chance such apparently minor incidents were, sooner or later, bound to end in tragedy.

The unthinkable finally happened on Thursday 22 November 1990 when the 45-foot Scottish trawler *Antares* sunk off the Isle of Arran after being dragged beneath the surface by the nuclear submarine *Trenchant* which had unwittingly run full tilt into her nets. Although *Trenchant* surfaced and tried to establish contact with two other vessels in the immediate area, both failed to respond. A report was therefore transmitted to the local coastguard station of a possible incident, but those aboard the submarine were completely unaware that they had accidently sunk an innocent fishing vessel and, closing the hatches, *Trenchant* returned to the depths.

When it became apparent that *Antares* was missing along with her four-man crew there was an outcry of protest from the fishing communities along the Clyde, led by the local member of parliament, George Foulkes. Feelings were running high because, over the years, numerous complaints had been lodged with the Ministry of Defence about incidents in which trawlers lost their nets or narrowly avoided collisions with submarines from Holy Loch, a danger exacerbated by the practice of submarines remaining submerged while entering and leaving the base to prevent Soviet spy-satellites from tracking their movements. In fact only the previous year, 1989, the American nuclear submarine *Will Rogers* had damaged the Ayr trawler *New Dawn* following a collision in the Firth of Clyde and it was firmly believed that *Antares* was an accident waiting to happen. It was a view not shared by the Armed Forces Minister Archie Hamilton who stated: 'We have never had a problem of loss of life before, and it does seem to have been a very freak accident.' Certainly there had been no lives lost in previous incidents, but it was misleading to imply that such episodes were rare. And in the light of the various encounters between submarines and trawlers listed in this book it was scarcely freakish.

The subsequent court-martial at *HMS Drake*, Devonport, failed to allay the fears of Scotland's fishermen, for it was revealed in evidence that, at the time of the collision, *Trenchant* was under the control of Lieutenant Peter McDonnell who was just completing an exhausting 21-day exercise – the deciding test to determine the outcome of his six-month command course, or, as it was known in the service, the 'Perisher'. *Trenchant*, it appeared, had passed close to the trawler at 2 am but McDonnell was not verbally informed of the fact and, unfortunately, failed to notice it on the submarine's manual plotter. When he turned the boat around he had relied totally on the information provided by *Trenchant*'s navigational computer which showed, reassuringly, that he was at least three miles away from the other vessel. His reliance on the computer was, however, argued to be tantamount to negligence as he had failed to follow the prescribed procedures for underwater pilotage.

In his defence it was submitted that: 'He was tired. It was the middle of the graveyard watch. It was dark and he really had been through it [during the intensive command exercise]. Although he was in charge, it is fair to say that he was not well supported.' But the Royal Navy is a hard master. While ruling that his alleged negligence was not necessarily the cause of *Antares'* loss, the court nevertheless still adjudged him guilty of negligence and McDonnell was given a severe reprimand.

The Scottish fishing industry regarded the verdict as a 'whitewash' and accused the Navy of producing a scapegoat. Indeed the solicitor representing the bereaved families of the trawler's crew was moved to comment that he had observed the court-martial with 'a growing sense of anger and sympathy [for the man chosen] to save the face' of the Royal Navy. 'The court-martial's purpose appears to get the Navy off the hook by prosecuting the most junior member of the command crew.' Mr Hynd's comments were reported in the *Daily Telegraph* of 6 June 1992.

But whoever may have been responsible for the tragedy on the Clyde that day, the dangerous cat-and-mouse game continued without respite in Arctic waters. America's *Baton Rouge* collided with a *Sierra*-class submarine off Murmansk on 11 February 1992 and, contrary to its usual reticence about such encounters, the Pentagon admitted to United States involvement under pressure from Boris Yeltsin's new government which had accused the American vessel of being inside Russian territorial waters. The following June saw media reports of an internal explosion aboard a Russian nuclear submarine while under repair at its base on the Kola Peninsula which had left one crewman dead, while another officially unconfirmed story the same year claimed that twenty-one sailors had died as the result of a fire in another Russian nuclear submarine although the boat was coaxed safely back to harbour after the flames had been extinguished. On 30 March 1994 it was France's turn to experience tragedy when ten crewmen of *Emeraude* lost their lives following an internal explosion off Toulon caused by water leaking into one of the nuclear submarine's power rooms. No serious structural damage to the vessel was reported.

As the tensions of the Cold War faded following the collapse of the old Soviet régime the frequency of collisions and near-misses also diminished dramatically. Accidents occurring since then have often been very different in both cause and effect. Indeed some could even be classed as downright bizarre.

The first such incident began on 17 September 1996 when a 375-ton North Korean *Shark*-class submarine ran aground on a reef inside neighboring South Korea's territorial waters during what was thought to be an infiltration mission. The men on board waded ashore and, seemingly working to a pre-arranged emergency plan, dispersed into groups and promptly went to ground. Within hours of finding the vessel wallowing in the surf South Korean troops and police began a massive manhunt to track them down – probably the first occasion on which survivors from a peacetime submarine accident have found themselves facing the wrong end of a gun. The drama heightened when warships were brought in to patrol the area to seaward of the wreck to frustrate any attempt by the North Korean navy to stage a rescue and salvage operation. In an additional show of strength fully-armed jet aircraft were placed on stand-by.

The authorities were first alerted by a taxi driver who had seen a group of men wearing orange-coloured lifejackets huddled at the side of a mountain road in heavy rain and the following day eleven of the survivors were found dead close to where he had sighted them. Ten lay in a semi-circle on the ground and each had been killed by a single gunshot to the head. An eleventh, thought to have been their executioner, was discovered a short distance away with a pistol at his side having apparently committed suicide. All eleven men were wearing civilians clothes complete with South Korean labels. A lone survivor, Lee Kwang-su was taken prisoner the same day and, after intensive interrogation, admitted that the submarine had suffered engine trouble and run aground while engaged on a mission to pick up secret agents. His statement was confirmed by a police report that the boat's conning-tower was blackened with fire.

The manhunt continued on Thursday 19 September and during the early hours of the morning a commando unit tracked down another four North Korean fugitives. A fierce firefight followed, in which three of the survivors were killed, although a fourth was said to have made his escape. Some hours later four more were found near the town of Kangnung and were disposed of with hand grenades by South Korean soldiers. The total number on board the submarine remains uncertain, but on 31 December 1996 media reports confirmed that the ashes of twenty-four crewmen had been returned to North Korea after Kim Jong-il's communist régime issued a formal admission and apology for the incident. Only two people seem to have benefited from this bizarre episode. The taxi driver, Lee Jin Kyu, received a £120,000 reward from the government for raising the alarm, while the only known survivor from the submarine, Lee Kwang-su, was recruited into the South Korean navy where his inside knowledge of the North's infiltration tactics and subversive operations were to prove invaluable.

He was to emerge briefly from the shadows again two years later when, on the night of 25 June 1998, a second North Korean submarine came to grief in South Korean waters. The unidentified 70-ton *Yugo*-class vessel became entangled in fishing nets during another suspected clandestine operation and subsequently sank while being towed back to the South's Donghae naval base. Salvage teams raised the submarine with the aid of frogmen and large air balloons, and troops were soon clambering over their unexpected prize.

Lee Kwang-su, however, counselled caution. He knew from experience that the submarine could be booby-trapped and he insisted on a very careful security check being carried out. Indeed, before the South Koreans entered the vessel, a miniature television camera was employed to search the interior of the submarine for explosives. When the hatch was finally opened the soldiers found the bodies of nine victims inside, five being identified as sailors, while the remaining four were assumed to be agents. It was reported that the five crewmen had been shot by machine guns, whereas the suspected landing-party had died from self-inflicted gunshot wounds. The scenario looked starkly simple and Lee Kwang-su concluded that the commando unit had murdered the crew following a dispute about surrendering the crippled submarine to the South Koreans.

If these two incidents were like nothing that had ever gone before, the drama that followed nearly three months later was, perhaps, even more bizarre. A Russian conscript, Alexander Kuzminkyh, being detained at Skalisty, an arctic base of the Northern Fleet, for acts of insubordination and general indiscipline, broke out of his cell and headed for the quay where a number of Russia's latest *Akula*-class nuclear-powered attack submarines were berthed. Overpowering the sentry guarding the gangplank to *Snow Leopard* (*K.971*), he seized the man's assault rifle and shot him dead with his own weapon before running up the companionway into the submarine. Once aboard, he made his way towards the bows of the vessel, killing a further seven members of the crew before locking himself inside the forward torpedo compartment. He then threatened to blow up himself and the submarine.

The 19-year-old seaman offered no explanation nor motive for his actions, although, later, Russian authorities alleged he had been suffering from a psychiatric disorder. Unable to bring the situation under control, and concerned about the dangers of radiation poisoning that might result if Kuzminkyh tampered with the nuclear reactor – although the lead-lined compartment was some distance from where the sailor had barricaded himself in – the local admirals called in Russia's anti-terrorist special forces to resolve the situation. A stand-off followed while trained negotiators attempted to defuse the tension by trying to establish a voice link to the young seaman who was holding them all to ransom. After some hours they persuaded him to accept a telephone which would make communication easier. They did not inform him that the instrument was a product of the Israeli secret service, *Mossad*. Neither did they tell him that it was a booby-trapped device designed to explode when he used it. Minutes later the telephone detonated as Kuzminhkh tried to make his first call. The siege of *Snow Leopard*, which had now claimed nine lives, was over.

There was a poignant return to a past tragedy on Tuesday

8 August 2002 when the remains of the Confederate submarine *Hunley*, lost in 1864 when she sank with her victim *Housatonic*, were finally raised to the surface. The wreck of this pioneering submersible death-trap had been located in 1995 by a team of divers sponsored by the best-selling author Clive Cussler. Covered by a thick layer of silt, *Hunley* was resting in thirty feet of water on the bottom of Charleston Bay approximately four miles from Sullivan's Island and it required considerable expertise and care to bring the rusted hulk up without causing further damage. Saluted by a salvo from a battery of re-enactment Civil War cannons, the historical Confederate vessel was taken to the old Navy Yard at Charleston for conservation and restoration – a process likely to extend over a number of years at an estimated cost of $17 million.

Marine archeologists hope that when the work is completed they will be able to establish the precise cause for the boat's loss, a matter of dispute among historians for some 138 years. Their findings will also settle the question of how many men were actually on board *Hunley* when she went down. The names of eight victims are recorded, but it is believed that a ninth unidentified man died with them.

*   *   *

At 07.29.34 GMT on the morning of Saturday 12 August 2000 the Norwegian NORSAR seismic observation service detected an explosion measuring 1.5 on the Richter scale north of the Arctic Circle in the Barents Sea. Just over two minutes later, at precisely 07.31.48 GMT, the needles of the seismographs juddered violently for a second time as they recorded a further explosion from the same location which this time registered 3.5 on the Richter scale. The twin detonations were also detected by the Russian flagship *Petr Velikiy* (*Peter the Great*) which at the time was leading a major exercise with Russia's Northern Fleet and by two American nuclear submarines, *Memphis* and *Toledo*, as well as the Royal Navy's *Splendid*, plus other NATO intelligence vessels in the area. Such was the intensity of the second explosion that it even registered on instruments as far away as Canada and Alaska.

Western observers were convinced that one of Russia's biggest and most modern submarines, *Kursk* (*K.141*), had gone to the bottom as the result of an internal explosion probably resulting from a missile or torpedo accident. The Russians, however, seemed less certain. For, although over the course of the next twenty hours *Kursk* twice failed to transmit a routine report of its position to the flagship in accordance with pre-arranged instructions, the Northern Fleet's admirals apparently showed no signs of alarm. The exact sequence of events on board the flagship remain obscure even now, two and a half years later, but it is generally accepted that little happened until 03.21 on Sunday 13 August when a sonar operator aboard *Petr Velikiy* reported an 'abnormality' on the seabed which appeared to be a large submarine. Even then a further four days were to pass before Admiral Vyacheslav Popov informed President Vladimir Putin that the submarine had probably met with disaster. Holidaying in a government *dacha* at Sochi on the Black Sea coast, Putin listened to the news, but did not consider it required him to curtail his vacation and return to Moscow.

Kursk was a massive war machine. A member of the *Project 949A*-class, she was commissioned in 1995 and immediately assigned to the underwater arm of the strategically important Northern Fleet. According to Russian sources her surface displacement was 14,700 tons and 24,000 tons when submerged, which would have made her the world's heaviest submarine. Western pundits, however, rated her at 13,900 tons in surface trim and 18,300 tons when dived. Smaller perhaps, but still impressively large.

With a submerged speed of around 30 knots, *Kursk* had been designed to attack American aircraft carrier battle groups at long range and to this end she was equipped with twenty-four P-700 (Granit) cruise missiles fitted with either nuclear or conventional warheads, together with four 650mm torpedo tubes for launching shorter-range anti-ship weapons, with a further two 533mm tubes for anti-submarine torpedoes. It was rumoured that her weapon outfit included the new top-secret *VA-111 Shkval* supercavitating torpedo – NATO name *Squall* – a revolutionary weapon with a submerged speed of at least 200 knots achieved by venting its rocket exhaust gases through the nose so that the module travelled through the water inside an air bubble. All in all, *Kursk* was a formidable weapons platform. She was also a death trap.

Her regular crew comprised 111 men, a total which included no fewer than forty-eight commissioned officers, although, in Western fleets, many of these would have been ranked as warrant and petty officers. She was, in addition, carrying two weapon experts from the Dagdizel armaments plant on the Caspian Sea, identified in the casualty list as Arnold Borisov and Mamed Gadshiyet, who were on board to evaluate tests on a new unidentified weapon thought to have been the *Squall* rocket torpedo. Also embarked as observers were five Navy captains of varying seniority drawn from the staff of the 7th Division Submarine headquarters. Their names were recorded as Vladimir Bagriantsev, Yuriy Shepernov, Viktor Belogun, Vasiliy Isayenko and Marat Baygarin.

It is now accepted that *Kursk*'s commander, Captain Gennadiy Liachin, and all but twenty-three of the men on board the submarine died within minutes of the two explosions. But the handful of survivors found safety in Section 9 where, having secured and clipped the watertight door, they huddled together in the pitch darkness of the unlit compartment where they remained trapped but alive for several days.

Bitter experience had already taught Western navies of the necessity of speed when responding to a submarine disaster and emergency arrangements were in place to ensure that rescue vessels were on the scene in the shortest possible time. For some reason, however, the Russian admirals took a more leisurely view of the situation and, as already noted, it was Sunday afternoon before rescue operations began in earnest, some thirty hours after the submarine had gone to the bottom. No intelligible reasons for the delay have been offered, although some of the subsequent press releases try to suggest that rescue ships were on the scene much earlier. The shambles that followed was a public relations disaster. The Russian media was not officially told of the sinking until Sunday and false hopes were raised by announcements that contact had been made with the survivors and air was being pumped into the stricken vessel.

Creating excuses and placing the blame on outside sources soon became a greater priority than rescuing any of the crew who might still be alive and there were government-inspired allegations that *Kursk* had sunk after she had been struck by a NATO submarine, a not unbelievable scenario in view of the many Cold War collisions already reviewed in this chapter. It was also claimed that a Western submarine had radioed an SOS call soon after the explosions in which it had sought permission to make an emergency docking in Norway to repair accident damage. Quite fortuitously, from Russia's point of view, *USS Memphis* arrived in Bergen on 18 August. But it proved to be a routine replenishment visit arranged months earlier and photographs of the submarine taken by eager pressmen with the active cooperation of the US Navy revealed no signs of a recent collision. Nevertheless the Russian media tenaciously stuck to their account of NATO responsibility for *Kursk*'s sinking.

Western experts, however, were now starting to place the blame on the secret *Squall* rocket torpedo which the submarine was known to be carrying. This unusual weapon had to swim out of the torpedo tube on electric motors and only when it was at a safe distance were its powerful rocket engines ignited. The presence of the two experienced rocket engineers on board *and* the party of senior staff officers which had joined *Kursk* to observe secret weapon experiments only served to compound their suspicions. The first explosion, the pundits surmised, occurred when the *Squall* missile failed to leave the tube. The second detonation was the result of the rocket engines igniting while still inside the submarine. American observers were less than convinced by this theory and preferred to blame *Kursk*'s thermal-fuelled torpedoes which, for reasons of financial economy, were powered by the inherently unstable mixture of kerosene and high-test hydrogen peroxide, which, if spontaneously ignited, could have triggered the detonation of other weapons. It will be remembered that a high-test peroxide torpedo had sunk *Sidon* at Portland in 1955. And anyone familiar with them knew they were dangerous animals.

Putting all rivalries aside, the West immediately offered its expert assistance, together with the necessary advanced hardware in a bid to rescue survivors, but Russia's admirals seemed reluctant to accept help from outside as a matter of pride, an attitude which may well have cost the lives of the twenty-three men trapped in the stern. They had by now lowered a rather old-fashioned diving-bell on to the sunken boat, but sea conditions made it impossible to lock on to the escape hatches. According to Moscow sources the support ship *Mikhail Rudnitskiy* arrived in the area on the night of 12 August, although other evidence suggests that the date was more probably the 13th. Her two Deep Submergence Rescue Vehicles (DSRVs), which examined the wreck on 14 August, established that only one of the escape hatches was operational, although they too failed to lock on, due to the submarine's sharply angled list, the strong undercurrents and the inability of *Kursk*'s crew to assist from inside the boat.

It would be tedious and unhelpful to detail the repeated dives

244

made by the DSRVs, which by now seemed to have totalled at least five in number, as every attempt to reach the survivors failed. The authorities, however, were still feeding misleading information to the world's press and, in one instance, claimed that 'there was a malfunction [in the submarine] which compels her to remain temporarily on the seabed'. This statement implied that the majority, if not all, of the crew were still alive and safe, even though the Northern Fleet's admirals knew by now that *Kursk* would never rise to the surface again by her own efforts and there was no hope of finding survivors. Finally President Putin, losing patience and concerned by the growing groundswell of adverse opinion against his régime, authorized the employment of foreign assistance over the heads of his reluctant admirals and the next day Britain's DSRV *LR-5* left Trondheim on *Normand Pioneer*, together with another support vessel carrying a Norwegian diving team. *LR-5* had been offered to the Russian navy very soon after *Kursk* had first sunk, but, as usual, had only met with procrastination.*

Even at this stage the Russians found reasons for not using *LR-5*, but the team of Norwegian salvage divers finally prised open the stern escape hatch which they found had been damaged in the earlier attempt of the diving-bell to dock with the submarine. The air-lock compartment was flooded and the lower section was thought to be blocked by the body of a survivor who failed to get out. It was a grim task carried out in dreadful conditions and tempers were fraying. Both the Norwegians and *LR-5*'s British team accused Russia's naval authorities of impeding their attempts to get inside the submarine. And Norway's Vice Admiral Einar Skorgen told a journalist angrily, 'The information given [to the divers by the Russians] was so unreliable it threatened their safety.'

The storm quickly subsided and on Monday 21 August, nine days after *Kursk* had gone to the bottom of the Barents Sea, Norwegian divers finally entered the submarine and Moscow officially confirmed that the entire crew had died in the disaster. Within hours angry relatives were demanding explanations and, for a short period, the stability of Putin's government appeared to be under threat. One television news sequence which showed a grieving mother being openly sedated with a drug-filled syringe to silence her protests during a public meeting shocked the world and for a time it was feared that the new democratic Russian Federation had

* Details of *LR-5* will be found in Chapter 16.

returned to the dark era of Soviet-style intimidation and state-inspired public deceit.

As the furore gradually faded, the grim task of recovering the bodies began – the first twelve being winched by cradle from Section 9 on 21 October before the operations were again halted by fierce arctic gales for several days. On 27 October the remains of 27-year-old Lieutenant-Captain Dmitry Kolesnikov were lifted by the divers and an oil-stained note, protected inside a plastic cover, was found in his top pocket. The naval authorities at first refused to release its contents, but, responding to pressure, allowed Dmitry's father, himself a former submariner in the Soviet fleet, to read it. He was, however, only allowed to make notes and copying was forbidden.

Part of the note read, 'All personnel from Sections 6, 7 and 8 moved to the 9th [section]. There are 23 of us here.' There then followed a list of names, together with the time, 13.58 [presumably Moscow time]. Nearly two hours later he penned a personal message to his wife and family. Later still, possibly as much as a day or more, he added, 'It is too dark to write here but I will try to write by touch. It looks like there is no chance . . .'. This comment suggests that, at first, the survivors were able to make use of the submarine's emergency lighting system while they awaited rescue. And when that failed any realistic hope of rescue died with it.

The note confirmed that one man had tried to leave the submarine by the aft escape hatch but became trapped in the air-lock chamber. It also indicated that *Kursk* was initially lying at an acute bow-down angle which meant the stern section, in which Kolesnikov and his party of survivors were trapped, would have been much closer to the surface – possibly no more than a hundred feet – than the rest of the submarine. In such circumstances rescuers would have stood a good chance of bringing them out *if the rescue ships had reached the scene quickly*. Once again speed of response was vital if lives were to be saved and the initial 30-hour delay had proved fatal.

Dmitry Kolesnikov's final words scrawled blindly and painfully on the precious piece of paper read: 'Hello to all. Don't lose hope!'

* * *

Kursk was finally raised to the surface on 8 October 2001 in a £90 million salvage operation spearheaded by the Dutch heavy-lift

246

barge *Giant 4* and taken to Roslyakovo near Murmansk for dry-docking and inspection. By the end of the month forty-five bodies had been recovered and three of *Kursk*'s cruise missiles removed from their silos – weapons that had posed a continual threat to the teams of men working their way through the debris inside the submarine. On 7 February 2002 it was announced that ninety-four crewmen had been brought out and recovery of any further remains was unlikely. The last of the missing sailors were probably located in the tangled wreckage that had once been Sections 1 and 2.

In July 2002 the Russian navy realized that prevarication was no longer possible and, reluctantly, admitted the truth. There had been no collision with a NATO submarine. *Kursk* had not been sunk by a missile from the flagship *Petr Velinkiy*. The cause for the submarine's loss had simply been due to leaking fuel from a hydrogen-peroxide torpedo which had ignited and detonated with catastrophic consequences. It is impossible not to ask why the admirals found it necessary to cover up what was, in the end, a perfectly explicable accident and one which the Royal Navy had experienced thirty-seven years earlier. But it is impossible, in such circumstances, to understand the Russian enigma.

* * *

The sage of *Kursk* had still not entirely faded from the headlines when tragedy struck again, this time in the warmer waters of the central Pacific, nine miles south of Honolulu's Diamond Head. And following so soon after the disaster in the Barents Sea the sinking of the Japanese oceanic research trawler *Ehime Maru* by *USS Greenville* was a chilling reminder that danger is ever-present beneath the waves. Submarines may now be safer than they used to be and rescue know-how more sophisticated, but the twin threats of human error or a systems malfunction can still, on the wrong day, bring death and destruction in their wake, while the chain of events that led to the sinking of *Ehime Maru* demonstrated that mankind's inherent foolishness could still lead to unintended tragedy. For, despite the lessons gleaned from a century of submarine history mistakes, unfortunately, can still be made.

Cruising submerged off Hawaii on Friday 9 February 2001 Commander Scott Waddle, skipper of the 6,082-ton nuclear submarine *Greenville*, was entertaining a party of sixteen VIP guests

247

when he decided to throw in an extra thrill: an emergency blow during which the submarine would shoot to the surface from a depth of 400 feet after high-pressure air was released into her ballast tanks. It can be an impressive exercise culminating in the submarine erupting on the surface in a maelstrom of air bubbles and emerging at such velocity that she almost leaps clear of the sea like a playful salmon.

Spectacular – without question. Showing off – well probably. An unwise way to entertain passengers? Only the court-martial can decide. But to aggravate an already doubtful decision and to add additional spice to the excitement one guest was invited to pull the levers actuating the release of the compressed air into the tanks while a second *sat at the helm*. US Navy spokesmen stressed that both civilians were closely supervised and no doubt they were. But members of *Greenville*'s crew alleged that the control room was overcrowded with bystanders who got in the way of the enlisted men who were trying to carry out their routine surfacing duties. The initial report on the accident conceded that the guests had disrupted 'vital communications' between Waddle and the sonar operator who was tracking the Japanese vessel. And, equally damning, it also admitted that the executive officer, Lieutenant-Commander Gerald Pfeifer, thought the captain's periscope search before surfacing had been too brief but did not voice his opinion to Waddle because he did not want to cause him any embarrassment in front of their VIP guests. In the circumstances the Tokyo government's accusation of 'slackness' on the part of the US Navy was hardly surprising, neither was the adjective 'outrageous' when employed in reference to joy-riding civilians being at the submarine's controls.

Greenville's emergency blow brought her to the surface directly under the keel of *Ehime Maru* and the trawler sank like a stone. Twenty-six of the crew and passengers managed to grab life-rafts as it went down and were picked up within an hour. But three seamen, two teachers and four teenage students from the Uwajima Marine High School lost their lives and their bodies were never recovered.

The US Navy blamed adverse weather conditions for *Greenville*'s failure to open her hatches and help drag the victims to safety. The Japanese media, however, took the view that the submarine had done nothing to rescue survivors from the water. The verdict on this, too, must await the result of the court-martial.

The diplomatic row reached as far as the White House and President George W. Bush ordered the Pentagon to review its regulations for embarking civilian guests on operational submarines, although he did not go so far as banning the practice completely. However, despite the tragic outcome of the accident, it is clear that a substantial amount of the furore was stirred up by anti-American politicians eager to see all US servicemen evicted from Japan's mainland islands where they have been since 1945.

One near-victim of the agitation was the Japanese Prime Minister, Yoshiro Mori, who became a target for public anger for deciding to continue playing a game of golf for two hours after learning of the accident, a scenario similar to Putin's decision to remain at his Black Sea holiday *dacha* after *Kursk* went down. This account of the tragedy must end here for, unfortunately, the result of the court-martial convened in the wake of the accident was not available when this book went to press.

By way of postscript: on 28 January 2002 *USS Greenville* collided with the amphibious warfare dock-landing ship *Ogden* off Oman in the Arabian Sea. With a displacement of 17,244 tons and an overall length of 570 feet, she must have been difficult to miss. Happily, this time there were no casualties and little damage. Neither, it must be added, did *Greenville* have any civilian passengers aboard.

Stop Press

At approximately 08.00 hrs on the morning of Wednesday 6 November 2002 Britain's nuclear-powered *Trafalgar* struck a submerged rock while running at 15 knots below the surface off the Isle of Skye. She suffered minor damage to her lower bows and sonar equipment, and two members of the crew were slightly injured by the shock of the impact. She returned to Faslane under her own power, but, as a precaution, was escorted back by tugs.

It was reported officially that the boat was under the control of an officer completing the final arduous 14-day exercise that marked the end of his qualification training course as a potential submarine commander. A senior officer observed that he would have been 'stretched to the limit to see [if he] was capable of doing the job'.

Recalling the circumstances that led to the tragedy of the trawler *Antares* when it was sunk by *Trenchant* (a sister-submarine of *Trafalgar*) in 1990, it is difficult not to feel a sense of *déjà-vu*.

—FIFTEEN—

Affray – The Last Word

It is now more than fifty years since *Affray* sank and we need to remind ourselves that she literally vanished off the face of the earth for a total of fifty-eight days before being found and identified on 14 June 1951, a period more than long enough for a succession of ridiculous rumours to germinate and spread with the speed of a biblical plague. Occultists, ufologists, para-psychologists and an assorted host of cranks and weirdos were quick to advocate their own pet theories. One even suggested that the Russians had spirited the submarine away, a story very much in line with later reports that the frogman, Commander Lionel Crabb, was in the Soviet Union instructing Russia's naval divers in the arts of underwater sabotage.

In this climate of speculation and fantasy the decision to close the Admiralty files relating to *Affray* to public scrutiny for 30 years – and in the case of two sets of papers 75 years – inevitably triggered fresh accusations of a cover up, together with claims of a high-level conspiracy to conceal the true facts. These files are now open for inspection, yet even this has failed to silence the sensationalists. And there still remains a small coterie of malcontents who continue to allege that the contents of the board of enquiry's transcripts were tampered with and doctored before their release.

As already noted, the loss of the submarine was attributed to the snort mast breaking away due to metal fatigue. This led to the sea flooding into the hull, although an automatic induction valve at the inboard end of the tube should have closed to prevent this

250

happening. Whether this valve was open or closed has never been established. It was, however, officially accepted that, as an alternative hypothesis, a battery explosion may have resulted in fatal damage to the external battery ventilation system which could also lead to catastrophic flooding. It should be noted that there was no evidence of such damage on the outside of the hull.

Finally, and very reluctantly, it was acknowledged that *Affray* might have been in collision with another ship, although, again, there was no external evidence to support such a theory.

Those favouring the cover-up theory claimed that, despite her recent construction – she was barely six years old – *Affray* had been overworked and boasted a tally of sea-miles far in excess of an average *A*-class boat. She was said to be in a poor condition and there were claims of engine problems, oil leaks and minor explosions in the battery compartment, the latter being a common fault in this class of submarine. It was also alleged that the 'top brass' had insisted on *Affray* going to sea despite her commander's misgivings about her mechanical and structural integrity. As a final trump card, she was overloaded. This latter claim is difficult to dispute for she sailed with seventy-five men aboard, which was fourteen more than her normal complement. Among those embarked was a twenty-strong instructional class of sub-lieutenants and a four-man Royal Marine landing-party. To balance these passengers, ten members of the regular crew were left ashore at Portsmouth, although this was less than a half of the additional personnel crammed on board when she sailed.

There is little real evidence to support claims of serious mechanical or structural faults, although Lieutenant John Goddard, in 1951 a Leading Seaman and one of the fortunate ten men left ashore, insists that he gave evidence to the subsequent board of enquiry that *Affray*'s captain had told him that there were problems with oil leaks and 'some trouble in the No 1 battery tank' before the submarine set out on her final journey. He later alleged that this statement was amended in the transcript to the effect that he, Goddard, was aware of 'no problems' with the vessel. In a radio programme about the tragedy in 1999 the widow of *Affray*'s commanding officer, Lieutenant John Blackburn DSC, said that, for the only time in his life, her husband had not wanted to go to sea on that particular occasion, although he gave her no reasons for his misgivings. But apart from the not unusual grumbling letters to their loved ones at home while the submarine was in the Far East, not a solitary piece of corroborative evidence has been produced to indicate any official motive for a cover-up.

One possible reason for the surprise closure of the files emerged in 1975 when Rear Admiral E.N. Poland's book *The Torpedomen* made its appearance. In this he revealed that the Admiralty Underwater Countermeasures & Weapons Establishment at Weymouth had been 'radiographing' mines using a cobalt-60 source and it is very probable that, during that particular period of the Cold War, the government did not want the Soviet navy to know they were employing X-ray technology for mine clearance. All attempts to photograph the snort mast induction valve in the months immediately following discovery of *Affray* had failed and, as a last resort, it was decided to employ the special cameras and radioactive isotopes from the Weymouth establishment to X-ray through the hull in the hope of obtaining a photographic image of the suspect valve.

Such a project would have had a top-secret classification which could explain why certain Admiralty papers were subject to a 75-year closure period. In the event, however, everything went wrong for, according to Rear-Admiral Poland, while divers were preparing to take the X-ray pictures the cobalt-60 isotope slipped out of its extemporised cradle and rolled under the submarine's hull where it proved too dangerous to recover. The Rear-Admiral's account concluded: 'It still lies in close proximity to *Affray*, providing a hazard to anyone venturing too near for generations to come. At least it ensures that . . . *Affray* will be left in peace.'

Many sceptics seized on this last sentence and claimed that the incident had been contrived to frighten off unofficial divers from examining the wreck and possibly finding something which the Admiralty wished to hide. The fact that Royal Navy teams continued to dive on the submarine into the 1990s certainly suggests that the area was not as dangerous as official sources alleged. However, the enactment of the *Protection of Military Remains Bill* in 1986 now provides the authorities with legal powers to prevent illicit interference with wrecked ships and aircraft, and such subterfuge, if the isotope story was untrue, is no longer required.

Before moving on from the use of radiography this seems an appropriate moment to dispose of another rather distasteful story promulgated by a contemporary author which must have upset the families and friends of those lost in the submarine. According to his account: 'The task [of X-raying] proved harder than expected and great chunks of *Affray*'s casing had to be ripped away using a grab before the valve could be exposed.' An experienced and completely independent diver who examined the wreck shortly before the statutory ban on such expeditions was imposed confirmed to me personally that, as the Admiralty had already stated, there was no external damage visible on *Affray*'s hull other than that caused by the failure of the snorkel mast. Unless evidence to the contrary can be produced it seems safe to conclude that this rather unedifying story is apocryphal.

Nevertheless several puzzling facts remain. The A-class submarines were notorious for minor battery explosions, due, probably, to a design flaw in their ventilation systems. The remote possibility of such an explosion on board *Affray* was offered as an alternative cause for her loss by First Lord of the Admiralty James Callaghan when he made a statement to the House of Commons in the aftermath of the tragedy. However, it is generally agreed that an internal explosion powerful enough to sink the submarine would have normally left visible hull damage. Another interesting point was made in *The Engineer* (18 May 1951): 'The *Affray*-class [submarines], if extensively flooded . . . tend to lie at a large angle on the bottom.' In this instance the allegedly flooded boat was resting on an even keel with only a slight list. Such matters, however, are puzzles and not mysteries, and they certainly do not constitute grounds for accusations of cover-ups and conspiracies.

The feasibility of collision with another vessel was virtually ruled out by official sources, especially in view of the absence of damage to the submarine. But a few years ago I received a letter from a correspondent who wished to remain anonymous, the contents of which merit being placed on record. The writer's friend had been an officer on a British freighter, the name of which I prefer to with-hold. On the night *Affray* went down he was on watch duty but had dozed off to sleep, leaving only the ship's Chinese coxswain at the helm. He was awakened by a 'sudden bump' and was convinced that the vessel had struck a submerged object. A deeply religious man, he was so upset by the incident that he sought the advice of a priest who told him to give up the sea for a year as a penance for his dereliction of duty. Convinced that he had been responsible for sinking *Affray*, he obeyed the priest's instructions and went to North America where, sadly, he and his wife were killed in a light aircraft crash a few months later.

A check on the ship's movements during the night in question revealed a distinct possibility of it being in the vicinity of Hurd Deep at the relevant time, although this conclusion relied on a number of unconfirmed assumptions. Unfortunately the vessel's logbook could not be traced as the merchantman had changed ownership several times since 1951 and is now registered with a South American company which failed to respond to my enquiries. It is thus possible that the freighter grazed the snort mast of *Affray* as Lieutenant Blackburn rose to periscope depth around dawn to fix his position and that, weakened by metal fatigue, this glancing impact was sufficient to snap it off and allow the sea to flood the submarine. I can offer no factual evidence to support this account and the central figure is now dead. In addition the number of unconfirmed assumptions involved make the scenario highly improbable. Nevertheless, it is a plausible explanation of how *Affray* met her end.

The only real mystery in the entire tragedy is the identity of the man who finally located the submarine on 14 June 1951. In his book *Subsunk* Captain Shelford implies that it was found by routine, in police parlance, leg-work. All the asdic contacts in the area were marked on the chart and the diving ship *Reclaim* methodically examined the wrecks one by one. In his own words: 'On 14 June *Reclaim* put down a diver in an observation chamber on what was known as *Contact J for Jig*. Although visibility was bad he reported he could see a gleaming white rail, the first time we had seen anything not covered in rust . . . the television camera was sent down [and] it immediately threw a picture on the screen of the rails around the submarine's gun-tower and, one by one, the letters Y-A-R-F-F-A appeared.' Shelford gives no indication that *Reclaim* was specifically directed to the wreck site and, as noted in my original text on page 202, he had identified Captain Foster-Brown's asdic contact which had 'nearly knocked him off the bridge' as being some 75 miles from where *Affray* lay on the bottom.

Captain (later Rear-Admiral) Roy Foster-Brown, in command of the 6th Frigate Squadron, told a very different story. Having spend weeks fruitlessly searching the English Channel with asdic detection equipment, the former submarine officer tried to visualize the intentions of Lieutenant Blackburn on the night of 16/17 April and concluded that *Affray* would have probably been in the vicinity of Hurd Deep at around dawn. He therefore directed his four *Loch*-class frigates to carry out a further search of the area the following day, but told them that this time they should use Type 162 echo-sounding gear rather than the asdic equipment they had employed previously.

Within hours of resuming the search Foster-Brown's own ship, *Loch Insh*, picked up a contact so powerful that 'it nearly blew me out of my chair [on the bridge]'. It was unquestionably the echo of a submarine and the captain promptly radioed his discovery to C-in-C Plymouth with an urgent request for *Reclaim* to be despatched to the scene so that her divers could investigate the contact with their new underwater television camera.

Rather strangely, this radio message was not referred to by Shelford who had, as we have seen, implied that *Reclaim* had sent her divers down during a routine process of elimination. Even more odd, and literally quoting Foster-Brown's own words, he had attributed the echo-sounding contact – which he referred to as an asdic echo – to a false alarm some days previously approximately 75 miles away from *Affray*'s true resting place. Furthermore he said that he had personally sent Foster-Brown on this wild goose chase as the result of 'evidence [sic] coming in from every sort of clair-voyant, mystic or dreamer in the country'. To be taken in by such mumbo jumbo suggests that Bill Shelford was by then a desperate man clutching at straws. This false trail has only served to muddy the waters, for, if Shelford's account was accurate, what had caused Foster-Brown to pick up such a strong echo in the wrong place? Only one conclusion can be inferred from these apparent contra-dictions. The incident, as described by Shelford, was for some obscure reason a total fiction.

In a letter to the press some forty years later Rear-Admiral Roy Foster-Brown revealed something rather more disturbing. When appointed as Director of Signals two years after the *Affray* disaster he had asked to see the relevant files on the tragedy. He told a journalist that, when they had been put on his desk, 'I was shocked and disgusted' by what he had found. It appeared that another officer, whom he refused to name but identified as the Director of Training and Anti-submarine Warfare, had stolen the credit for finding *Affray*, even though he had played no role in the search operation. To make matters worse he had even alleged that Foster-Brown's return to Hurd Deep was the direct result of orders which he had personally issued.

The Rear-Admiral also failed to find any trace of his radio signal to C-in-C Plymouth which had been transmitted from *Loch Insh* very shortly after the vital echo-sounding contact. The *Daily Mail* gave the name of the officer concerned, but it will not be repeated here as doubts exist about his correct identity. The newspaper's report claimed that the suspected person had been elevated to flag-rank ahead of Foster-Brown. The latter's obituary in the *Daily Telegraph*, however, stated that, despite these alleged behind-the-scenes machinations, the culprit failed to gain promotion.

Roy Foster-Brown admitted that he had been deeply hurt by the Admiralty's refusal to acknowledge his pivotal role in finding *Affray*, although he tried to have the record corrected on several occasions. But right up to his death at the age of 94, like the true gentleman that he was, the Rear-Admiral refused to identify the officer who denied him the credit for what he had achieved. Let us respect his discretion by doing the same.

As Rear-Admiral Poland observed in *The Torpedomen* may we also hope 'that *Affray* will [now] be left in peace'.

—SIXTEEN—

'Deliver us, O Lord'

In the preceding pages we have examined more than two hundred submarine disasters ranging from such tragedies as *Thresher*, *Thetis*, *Komsomolets* and *Kursk* to the often hilarious antics of the steam-driven K-boats and John Philip Holland's running battle with the Fenian Brotherhood. They resulted from a whole gamut of causes: human error, structural failures, mechanical faults, ignorance, collisions, the accidental detonation of torpedoes and mines, battery explosions, negligence, chlorine gas, carbon dioxide poisoning and destruction in error by friendly forces. The list seems endless in its variation and infinite in its permutations.

We have seen, too, the courage of men fighting for survival in the face of terrifying death. We have read of long hours trapped inside a flooded submarine breathing air so poisoned and contaminated that the human brain can no longer function coherently; of the men rescued from the *Squalus* after forty hours on the bottom and the crew of *K.13* released from entombment after their incredible fifty-seven hour ordeal in Gareloch; and the unlucky ones who survived only to die in the moment of their deliverance; the men from *Truculent* swept to oblivion by the tide; the crew of *K.17* cut to pieces by the destroyers speeding through the darkness of night; and the gallant fighters of the *USS Tang* tortured and killed by those who had dragged them from the sea.

What, then, of the years that lie ahead? Lacking reliable up-to-date information and hamstrung by the demands of security, the historian is in a difficult situation when he attempts to relate the

257

events of the past to the conjectural happenings of the future. But by making use of the facts available it is possible to reach some conclusions and to make a few tentative predictions.

One immediate inference is that the frequency of accidents is directly related to the number of submarines in service. This, however, is a fallacy as the statistics of peacetime disasters demonstrate. In very round figures there were some 350 submarines at sea in 1915 and in the preceding period (1910-1914) losses averaged 2.6 boats per year. By 1939 the world total of submarines had risen to approximately 650 with a loss-rate in the twenty years 1919-1939 of 2.2 per annum – only marginally less that the pre-World War One era when there were far fewer boats. Yet by 1975, when there were more than 850 submarines in service, the annual accident rate over the preceding fifteen-year period had fallen to 1.6

Many of the reasons for this welcome decline have their origins in history. In the early days, for example, much less was known about the construction of underwater vessels. Design technology was frequently no more than trial and error – a situation analogous to pioneer aircraft manufacturers who also had to learn the hard way. The crews, as we have seen, were often only semi-trained and their officers lacked the necessary experience. Indeed, even today, some experts attribute Russia's alarming disaster rate in recent years to inadequate training and the poor educational standards of conscripted crews. Finally, the early vessels were not always operated to best advantage or with sufficient regard for safety.

The prime function of the submarine in the 1900s was coastal defence and this meant working in shallow inshore waters where the crowded shipping lanes increased the risk of collision with surface vessels. Such dangers were unavoidable in the initial stages of development as the early submarines were cranky, unreliable boats totally unsuited to the rigors of the open sea and it would be unfair to blame flag officers and flotilla captains on this account. But, having said this, there is little doubt that senior officers misunderstood the true role of the submarine as a lone predator and tried to operate them in tidy disciplined groups under the control of a flotilla commander in a cruiser or a destroyer. The multiple collision off May Island in 1918 in which two K-boats were lost is perhaps the prime example of this ill-conceived theory.

There were, of course, many other less dramatic but equally valid reasons why the pioneer submarines were so vulnerable. Until the advent of nuclear-powered boats the submarine could not live beneath the sea. Its underwater endurance was relatively brief and it was forced to regain the upper air at frequent intervals to recharge its batteries. In addition the capacity of its electric motors, limited by the amp-hour life of the accumulators, was not much more than an hour and, even in later designs, twelve hours at the most. Submarines which remained submerged for long periods during the war – *Tetrarch* stayed down for forty-three hours on one occasion in the Second World War – spent most of the time resting on the seabed with their motors switched off. Thus an in-built feature of the earlier submarines was the necessity to return to the surface at frequent intervals.

It will have been apparent from the many incidents described in these pages that a high proportion of disasters have resulted from collisions while the submarine was either rising to, or running on, the surface. And it follows that the more often a submarine has to seek the upper air the greater the risk of its involvement with another vessel. In addition the older boats spent a good deal of their submerged time at periscope depth and, as we have seen, there were many instances when a deep-laden surface ship had sufficient draught to strike the conning-tower and even the pressure hull of a submarine when it was running submerged and maintaining periscope watch.

By contrast the nuclear submarine can run forty or fifty days without once rising to the surface and, thanks to the snorkel tube which draws air into the diesel engines while submerged, even conventionally powered boats no longer have to come up to recharge their batteries. Both factors have greatly reduced the risk of collision, although, ironically, this was not the prime intention of the designers, who were only seeking to improve the submarine as a weapon of war. The safety factor was an unplanned bonus.

It is chastening to discover that tests on *Thresher*'s class-mate, *Tinosa,* which were made *after* the disaster in 1963, revealed that when the submarine was under deep submergence conditions the high-pressure air system iced up and cut off the air flowing into the main ballast tanks. That is to say it was unable to expel the water ballast so that positive buoyancy could be restored in the event of a power failure, and even when the offending filters were removed the compressed air reserves proved to be only sufficient to blow *half* of the tanks!

These findings were a damning indictment of so-called high technology and a poor return for the unlimited funds made available for the development of America's nuclear-powered submarine programme. They were design failures that should never have been allowed to happen. But they *did* and it is difficult to understand how or why. The fault, we are told, has now been eliminated.

The *Thresher* and *Scorpion* disasters hit the scientists and top brass of the US Navy like a bombshell and did much to destroy the outdated 19th Century complacency of modern high-technology. As a result submarines are now subject to the most stringent tests at all stages of design and construction including ultra-sonic and X-ray examination of their hulls. For the sake of the men who go down to the sea in the world's nuclear submarine fleets it is reassuring to know that the scientists are now actively thinking in terms of safety and are no longer solely concerned with producing bigger submarines capable of making larger and louder bangs on targets that are at greater and greater distances from the firing point.

* * * * * * *

Rescue operations and escapes from sunken submarines have made up an important part of this history of underwater disaster, and rightly so. For it is man's steadfast fortitude in the face of impossible odds that gives purpose to what would otherwise be no more than a macabre catalogue of material and human destruction.

Until 1939 the United States had, in general, adopted escape routines similar to those employed by the Royal Navy with the emphasis on individual survival. But the success of the *Squalus* rescue turned thoughts towards multiple escapes with the aid of externally controlled diving bells. And this aspect of underwater survival was given additional impetus in the post-war period with the advent of nuclear-powered vessels and the greater depths at which they are designed to operate. Development, however, was slow. And it was only after a major disaster that the necessary funds were made available.

Within days of the *Thresher* tragedy a Deep Submergence Systems Review Group was set up to assess the situation and it was given a generous five-year period in which to come up with the answer. Its brief was to 'develop a deep-submergence rescue vehicle (DSRV) which could operate below the collapse depth of our fleet submarines and which could search for and rescue surviving personnel.'

The value of the bathyscaphe *Trieste* had already been recognized a number of years before the *Thresher* went down and the US Navy had purchased the vessel from Professor Jacques Piccard in 1957. Its potential was vividly illustrated in 1960 when it reached a depth of 35,800 feet in the Challenger Deep in a Marianas and it was clear that the new DSRV must be based on a combination of the bathyscaphe and the McCann rescue-bell. By 1966 the Review Group's plans had matured sufficiently for orders to be placed with Lockheed for the first two Deep Submergence Rescue Vessels. *DSRV-1* was laid down on 24 January, 1970.

On delivery in August, 1971, it was found that *DSRV-1* had cost a staggering $41,000,000 to develop and it was small consolation that *DSRV-2*, completed the following year, had halved this prodigious expenditure to a mere $23,000,000. Both vessels carry a crew of three and are capable of lifting twenty-four survivors on each ascent. Like the McCann bell the DSRV seats itself onto a special escape hatch on the submarine's hull and, thanks to improvements in technology, a watertight coupling can be obtained with the sunken boat listing up to 45° from the horizontal.

The two prototype DSRVs weigh 35 tons, have an overall length of 49.2 feet, and diameter of 8 feet. Their conventional cigar-shaped sppearance is misleading, for the onlooker sees only the outer shell. Inside this fibreglass casing are three interconnected spheres made from HY-140 steel which contain the operating crew, the rescue chamber and airlock, and the passenger space. Using a combination of propellers and thrusters the vessels can make a 5-knot maximum on their special electric motors and have a diving endurance of 12 hours at 3 knots. Their depth limit is stated to be 5,000 feet.

Unlike the McCann rescue diving-bell, which has itself been updated and can now accommodate eight survivors from a maximum depth of 800 feet, the DSRV is launched from a *submerged* mother submarine and survivors are transhipped to the parent vessel under water instead of being returned directly to the surface. Both launching and recovery take place at approximately 500 feet but the technical thinking behind this rather unusual system of operation is not known.

It was planned to put six DSRVs into service and they were to be supported by three mother-ships – the submarines *Halibut, Finback,* and *Hawkbill.* Two DSRVs were to be based at each of San Diego, Charleston and New London and, in the event of a *Subsunk* emergency, one vessel would be flown to the mothership nearest to the disaster in a giant Lockheed C-5 jet cargo aircraft backed by a specialized road transport unit.

But despite the grandiose programme set out by the Deep Submergence Systems Review Group only two of the original DSRVs, now named *Mystic* and *Avalon,* were built and nothing more has been heard of the other projected units. One reason for this failure to construct any further DSRVs was officially attributed to a cost over-run of 1,500%. Sceptics, however, questioned the value of the DSRV on other grounds, pointing out that as they were intended to operate *below* the crushing depth of the crippled submarine there were unlikely to be any survivors still alive to be rescued. However, within the limits of safe submergence, that is to say where the hull of the submarine remains intact, there is little doubt that the DSRV will prove to be a useful rescue vehicle, especially at depths below 800 feet, the maximum safe diving limit of the latest McCann-type rescue bell.

As it happens there have been no disasters in recent years to test the practical viability of the DSRV under operational conditions, but in September, 1986, *Mystic* took part in an exercise off Stavanger during which she evacuated a substantial number of 'survivors' from an American submarine as it lay 'disabled' on the floor of the Norwegian Sea. The exercise, which included a piggy-back ride to the rescue zone by the *Mystic* clamped to the outer casing of the submarine *Billfish,* proved a complete success. As similar exercises now take place on a regular basis and include both American and NATO naval forces the prognosis for survival in the event of a major underwater accident is decidedly better than it was even a decade ago.

Until the recent establishment of the UK Submarine Rescue Service the Royal Navy continued to put its trust in the free-escape system and the collapsible twill trunk which, it will be recalled, Ruck-Keene had wanted to scrap nearly fifty years ago. As this history of underwater disasters has demonstrated it is a system that has had both successes and failures. But instruction in free escape procedures still remains an important and integral part of the submarine training programme at Fort Blockhouse where every prospective submariner is required to make a free ascent in the escape tank that forms such a prominent feature of the Gosport landscape. Training is for real and, although all possible safety precautions are taken, the occasional tragic accident still occurs. And even as these words are being written British newspapers are carrying reports of a fatality during a routine underwater escape simulation in the Fort Blockhouse training tank.*

Immersion suits have been updated in design and remain standard issue, and it is interesting to note that Britain's first nuclear submarine, *Dreadnought*, was designed to incorporate one-man escape chambers similar in concept to those suggested by the Ruck-Keene Committee back in 1946. Clearly, even at that time, individual escape was still the Admiralty's preferred policy in the event of an underwater accident.

Until recently the only significant change in the Royal Navy's approach to submarine survival was the switch to BIBS – Built-in Breathing System – similar in principle to Momsen's pre-war central oxygen manifold pioneered by the US Navy. This obviates the necessity for individual breathing apparatus and is intended for use during the dangerous flooding-up period. A mixture composed of 60% oxygen and 40% nitrogen is fed into the central manifold from pressurised cylinders and survivors can draw their requirements through flexible rubber mouthpieces. A demand valve ensures that the mixture is not wasted and there is also provision to tap into the manifold for the inflation of life-jackets.

But despite the elaborate equipment and the rigorous training that goes with it, the free-escape method is of doubtful utility at depths approaching 300 feet. And it needs hardly be added that most nuclear submarines habitually operate a depths far below 300 feet.

The Royal Navy, however, is now following in the footsteps of its American cousin and since 1983 has retained on permenant contract a manned submersible, *LR5*, owned by a commercial company, Cable & Wireless Marine, with technological backing from another private concern, Rumic Ltd. *LR5* is 9.8 metres in length and has a beam of 3 metres. Its pressure hull is constructed

*Able Seaman Adam Twells was accidently drowned during an exercise on 14 July, 1995]

from glass-reinforced plastic and it is powered by a 10 HP 120-volt DC motor with an endurance range of six to ten hours and a maximum speed of two knots. The vessel's four-man crew are all civilian specialists.

LR5 is intended to form an integral part of the NATO submarine rescue organization and may find itself working alongside the Italian mini-submersible *MSM1* or one of the American DSRVs. In addition to this manned submersible the Royal Navy also owns and operates *Scorpio 45*, a remotely controlled unmanned underwater vehicle whose primary function is to carry out television and video surveys of a sunken submarine and to transfer life-support stores and equipment to survivors via the boat's escape hatch. Such stores would include oxygen candles and carbon-dioxide absorbant to keep the air inside the submarine breathable for the duration of the rescue operation.

The Royal Navy's Submarine Escape and Rescue Project only came into being in 1992 and at this early stage it is not possible to provide a detailed account of its work. Its stated purpose is to support the Flag Officer Submarines and the Submarine Escape Training Tank at Fort Blockhouse (*HMS Dolphin*); to provide rescue facilities and develop escape and rescue equipment; and to act as the focal point for all operational and material aspects of submarine rescue. Suffice it to say that the establishment of such a service by the Ministry of Defence Support Command demonstrates that the authorities now recognize the need for instant response and the application of advanced technology in the pursuit of submarine safety. And so far as the Royal Navy and NATO are concerned it augers well for the future.

Before closing this review of the latest developments it must be added that several other navies are now organizing search and rescue systems on the lines of those being pioneered by Britain and the United States. Italy, as befits the nation that first created the mini-submarine and the human torpedo, has its own submersible *MSM1*; Russia and Japan are both building their own DSRVs; while Korea is procuring an *LR5K* from Britain. Australia, Libya, Finland, Pakistan and Taiwan are all in the process of acquiring some form of underwater rescue vehicle in the near future.

* * * * * * * * *

Despite the end of the Cold War there are still some 30,000 men living and working beneath the surface of the sea every hour of the day and night as the submarines of the world's navies ply their lawful occasions. At this precise moment submarines are cruising beneath the icecaps of the North Pole seeking each other out in a monstrous game of hide-and-seek. Others are stalking the depths of the Atlantic and Pacific Oceans ready to release their megaton missiles on receipt of a coded signal from Washington, Moscow, London, Paris and, in all probablity, Beijing. Still more are nosing the warm waters of the Mediterranean and the Caribbean, patrolling the coastlines of Latin America, guarding the shipping routes of southern Africa, moving stealthily through the China Sea and carefully quartering the vast wastes of the Indian Ocean.

All, regardless of nationality, run the same risks of death and disaster. For the submariner of 2002 shares the self-same dangers as the submariner of 1902. And like his predecessors in history he carries out his duties with the same dedicated vigilance remembering always that 'a trifling mistake can be a possible cause of serious danger'.

In the words of the old naval prayer: *Deliver us, O Lord, from the perils of the sea and the violence of the enemy.* As we recall the disasters of the past let us all say a fervent amen to that.

AUTHOR'S NOTE TO APPENDICES

It is not always easy to classify certain types of accident. Does a submarine that runs aground, or founders in harbour, without casualties and which is subsequently refloated and returned to service qualify as an accidental loss? And should a submarine that loses half its crew in an engine-room or battery explosion and yet remains afloat be excluded? I have had to apply my personal judgement in such cases and, in some instances, the reader may disagree with my classification. But, subject to these reservations, Appendix Two can be regarded as definitive. In the nature of things Appendix One can only be speculative, although it is the result of exhaustive research.

Statistics are often misleading and the totals shown in the war loss sections of other appendices are only as accurate as the official records on which they are based.

In wartime many submarines are simply posted as 'overdue and presumed lost'. A high proportion of such losses are almost certainly attributable to minefields and enemy action. But, equally, accidents and human error will have accounted for some of the casualties. Sadly, the true fate of these missing submarines will never be known. This qualification should be borne in mind when examining the loss statistics in the later appendices.

Finally, and a cause of great difficulty during research, many submarines lost by accident were salvaged and returned to service. As a result reference books frequently show a disposal date considerably later than the loss date ascribed to it in these appendices. This fact does not, of course, invalidate the entry in the relative appendix nor the statistical analyses.

APPENDIX 1 Pioneer & experimental submarines lost before 1 January 1900

Date	Submarine	Origin	Location	Cause	Lost	Survived
1719	Timsah [Crocodile] a	Turkey	Off Seraglio Point	Not known	0	5
20 Jun 1774	John Day's Maria	Britain	Plymouth Sound	Design fault	1	0
1831	Cervo's submarine	Spain	?	Design fault	1	0
1834	Dr Petit's submarine	France	St Valery-sur-Somme	Design fault	1	0
1 Feb 1851	Bauer's Brandtaucher	Germany	Kiel harbour	Human error	0	3
1851	Philip's submarine	USA	Lake Erie	Dived too deeply	1	0
1855	Scott Russell's submarine	Britain	River Thames	Design fault	3 ?	0
2 Oct 1856	Bauer's Diable Marin b	Russia	Kronstadt harbour	Navigational hazard (Salvaged)	0	14
1856	Bauer's Diable Marin b	Russia	Orchada	No details available	–	–
Feb 1863	Pioneer	US Confed	Lake Pontchartrain	Foundered c	?	?
2 Apr 1863	Alligator	US Union	Chesapeake Bay	Foundered in storm	?	?
1863	McLintock's American Diver	US Confed	Mobile Bay	Foundered while under tow	–	–
1863	H.L. Hunley	US Confed	Charleston harbour	Swamped (Salvaged)	8	1
Aug 1863	H.L. Hunley	US Confed	Charleston	Foundered in storm (Salvaged)	6	3
1863	H.L. Hunley	US Confed	Ft Johnson, Charleston	Capsized in collision (Salvaged)	5	4
15 Oct 1863	H.L. Hunley	US Confed	Stone river, Charleston	Diving error (Salvaged)	9	0
1863	H.L. Hunley	US Confed	Charleston harbour	Fouled lines (Salvaged)	7	0
17 Feb 1864	H.L. Hunley	US Confed	Charleston Roads	Entangled with target (Raised in 2000)	9	0
Apr 1865	Plongeur	France	Rochefort	Design fault	0	12
1866	Flach's submarine	Chile–Peru	Valpariso Bay	Design fault	8	0
1868	Potpourri	Russia	St Petersburg	Design fault	1 ?	0

APPENDIX 1 (Continued)

Date	Submarine	Origin	Location	Cause	Lost	Survived
1871	Aleksandrovski-type	Russia	Near St Petersburg	Crushed during diving tests d	?	?
1872	Intelligent Whale	USA	Newark, NJ	Design fault (Salvaged)	13	0
1872	Intelligent Whale	USA	Newark, NJ	Design fault (Salvaged)	13	0
1872	Intelligent Whale	USA	Newark, NJ	Design fault (Raised later)	13	0
22 May 1878	Holland II	USA	Upper Passiac River, NJ (Salvaged)	Human error on launching	–	–
26 Feb 1880	Resurgam	Britain	Off Rhyl	Foundered in tow	–	–
Nov 1883	Holland IV	US	Long Island Sound	Foundered in tow	–	–
Nov 1883	Fenian Ram (Holland III)	US	Mill River, New Haven, Conn.	Swamped while under tow	0	1
1885	Peacemaker	US	Hudson River	Design fault	0	3
1886	Holland V (Zalinsky boat)	US	Fort Hamilton, NY	Design fault	–	–
1887	Nautilus (Campbell & Ash)	Britain	Tilbury docks, Essex	Design fault. Regained surface	0	All
18 Sep 1888	Nordenfelt II	Britain e	Coast of Jutland	Ran aground under tow	–	–
1897	Plunger (Holland VII)	US	New York	Capsized on launching	–	–

Notes: While every effort has been made to check these entries they should not, for obvious reasons, be regarded as definitive.

a Designed by Ibrahim Effendi. Oar-powered and probably similar to Van Drebbel's vessel. (See text)

b German name Seeteufel [Sea Devil]

c An earlier Confederate submarine, sometimes named as Pioneer, was scuttled to avoid capture at New Orleans in 1861. This has been classified as lost by enemy action.

d This might be the same vessel as Potpourri shown earlier as lost in 1868. Russian sources are often unreliable.

e Purchased by Russia but never paid for after sinking.

268

APPENDIX 2 Naval submarines lost by accident or error since 1900

Date	Submarine	Origin	Location	Cause	Lost	Survived
1903	Adder	USA	?	Lost while under tow to exercise area	–	–
1903	Moccasin	USA	?	Lost while under tow to exercise area	–	–
1904	Plunger	USA	Watch Hill, RI	Lost while under tow to exercise area. Ran ashore	–	–
18 Mar 1904	A.1	Britain	Spithead, Portsmouth	Collision with SS Berwick Castle	11	0
20 Jun 1904	Delfin	Russia	River Neva	Swamped by passing ship	26	6
8 Jul 1905	A.8	Britain	Plymouth Sound	Foundered while changing crews	15	4
6 Jul 1905	Farfadet	France	Lake Bizerta	Human error. Hatch not secured	14	3
16 Oct 1905	A.4	Britain	Stokes Bay, Portsmouth	Human error. Swamped by passing vessel	0	11
13 Aug 1906	Esturgeon	France	Saigon, Indo-China	Sank in dock	0	5
17 Oct 1906	Lutin	France	Lake Bizerta	Flooded due to leaks in hull plating	14	0
17 Jan 1907	Algerien	France	Cherbourg dockyard	Flooded due to mooring error	–	–
19 Jun 1907	Gymnote	France	Toulon	Flooded in dock. Human error	2	2
5 Jul 1907	Bonite	France	?	Flooded in dock. Human error	–	–
6 Aug 1907	Castor	France	?	Unspecified accident	0	5
15 Oct 1908	Fresnel	France	?	Unspecified accident	0	5
26 Apr 1909	Foca	Italy	Naples harbour	Internal explosion	14	12
12 Jun 1909	Kambala	Russia	Off Sevastopol	Rammed by battleship Rostislav	20	4
14 Jul 1909	C.11	Britain	Off Cromer	Collision with SS Eddystone	13	2
15 Apr 1910	No 6	Japan	Off Kure, Hiroshima Bay	Diving error	14	0
26 May 1910	Pluviose	France	2 miles from Calais	Collision with SS Pas de Calais	27	0
1 Jun 1910	Forel	Russia	?	Sank while being towed	–	–
17 Nov 1911	U-3	Germany	Kiel harbour	Submerged with ventilator open	3	28
2 Feb 1912	A.3	Britain	Off Isle of Wight	Collision with HMS Hazard	14	0
8 Jun 1912	Vendemiaire	France	Near Cherbourg	Rammed by battleship St Louis	24	0

APPENDIX 2 (Continued)

Date	Submarine	Origin	Location	Cause	Lost	Survived
4 Oct 1912	B.2	Britain	Near Dover	Collision with German SS Amerika	15	1
11 Oct 1912	F.1	USA	Port Watsonville, Calif.	Broke moorings in heavy seas	2	0
10 Dec 1913	C.14	Britain	Plymouth Sound	Collision with Hopper No 27	0	20
16 Jan 1914	A.7	Britain	Whitesand Bay	Diving failure. Cause never established	11	0
31 Jan 1914	0-5	Holland	Scheldt Quay	Mechanical failure – tube doors open	1	19
Mar 1914	Minoga	Russia	Off Libau	Ventilator open while diving	0	20
7 Jul 1914	Calypso	France	Off Cape Lardier	Rammed by submarine Circe	3	23
14 Sep 1914	AE-1	Australia	Bismarck Sea	Disappeared. Reason not established	30 d	0
17 Jan 1915	Saphir	France	Dardanelles	Ran aground while detouring minefield	14	13
21 Jan 1915	U-7	Germany	North Sea	Torpedoed in error by U-22	28	1
25 Mar 1915	F.4	USA	Honolulu	Corroded battery tank caused flooding	21	0
17 Apr 1915	E.15	Britain	Dardanelles	Ran aground due to navigational hazards	7	23
22 Jun 1915	U-30	Germany	Off Ems River	Diving accident	32	3
2 Jul 1915	UC-2	Germany	North Sea	Ran aground	0	14 e
18 Aug 1915	E.13	Britain	Saltholm Flat	Ran aground – compass failure. Sunk by enemy later	15	16
15 Oct 1915	No 2	Russia	Svjatoj Nos	Ran aground	?	?
21 Oct 1915	UC-9	Germany	North Sea	Blown up by own mines	16	0
30 Oct 1915	Turquoise	France	Dardanelles	Ran aground. Later sunk by gunfire	0	25
4 Nov 1915	UC-8	Germany	Terschelling	Ran aground	0	14
11 Nov 1915	Gepard	Russia	Baltic	Collision with British submarine E.8	?	?
19 Nov 1915	UC-13	Germany	Black Sea	Stranded and foundered in heavy seas	0	14
5 Dec 1915	Fresnel	France	Off coast of Albania	Stranded in fog. Subsequently sunk by enemy	0	26
6 Jan 1916	E.17	Britain	Dutch coast – Texel	Grounded & foundered in heavy seas	0	30

APPENDIX 2 (Continued)

Date	Submarine	Origin	Location	Cause	Lost	Survived
15 Jan 1916	E.2	USA	Brooklyn Navy Yard	Internal explosion. Probably battery gas	5	15 e
19 Jan 1916	H.6	Britain	Schiermonnikoog	Stranded in shallow water. Salvaged by Dutch	0	22
16 Mar 1916	UC-12	Germany	Off Taranto	Blown up on own mines. Seconded to Austria as U-24	12	0
27 Apr 1916	UC-5	Germany	Off Harwich	Stranded on mudbank	0	14
23 May 1916	Som	Russia	Aaland Strait	Collison with SS A.K. Angermanland	?	?
30 Jul 1916	Pullino	Italy	Galiola Island	Beached. Salvaged but subsequently sank in tow	0	21
15 Aug 1916	E.41	Britain	Off Harwich	Collied with E.4 (qv)	16	15
15 Aug 1916	E.4	Britain	Off Harwich	Collided with E.41 (qv)	30 d	0
24 Aug 1916	Gustave Zede	France	?	Battery explosion	4	36
Sep 1916	Bremen	German	Off Norway	Foundered in heavy seas (possibly struck mine)	30 d	0
9 Oct 1916	Dykkeren	Denmark	Off Copenhagen	Collision with Norwegian SS Vesla	1	8
5 Nov 1916	U-20	Germany	Danish coast	Ran aground	0	35
14 Nov 1916	No 4	Japan	Inland Sea	Unspecified accident	2	14
19 Jan 1917	E.36	Britain	North Sea	Collision with submarine E.43	30 d	0
29 Jan 1917	K.13	Britain	Gareloch	Submerged with ventilators open	32	48
14 Feb 1917	F.8	Italy	Two miles off Spezia	Sank during trials	?	26 ?
23 Feb 1917	UC-32	Germany	Off Sunderland	Blown up on own mines	22	4 e
25 Feb 1917	UB-30	Germany	Walcheren	Stranded in shallow water and interned	0	23
10 Mar 1917	Guglielmotti	Italy	NW of Capraia Island	Sunk in error by HMS Cyclamen	14	25 ?
12 Mar 1917	UB-6	Germany	Voorne Island	Stranded and salvaged by Dutch	0	14
17 Mar 1917	A.10	Britain	Ardrossan	Foundered at moorings	–	–
19 Mar 1917	UB-25	Germany	Kiel	Collision with destroyer V.6	16	0

APPENDIX 2 (Continued)

Date	Submarine	Origin	Location	Cause	Lost	Survived
15 Apr 1917	A.5	USA	Cavite, Phillipines	Internal explosion	0	7
16 Apr 1917	C.16	Britain	North Sea	Collision with destroyer *Melampus*	16	0
26 Apr 1917	No 1	Russia	Murmansk	Collision with submarine *Delfin* (qv)	?	?
10 May 1917	UC-76	Germany	Off Heligoland	Blown up by own mines	16	0
19 May 1917	Bars	Russia	Baltic. N of Dago	Sunk in error by Russian destroyer	?	?
26 Jul 1917	UC-61	Germany	Near Cape Gris Nez	Stranded and later scuttled	1	25 e
10 Aug 1917	Delfin	Russia	Murmansk harbour	Foundered after damage incurred on 19 May (qv)	?	?
10 Sep 1917	UC-42	Germany	Irish Sea, S of Cork	Blown up on own mines	27	0
14 Sep 1917	D.2	USA	New London	Sank alongside quay	0	15 e
16 Sep 1917	G.9	Britain	Off Norway	Sunk in error by *HMS Petard*	30	1
17 Sep 1917	UC-45	Germany	North Sea	Diving failure	0	26 e
28 Oct 1917	C.32	Britain	Gulf of Riga	Ran aground. Blown up to avoid capture	0	16 e
29 Oct 1917	U-52	Germany	Kiel dockyard	Accidental torpedo explosion	5	30 e
17 Nov 1917	K.1	Britain	North Sea	Collision with submarine *K.4*	0	56
24 Nov 1917	U-48	Germany	Goodwin Sands	Ran aground & stranded. Sunk by gunfire	0	35
6 Dec 1917	UC-69	Germany	Off Barfleur	Collision with *U-96*	11	18
7 Dec 1917	UB-84	Germany	Baltic	Collision	0	34 e
17 Dec 1917	F.1	USA	Off Point Loma, Calif.	Collision with submarine *F.3* in fog	19	5
1 Feb 1918	K.4	Britain	Firth of Forth	Collision with submarine *K.6*	55	0
1 Feb 1918	K.17	Britain	Firth of Forth	Collision with cruiser *Fearless*	48	8
Feb 1918	Igor	Russia	Near Reval	Submerged with hatch still open	16 d	2
2 Mar 1918	H.5	Britain	Irish Sea	Rammed in error by SS *Rutherglen*	22 d	0
15 Mar 1918	UB-106	Germany	Baltic	Unspecified accident	35	0

APPENDIX 2 (Continued)

Date	Submarine	Origin	Location	Cause	Lost	Survived
12 Mar 1918	D.3	Britain	Off coast of Flanders	Sunk in error by French airship	29	0
16 Apr 1918	H.5	Italy	Southern Adriatic	Sunk in error by British submarine H.1	20	5
28 Apr 1918	Prairial	France	Off Le Havre	Collision with SS Tropic at night	19	6
9 Jul 1918	U-10	Austria	Adriatic	Wrecked – hazard of the sea. (Ex-German UB-1)	0	14 e
10 Jul 1918	UB-65	Germany	Off Cape Clear	Premature torpedo explosion	48	0
2 Aug 1918	Floriel	France	Off Salonika	Collision with Armed Boarding Vessel Hazel	0	26
5 Sep 1918	UC-91	Germany	Baltic	Collision with SS Alexandra Woerman	0	32 e
6 Oct 1918	C.12	Britain	River Humber	Collision following engine failure	0	16
15 Oct 1918	J.6	Britain	North Sea	Sunk in error by British decoy ship Cymric	19	15
21 Oct 1918	UB-89	Germany	Off Kiel	Collision with cruiser Frankfurt	7	27 e
18 Nov 1918	U-165	Germany	River Weser	Collision. (Submarine still under construction ?)	0	39 e
22 Nov 1918	G.11	Britain	Howick	Wrecked by hazard of the sea	2	29
2 Jun 1919	Rucumilla	Chile	Off Talcahuana	Human error while diving	0	25
2 Jul 1919	G.2	USA	Long Island Sound	Foundered – hazard of the sea	3	1
18 Oct 1919	H.41	Britain	Blyth	Damaged by HMS Vulcan and subsequently sank	0	22
1919	C.5	USA	Colo Solo, Canal Zone	Flooded by negligence of dockyard workers	–	–
24 Mar 1920	H.1	USA	Magdalena Bay, Calif.	Ran aground and sank when refloated	4	0
1 Sep 1920	S.5	USA	Off Cape May, NJ	Flooded when pipe burst	0	38

273

Date	Submarine	Origin	Location	Cause	Lost	Survived
20 Jan 1921	K.5	Britain	WSW of Scilly Isles	Failed to surface after diving – reason unknown	57	0
25 Jun 1921	K.15	Britain	Portsmouth dockyard	Hydraulic failure due to hot weather	0	6
26 Sep 1921	R.6	USA	San Pedro, Calif.	Torpedo tubes opened in error	2	18
Oct 1921	O.8	Holland	Den Helder	Sea cock left open in error	0	26
7 Dec 1921	S.48	USA	Long Island Sound	Manhole left open through negligence	0	41
23 Mar 1922	H.42	Britain	Off Gibraltar	Rammed by destroyer HMS Versatile	26	0
17 Jul 1923	S.38	USA	Anchorage Bay, Alaska	Flooded by negligence while moored	0	38 e
18 Aug 1923	L.9	Britain	Hong Kong harbour	Foundered in typhoon	0	5
21 Aug 1923	Ro-31	Japan	Off Kobe	Hatch opened while submerged	88	5
28 Oct 1923	O.5	USA	Limon Bay, Canal Zone	Collision with SS Abangarez	3	18
29 Oct 1923	Ro-52	Japan	Kure harbour	Torpedo tubes opened in error while moored	0	?
10 Jan 1924	L.24	Britain	20m SW Portland Bill	Rammed by battleship HMS Resolution	43	0
19 Mar 1924	Ro-25	Japan	Off Sasebo	Collision with cruiser Tatsuta	46	0
13 Jan 1925	S.19	USA	Nauset, Mass.	Ran aground	0	42 e
29 Jan 1925	S.48	USA	Off Portsmouth, NH	Ran aground. (S.48 had also sunk in dock, 1921)	0	45 e
26 Aug 1925	Veniero	Italy	Off Cape Passero	Collision with SS Capena	54	0
25 Sep 1925	S.51	USA	Off Block Island	Collision with SS City of Rome	33	3
12 Nov 1925	M.1	Britain	Off Start Point, Devon	Collision with SS Vidar	69	0
9 Aug 1926	H.29	Britain	Devonport dockyard	Flooded – hatches left open in error	6	0
1927	Volk (Ex B.1)	Russia	?	Lost during exercise – cause unknown	52 d	0
Sep 1927	Bezhozhnik	Russia	?	Collision with a destroyer	18 f	7

APPENDIX 2 (Continued)

Date	Submarine	Origin	Location	Cause	Lost	Survived
17 Dec 1927	S.4	USA	Off Cape Cod	Rammed by Coast Guard cutter Paulding	40	0
6 Aug 1928	F.14	Italy	W of Brioni Island	Collision with destroyer G. Missori	27	0
3 Oct 1928	Ondine	France	Off Vigo	Collision with Greek SS Ekaterina Goulandris	43	0
9 Jul 1929	H.47	Britain	Off Pembroke coast	Collision with submarine L.2	21 +3 h	3
11 May 1931	Nereus	Greece	Off Pyrgos	Misunderstood order led to flooding	41 d	0
22 May 1931	Rabochiy	Russia	100 miles SE Helsingfors	Rammed by No 4	35	0
9 Jun 1931	Poseidon	Britain	21 miles of Wei-Hai-Wei	Collision with SS Yuta	20	35
Oct 1931	Unidentified	Russia	?	Lost during acceptance trials but salvaged	?	?
24 Oct 1931	L.55	Russia	W of Leningrad	Collision with German SS Grattia	50	0
26 Jan 1932	M.2	Britain	West Bay, Portland	Hangar door opened before fully surfaced	60	0
8 Jul 1932	Promethee	France	Off Cherbourg	Hydraulic failure	66	7
1934	Proletary	Russia	?	Unknown	?	?
1934	Metallist	Russia	?	Unknown	?	?
25 Jul 1935	Tovarich	Russia	Gulf of Finland	Collision with battleship Marat	66	0
Sep 1935	Bolshevik (Ex Rys & B.7)	Russia	?	Unknown	?	?
20 Nov 1936	U-18	Germany	Bight of Lübeck	Collision with tender T.156	8	12
Nov 1937	M-type	Russia	?	?	?	?
1938	M-90	Russia	Off Leningrad	Rammed by tug	?	?
Nov 1938	M-174 (Ex M-91)	Russia	?	Failed to surface during exercises	?	0
Feb 1939	I-63	Japan	Off Bungo Suido	Collision with submarine I-60	81	6

APPENDIX 2 (Continued)

Date	Submarine	Origin	Location	Cause	Lost	Survived
23 May 1939	*Squalus*	USA	Off Isle of Shoals	Failure of main induction valve	26	33
1 Jun 1939	*Thetis*	Britain	Liverpool Bay	Flooded by human error	99	4
15 Jun 1939	*Phenix*	France	NE of Saigon, Indo-China	Diving accident – cause unknown	71	0
24 Jul 1939	*Shch-424*	Russia	Off Murmansk	Collision with trawler	34	0
10 Sep 1939	*Oxley*	Britain	Off Norway	Torpedoed in error by *HMS Triton*	53	2
3 Jan 1940	*S.2*	Russia	?	?	?	?
31 Jan 1940	*U-15*	Germany	Baltic	Collision with torpedo-boat *Iltis*	25	0
6 Mar 1940	*O.11*	Holland	Off Den Helder	Rammed by naval tug	3	27
29 Apr 1940	*Unity*	Britain	Off river Tyne	Collision with SS *Atle Jarl*	2	25
15 Jun 1940	*Macalle*	Italy	Red Sea. Barr Musa Seghir	Ran aground and abandoned due to poisonous fumes	0	44
20 Jun 1940	*O.13*	Holland	Off Norway	Sunk in error by Polish submarine *Wilk*	?	?
3 Aug 1940	*U-25*	Germany	N of Terschelling	Blown up by own mines	49	0
29 Aug 1940	*I-67*	Japan	Off Bonin Island	Foundered in storm	89	0
3 Sep 1940	*U-57*	Germany	Brunsbuttel	Collision with Norwegian SS *Rona*	6	38
8 Oct 1940	*Gemma*	Italy	Aegean Sea	Sunk in error by Italian submarine *Trichero*	44	0
Nov 1940	*Dekabrist (D-1)*	Russia	Arctic	Flooded by human error	?	?
19 Dec 1940	*Sfax*	France	Off Cape Juby	Sunk in error by *U-37*	61	4
20 Jun 1941	*O.9*	USA	Off Isle of Shoals	Foundered	33	0
19 Jul 1941	*Umpire*	Britain	Off The Wash	Collision with trawler *Peter Hendricks*	22	16
29 Sep 1941	*U-579*	Germany	?	Accidental torpedo detonation	2	42 e
2 Oct 1941	*I-61*	Japan	Off Iki Island	Collision with gunboat	70	0
11 Nov 1941	*U-580*	Germany	Off Memel	Collision with target vessel *Angelburg*	12	32 e
15 Nov 1941	*U-583*	Germany	Baltic	Collision with *U-153*	45	0

276

Date	Submarine	Origin	Location	Cause	Lost	Survived
Nov 1941	*Marconi*	Italy	Atlantic	Sunk in error by *U-67*	57	0
Nov 1941	*U-560*	Germany	Off Memel	Collision. Subsequently salvaged	0	45
4 Dec 1941	*U-43*	Germany	Base in Occupied France	Sank alongside. Subsequently salvaged	0	45 e
16 Dec 1941	*U-557*	Germany	SW of Crete	Collision with Italian torpedo-boat *Orione*	43	0
17 Dec 1941	*Ro-66*	Japan	Wake Island	Collision with submarine *Ro-62*	56	3
29 Dec 1941	*Ro-60*	Japan	Kwajalein Atoll	Stranded and wrecked	0	59
20 Jan 1942	*S.36*	USA	Taka Bakong Reef	Ran aground and wrecked	0	42 e
24 Jan 1942	*S.26*	USA	Gulf of Panama	Collision with *USS PC-460*	38	0
18 Feb 1942	*Surcouf*	France	Gulf of Mexico	Collision with American *SS Thompson Lykes*	159	0
Feb 1942	*I-23*	Japan	Off Hawaii	Marine casualty. No details known	96	0
14 Mar 1942	*U-133*	Germany	Off Salamis	Blown up by own mines	45	0
2 May 1942	*Jastrzab*	Poland	Off northern Norway	Sunk in error by British escorts *St Albans & Seagull*	5	37
19 Jun 1942	*S.27*	USA	Amchitka Island	Ran aground and wrecked in bad weather	0	42 e
21 Jun 1942	*P.514*	Britain	NW of Cape Breton	Sunk in error by *HMCS Georgian*	42 f	0
14 Jul 1942	*Atilay*	Turkey	Off Canakkale	Diving accident. Cause unknown	39	0
6 Aug 1942	*U-612*	Germany	Off Danzig	Rammed by *U-144* during training exercise	2	44
13 Aug 1942	*S.39*	USA	Off Rossel Island	Wrecked – hazard of the sea	0	42 e
2 Sep 1942	*U-222*	Germany	Off Danzig	Collision with *U-626* during training	41	4
4 Sep 1942	*Sjoborren*	Sweden	Baltic	Collision with *SS Virginia*	1	33
13 Oct 1942	*L.16*	Russia	Off W coast of USA	Sunk in error by Japanese submarine *I-25*	55f	?

277

APPENDIX 2 (Continued)

Date	Submarine	Origin	Location	Cause	Lost	Survived
Oct 1942	I-22	Japan	Solomon Islands	Marine casualty. Details not known	100	0
4 Nov 1942	RO-65	Japan	Kiska	Struck rocks while running submerged in harbour	19	40
11 Nov 1942	Unbeaten	Britain	Bay of Biscay	Sunk in error by RAF aircraft	36	0
12 Nov 1942	U-272	Germany	Off Hela	Collision with depot ship Hela	28	19
8 Dec 1942	U-254	Germany	Greenland	Collision with U-221 during convoy attack	41	4
1942	Zoea	Italy	Taranto	Sank at moorings	0	?
24 Feb 1943	Vandal	Britain	Off Isle of Arran	Diving failure – cause unknown	37	0
24 Feb 1943	U-649	Germany	Baltic	Collision with U-232	36	11
19 Mar 1943	U-5	Germany	W Of Pilau	Diving accident	20	16
23 Mar 1943	Delfino	Italy	Taranto	Collision with pilot boat	?	?
14 Apr 1943	Ulven	Sweden	Off Marstrand	Neutral vessel sunk by mine	33	?
4 May 1943	U-659	Germany	W of Cape Finisterre	Collision with U-439	44	3
4 May 1943	U-439	Germany	W of Cape Finisterre	Collision with U-659	40	9
30 May 1943	Untamed	Britain	W coast of Scotland	Equipment failure	36	0
12 Jun 1943	R.12	USA	Off Key West	Foundered	42	0
14 Jul 1943	I-179	Japan	Iyo Nada	Marine casualty. Details not known	85	0
5 Aug 1943	U-34	Germany	W of Memel	Collision with depot ship Lech	4	39
12 Aug 1943	Ilern	Sweden	Kalmarsund Strait	Collision with Swedish MS Birkaland	1	30
21 Aug 1943	U-670	Germany	Baltic	Collision with target-ship Bolkoburg	21	22
8 Sep 1943	U-983	Germany	N of Loba	Collision with U-988	5	42
12 Sep 1943	Topazio	Italy	SE of Sardinia	Sunk in error by RAF aircraft	44	0
20 Sep 1943	U-346	Germany	Off Hela	Diving accident [suspected sabotage]	37	0
12 Oct 1943	Dorado	USA	Panama Canal Zone	Sunk in error by US Navy aircraft	76	0
18 Nov 1943	U-718	Germany	Off Bjornholm	Collision with U-476 during training	43	7

APPENDIX 2 (Continued)

Date	Submarine	Origin	Location	Cause	Lost	Survived
20 Nov 1943	*U-768*	Germany	Off Pilau	Collision with *U-745* during training	49	0
21 Dec 1943	*U-284*	Germany	North Atlantic	Damaged by heavy seas and scuttled	0	49
28 Dec 1943	*Axum*	Italy	W coast of Morea	Ran aground and wrecked	0	44
21 Jan 1944	*U-263*	Germany	Off La Pallice	Lost trim and sank while being tested as flak-boat	51	0
14 Feb 1944	*U-738*	Germany	Off Gdynia	Collision with *SS Erna*	22	24
18 Feb 1944	*U-7*	Germany	W of Pilau	Collision during training exercises	26	0
17 Mar 1944	*U-1013*	Germany	Baltic	Collision with *U-286* during training	25	24
17 Mar 1944	*U-28*	Germany	Newsstadt	Sank alongside	1	0
20 Mar 1944	*Graph*	Britain	W coast of Scotland	Sank in tow after accident damage in dock	–	–
26 Mar 1944	*Tullibee*	USA	N of Palau	Struck by own torpedo	79	1
3 Apr 1944	*I-174*	Japan	Central Pacific	Unspecified accident	107	0
4 Apr 1944	*I-169*	Japan	Truk	Flooded in harbour by human error	103	1
6 Apr 1944	*U-455*	Germany	Off Spezia	Blown up by own mines	51	0
8 Apr 1944	*U-2*	Germany	W of Pilau	Collision with trawler *Frose*	16	18
15 May 1944	*U-1234*	Germany	Off Gdynia	Collision with tug	13	32
19 May 1944	*U-1015*	Germany	W of Pilau	Collision with *U-1014* during training	36	14
13 Jun 1944	*I-33*	Japan	E of Leyte	Unspecified accident	92	2
8 Jul 1944	*Perle*	France	North Atlantic	Sunk in error by British aircraft	57	1
27 Jul 1944	*B.1*	Russia	Arctic	Sunk in error by British aircraft	27 d	?
21 Aug 1944	*U-230*	Germany	Nr Toulon	Stranded and then scuttled	0	49
16 Sep 1944	*U-1054*	Germany	Off Hela Scrapped	Rammed by ferry *Peter Wessell.*	0	54
21 Sep 1944	*P-402* a	Russia	Barents Sea	Sunk in error by Russian aircraft	38 d	?
3 Oct 1944	*Seawolf*	USA	Off Morotai	Sunk in error by *USS Rowell*	99 c	0

279

Date	Submarine	Origin	Location	Cause	Lost	Survived
10 Oct 1944	U-2331	Germany	Baltic	Lost during training. (Salvaged)	15	4
21 Oct 1944	U-957	Germany	Lofoten Islands	Rammed by German transport. Written off	0	44 e
24 Oct 1944	U-673	Germany	N of Stavanger	Collision with U-382 (Salvaged)	0	47
24 Oct 1944	Tang	USA	NW of Formosa	Struck by own torpedo	73	15 i
24 Oct 1944	Darter	USA	Bombay Shoal	Navigational error – ran aground	0	80 e
Oct 1944	I-26	Japan	E of Leyte	Unspecified accident	105	0
4 Nov 1944	U-1226	Germany	Atlantic	Probable snorkel failure	56	0
14 Nov 1944	U-2508	Germany	Kattegat	Flooded by open diesel air intake (salvaged)	1	0
15 Nov 1944	Settembrini	Italy	Western Atlantic	Sunk in error by USS Frament	?	?
28 Nov 1944	U-80	Germany	Off Hela	Diving accident during training	48	0
12 Dec 1944	U-416	Germany	W of Pilau	Collision with minesweeper M-203	36	8 e
18 Dec 1944	U-1209	Germany	Wolf Rock	Seriously damaged by hitting rock & scuttled	9	44
19 Dec 1944	U-737	Germany	Lofoten Islands	Collision with minesweeper MRS-25	31	20
30 Dec 1944	U-382	Germany	Baltic	Collision during training	0	44 e
Jan 1945	I-12	Japan	Central Pacific	Unspecified accident	114	0
15 Feb 1945	U-1053	Germany	Off Bergen	Accident during diving exercises	45	0
18 Feb 1945	U-2344	Germany	Off Heiligendam	Collision with U-2336 (Salvaged)	7	0
20 Feb 1945	U-869	Germany	60m off New Jersey	Sunk by own torpedo	56	0
15 Mar 1945	Lancefish	USA	Boston	Foundered	0	80 e
14 Apr 1945	U-235	Germany	Kattegat	Sunk in error by Germany torpedo-boat T-17	46	0
14 Apr 1945	U-1206	Germany	Off Peterhead	Flooded by human error	4	44
8 Jul 1945	O-19	Holland	South China Sea	Wrecked	0	39

APPENDIX 2   (Continued)

Date	Submarine	Origin	Location	Cause	Lost	Survived
19 Sep 1945	*Minerve*	France	Portland Bill	Ran aground in bad weather	0	48 e
29 Oct 1945	*Ha-204*	Japan	?	Stranded and wrecked	0	32
27 Jun 1946	*C.4*	Spain	Off Balearic Islands	Rammed by destroyer *Lepanto*	46	0
5 Dec 1946	*Ex U-2326*	France	Off Toulon	Diving accident – cause unknown	26	0
26 Aug 1949	*Cochino*	USA	Off Northern Norway	Foundered after battery explosion	1 + 6 b	77
12 Jan 1950	*Truculent*	Britain	Thames estuary	Collision with Swedish tanker *Divinia*	64	15
16 Apr 1951	*Affray*	Britain	Hurd Deep N of Alderney	Cut-off valve of snorkel probably failed	75	0
23 Sep 1952	*Sibylle*	France	Off Toulon	Unexplained diving accident	47	0
4 Apr 1953	*Dumlupinar*	Turkey	Dardanelles	Collision with Swedish *SS Naboland*	81	5
16 Jun 1953	*Sidon*	Britain	Portland harbour	Hydrogen-peroxide torpedo explosion	13	43
1956	*Sazan (Shch 201)*	Russia	Poti	Wrecked. No details released	?	?
Sep 1957	*M.256*	Russia	?	Flooded by water used to douse engine fire	?	?
30 May 1958	*Stickleback*	USA	20m SW Pearl Harbor	Collision with *USS Silverstein*	0	82
May 1959	*S.99*	Russia	?	Explosion in fuel line. Constructive total loss	?	?
10 Apr 1963	*Thresher**	USA	220 miles E of Boston	Structural failure resulted in flooding	129	0
14 Sep 1966	*Hai*	W Germany	Dogger Bank, North Sea	Welding failure	19	1
3 Nov 1966	*Tiru*	USA	Frederick Reef	Ran aground	0	80 e
25 Jan 1968	*Dakar*	Israel	E Mediterranean	Disappeared – cause not known	69	0
27 Jan 1968	*Minerve*	France	W Mediterranean	Disappeared – cause not known	52	0
21 May 1968	*Scorpion**	USA	250m SW of Azores	Struck by own malfunctioning torpedo	99	0
1968	Unidentified*	Russia	Near Severomorsk	No information released. Media reports only	?	0

281

APPENDIX 2 (Continued)

Date	Submarine	Origin	Location	Cause	Lost	Survived
8 Mar 1968	K.129	Russia	1677m NW of Hawaii	Internal explosion. Partially salved by US	98	0
16 May 1969	Guitarro*	USA	Mare Island Navy Yard	Flooded in dock due to negligence	0	–
4 Mar 1970	Eurydice	France	East of Toulon	Internal explosion	57	0
12 Apr 1970	K.8 (November class)*	Russia	70m SW Land's End	Scuttled following reactor fire	52	?
1 Jul 1971	Artemis	Britain	Gosport submarine base	Sank at moorings. Human error	0	23
11 Oct 1972	Sirene	France	Lorient	Flooded through faulty torpedo tube	0	42
Dec 1979	Unidentified*	Russia	Mid-Atlantic	Scuttled following radiation accident	?	?
Sep 1983	Charlie-type*	Russia	Off Kamchatka	No information released	90 d	0
20 Feb 1985	Unidentified	N Korea	Korean waters	No information beyond media reports of sinking	56 d	0
3 Oct 1986	K.219*	Russia	North of Bermuda	Spontaneous explosion of RSM-25 missile	4	115
26 Aug 1988	Pacocha	Peru	4 miles W of Callao	Rammed by trawler Kyowa Maru	7	45
7 Apr 1989	Komsomolets* (K.278)	Russia	SW Bear Island, Barents Sea	Fire caused by short circuit	41	28
17 Sep 1996	Shark-type	N Korea	Kangnung, S Korea	Ran aground and abandoned	0 k	25 k
23 Jun 1998	Yugo-type	N Korea	Off Donghae, S Korea	Tangled in trawl net. Seized by S Koreans but sank in tow	9 l	01
12 Aug 2000	Kursk* (K.141)	Russia	60m north of Severmorsk	Spontaneous detonation of hydrogen-peroxide torpedo	118	0

Notes: * Indicates a nuclear-powered submarine.
  a Four other Russian submarines were lost by accidents during the Second World War period but no dates or details are known. They have been identified as: *Shch-136, Shch-410, M-20* and *M-51*.

282

b The additional six men were from the crew of the rescue submarine USS Tusk.

c Including 17 US Army personnel.

d Lost with all hands. Estimated figure based on official complement and other information.

e Number of survivors not recorded. Estimated figure based on known number lost and official complement.

f Estimated total.

g Although sailing under the Austrian flag, this was basically a German boat with a German captain and crew. One Austrian officer was embarked for reasons of international law.

h The additional three men were from the submarine L.2.

i Six survivors died as prisoners-of-war and only nine returned to the US after the war.

j Sinking unconfirmed by official sources but reported reliably by CBS News.

k Ran ashore while on clandestine infiltration mission. Ten survivors were shot by a member of the crew who then shot himself, seven were shot by South Korean troops, four were found shot, one was captured and two were listed as missing. (Details based on newspaper reports.)

l The entire nine-man crew were inside when the submarine foundered. It was subsequently established that all had died by self-inflicted (?) gunshot wounds.

– In lost and survived columns indicate that there was no one aboard when the submarine sank.

NB Submarines that sank under tow, or otherwise foundered, after surrendering at the end of both World Wars, and submarines which sank after being sold out of service, have been excluded from this list. So, too, have midget submarines, naval and civilian, lost by accident. Except for submarines of Russian origin, most of the data supplied has come from official sources.

Appendix 3 Submarine Losses from 1 January 1900 to 31 July 1914

	Lost by enemy action, by mines, scuttled to avoid capture or 'missing'	Lost by accident, shipwreck, friendly fire, negligence, or on own mines
France	–	11
Britain	–	8
Russia	–	4
USA	–	4
Italy	–	1
Germany	–	1
Japan	–	1
Holland	–	1

Appendix 4   Submarine Losses from 1 August 1914 to 11 November 1918

	Lost by enemy action, mines, scuttled to avoid capture and missing	*Lost by accident, shipwreck, friendly fire, negligence, or on own mines*
Germany a	177	26
Britain	37 b	19
Russia	16 d	7
Austria	15	1 e
France	9	6
Italy	6	4
Australia	1	1
USA	–	5 c
Denmark [neutral]	–	1

a   Excluding U-boats surrendered under the Armistice terms or scuttled en route to internment after 11 November. Includes *UC-12* blown up on own mines while masquerading under Austrian colours.

b   Excludes *C.3* blown up to destroy viaduct during the Zeebrugge operation.

c   Including three lost before entry into the war.

d   Excluding *Ersh* lost in action during the civil war in 1919.

e   Excludes *UC-12* which has been classified as German.

Appendix 5 Submarine Losses from 12 November 1918 to 31 August 1939

	Lost by enemy action, mines, scuttled to avoid capture and missing	Lost by accident, shipwreck, friendly fire, negligence or on own mines
Russia	1 a	13 d
Britain	1 b	13
USA	–	13
Japan	–	4
France	–	3
Italy	–	2
Germany	–	2 e
Holland	–	1
Spain	2 c	–
Greece	–	1
Chile	–	1

a   Including *Ersh* lost in action during civil war 1919.
b   Including *L.55* lost in action against Bolsheviks in 1919. (Subsequently salvaged by Russians and accidentally lost in 1931.)
c   *C.3* and *C.6* lost in action during civil war 1936–1939.
d   Russian statistics may not include unpublicized accidents.
e   Excludes U-boats surrendered under Armistice terms and scuttled or wrecked on route to internment as such losses were due to deliberate acts of sabotage.

Appendix 6   Submarine Losses from 1 September 1939 to 2 September 1945

	Lost by enemy action, by mines, scuttled to avoid capture or 'missing'	Lost by accident, shipwreck, friendly fire, negligence or own mines
Germany	783 a	51 b
Japan	117	13 c
Russia	94	9 d
Britain	69	8
Italy	63 h	8
France	52 g	3
United States	38	12 e
Denmark	9 i	–
Holland	7	3
Norway	5	–
Greece	4	–
Yugoslavia	3 j	–
Poland	1	1
Sweden (neutral)	–	3 f
Turkey (neutral)	–	1

a   Excludes U-boats surrendered at the end of the war or otherwise interned.

b   Excludes U-boats which foundered or were scuttled to avoid surrender in May 1945. *U-963* is now regarded as being deliberately wrecked on 9 May 1945 and has also been excluded.

c   Includes two submarines lost before 6 December 1941.

d   Russian losses probably greater than stated. Includes two submarines lost before 22 June 1941.

e   Includes one submarine lost before 6 December 1941.

f   One of these submarines was sunk by a mine of unknown origin.

g   French submarines were beset from all sides in the Second World War. The total given can be analysed as follows:

   (i)   Sunk by mines or in action against Axis forces   3

   (ii) Sunk by British and Allied forces in the course of operations against French African colonies. Some destroyed in harbour – others while engaged on defensive missions against these forces   24

   (iii) Scuttled to avoid capture by German occupying forces in June 1940 and November 1942   20

   (iv) Captured by Axis forces at Bizerta. (Captured boats which were later sunk have been included under (ii))   5

   NB Submarines seized in Britain or interned at Alexandria in 1940, seven boats, have been excluded. Most of these were taken over by Free French crews and continued combat operations against the Axis.

h   Excludes four taken over by Germany after the armistice of 8 September 1943 which were recommissioned into the *Kriegsmarine* with *UIT* prefixes.

Three of these were subsequently sunk or scuttled and are included in the appropriate column of the German losses. This figure also excludes 34 boats surrendered to the Allies following the armistice.

Nine submarines were scuttled to avoid capture when German forces occupied Denmark on 29 August 1940 after the initial invasion in May.

Three submarines were seized by Axis forces following Yugoslavia's surrender.

Appendix 7 3 September 1945 to 31 December 2001

	Lost by enemy action	Lost by accident
Argentina	1 a	–
Pakistan	1 b	–
Russia	–	11 c
USA	–	6 d
France	–	6
Britain	–	4
North Korea	–	3
Spain	–	1
Germany	–	1
Japan	–	1
Israel	–	1
Peru	–	1
Turkey	–	1

a *Santa Fe* lost in Falklands War 1982.
b *Ghazi* lost during the war with India December 1971.
c Includes seven nuclear-powered submarines.
d Includes three nuclear-powered submarines.

Appendix 8   World Submarine Losses 1719 to 31 December 2002

	Lost by enemy action, mines, capture, scuttling to avoid capture and 'missing'	Lost by accident, hazard of the sea, human error, or own mines	Total
Germany	960	81	1041
Britain	107	52	159
Russia	111	44	155
Japan	117	19	136
France	61	29	90
Italy	69	15	84
USA	38	40	78
Austria-Hungary	15	1	16
Holland	7	5	12
Denmark	9	1	10
Norway	5	–	5
Greece	4	1	5
Spain	2	1	3
Sweden	–	3	3
North Korea	–	3	3
Yugoslavia	3	–	3
Poland	1	1	2
Australia	1	1	2
Turkey	–	2	2
Pakistan	1	–	1
Israel	–	1	1
Peru	–	1	1
Argentina	1	–	1
Chile	–	1	1
Before 1900	1	34	35
	1513	336	1849

NB: Submarines surrendered or interned under terms of an armistice or peace treaty (including those deliberately sunk en route to surrender or internment) have been excluded from these totals. They are to be distinguished from those scuttled to avoid capture in combat conditions or scuttled to escape seizure by hostile forces which have been classified as 'lost in action'.

Index

Behnke, Lieutenant, 139
Belogun, Captain Viktor, 243
Beresford, Admiral Lord
    Charles, 40
Berlitz, Charles, 214
Berwick Castle, 48–50, 269
Bignell, Lt-Cdr Laurence, 83
Birkaland, 179, 278
Blackburn, Lt John, 251, 254
Blake, Christopher, 20–21
Blandy, 212
Blonde, 81–82
Bluebird, 207
Boase, Lt Harold, 83–85
Bolkoburg, 278
Bolshakov, Engineer, 186
Bolus, Lt-Cdr Guy, 154–156,
    158–162, 164–166, 168–169
Bontier, Lt-Cdr A.L., 175
Borelli, Abbe Giovanni-Alfonso,
    19, 37
Borgeois, Simeon, 34
Borisov, Arnold, 243
Bourne, William, 18, 19, 37
Bowerman, Lt-Cdr Harold,
    172–173
Bowers, Lt C.P., 196–197
Brazen, 157, 163–164, 166
Breslin, J.J., 43
Brock, Wreckmaster, 168
Brodie, Lt-Cdr T.S., 77
Brooklyn, 144
Brown, Stoker Petty Officer
    William, 88–90
Brun, Charles-Marie, 34
Brunel, Isambard Kingdom, 25
Buckingham, Electrical
    Artificer, 197–198

Bukhnikasvili, Seaman Nadari,
    226
Bulganin, Nikolai, 203
Bush, President George W., 249
Bushnell, David, 21
Bushnell, 124
Butler, Charles, 118

Cable & Wireless Marine Ltd,
    263
Callaghan, James, MP, 253
Camden, 112
Campbell, Mr, 39
Candy, Lt H.C., 52
Canterbury, 111–112
Capena, 120, 274
Carr, Ensign, 63
Carrie, Lt-Cdr., 122
Cervo, Senor, 21, 240
Chanticleer, 52
Chapman, Lt Harold, 156–162,
    165–166
Christaansen, Lieutenant, 85–86
Chuyo, 153
Cicogna, 171
City of Rome, 120, 274
Clayton, Edward, 151
Coath, 59
Cole, Rear Admiral Cyrus W.,
    143–145, 147
Coltart, Lieutenant, [*G.6*], 98
Coltart, Lt R.E., 156–157, 162
Comet, 4
Commonwealth, 52
Constantine, Grand Duke, 26
Conte, 58
Cooke, Lt-Cdr Charles W., 108
Cooper-Key, Rear Admiral Sir
    Ashley, 26

Hindes, Lt F.J., 197–199
Hine, Chief ERA Sam, 198
Hole, W.T., 165
Holland, John Philip, 35, 40–47, 72, 102
Holland, Michael, 41
Holt, Able Seaman, 131
Hommerberg, Captain, 196
Hopper No 27, 71, 270
Horton, Admiral Sir Max, 205
Housatonic, 33–34, 241
Hoxey, General, 36
Hughes, Howard, 218
Humphrey-Baker, Lieutenant, 195–197
Hunley, Horace L., 28, 29, 31–33, 37
Hynd, (Mr), 237

Ilena, 58
Iltis, 58
Inconstant, 110
Indian Chief, 33
Inflexible, 92
Isayenko, Captain Vasiliy, 243
Ithurial, 91, 92

Joanna C, 236
Jones, Lt-Cdr Vaughn, 111
Joubert, Dr Georges, 63
Juno, 48

Kattegat, 86–87
Kellet, Lt-Cdr Gilbert, 17
Kenny, T.W., 165
Khruschev, President Nikita, 203
Killen, Chief ERA, 182–183
King, Fleet Admiral Ernest, 121, 125

Kissinger, Henry, 217
Kittyhawk, 234
Kolesnikov, Lt-Captain Dmitry, 246
Kolyshkin, Rear Admiral Ivan, 185
Korth, Secretary, 213
Krashnogvardeysk, 224
Kuney, Yeoman Charles, 140
Kurtaran, 207
Kuzminkyh, Alexander, 240
Kwang-su, Lee, 239–240
Kyowa Maru, 225–226, 282
Kyu, Lee Jin, 239

L-2 (*Zeppelin*), 71n
Lake, Simon, 47
Lane, Engineer Lt Arthur, 5, 7, 16–17
Laubeuf, Maxime, 47
Laurence, Cdr Noel, 2
Layton, Lt-Cdr Geoffrey, 80–81, 93–95
Leander, 35
Leathes, Lt-Cdr, 134
Lech, 278
Lee, Lord, 104
Leir, Captain Ernest, 2, 91–94
Lepanto, 194, 281
Liachin, Captain Gennadiy, 243
Little, Captain Charles, 91, 93
Loch Insh, 255
Lockwood, Cdr Charles A., 138, 144
Lodestar, 39
Lovock, Able Seaman, 131
Low, Lt John, 180
LR-5, 245, 263–264
LR-5K, 264

300